To O.J.

With best wishes

to a clear thinker

Art 2/10/93

MANAGING YOUR INVESTMENT MANAGER

COMPLETE GUIDE TO SELECTION, MEASUREMENT, AND CONTROL

MANAGING YOUR INVESTMENT MANAGER

COMPLETE GUIDE TO SELECTION, MEASUREMENT, AND CONTROL

*THIRD
EDITION*

Arthur Williams III

BUSINESS ONE IRWIN
Homewood, Illinois 60430

Project editor: Karen J. Nelson
Production manager: Diane Palmer
Jacket designer: Ray Machura
Designer: Heidi J. Baughman
Art manager: Kim Meriwether
Compositor: BookMasters, Inc.
Typeface: 11/13 Times Roman
Printer: Arcata Graphics/Kingsport

Library of Congress Cataloging-in-Publication Data

Williams, Arthur
    Managing your investment manager : the complete guide to
selection, measurement, and control / Arthur Williams, III. — 3rd
ed.
        p.   cm.
    ISBN 1-55623-515-1
    1. Mutual funds. 2. Pension trusts—Investments. 3. Portfolio
management. I. Title.
HG4530.W54   1992
332.63'27—dc20   92–3318

Printed in the United States of America
1 2 3 4 5 6 7 8 9 0 AG-K 9 8 7 6 5 4 3 2

For Sandra, Art and Leigh, Mindy, and Tom
without whose patience, understanding and support
this book could not have been completed;
and for Torrie, who heralds the next generation

FOREWORD

I can name on the fingers of both hands the books about investing that contain distilled knowledge and technique and are not potboilers, junk, or worse. But those ten are worth their weight in gold because true insights can save the nonprofessional immense amounts of time and money. There is wisdom and experience out there about supervising money in a responsible and effective way, but its presentation lacks the best-selling drama of a mystic with an apocalyptic view of the world or of a technician who thinks he has found an infallible system in the squiggles of a relative strength line.

As the senior executive of an asset management firm, I continually see people who have suddenly assumed the responsibility for supervising serious money. They are bright souls and they know they need help. Suddenly, in effect, they have become fiduciaries. They have no intention of managing those funds themselves, but after speaking with some brokers, investment management firms, trust departments, and maybe a mutual salesman or two, they are confused and lost. Each party advises a solution to the investment process problem that serves his special self interest. There is literally nowhere to go for impartial judgment and advice.

What this new fiduciary needs is good advice on how to construct a framework in which to function with his money. This framework must include the nuts and bolts of investing from establishing reasonable goals to asset allocation and on to selecting and evaluating the performance of investment managers. It should even tell you how to be a good client. It should be a reference book that can give you as much or as little knowledge as you want.

I know of no good book on this subject other than the one whose pages you have opened. The author is an accomplished, practicing professional in the business. In other words, he knows of what he writies which is an unusual event in and of itself. It should be required reading, in my opinion, for both amateur and professional fiduciaries. The third edition is better, more complete, more up to date than the second.

And remember, buy low sell high.

Barton M. Biggs
Chairman
Morgan Stanley Asset Management

The 1980 first edition of Arthur Williams' book *Managing Your Investment Manager* represented a fundamental building block in the body of literature concerning pension investment. Art's volume filled a long-empty niche by focusing on a key and somewhat unique element of the investment challenge for a pension fund—the successful hiring and on-going management of outside investment advisers. As with most investment functions, successful results are not always sure, but Art's work has delineated a process which increases the probability that value will be added to a pension plan and its beneficiaries.

As the only volume known to me that focuses solely and competently on external manager matters, Art's book represents a significant contribution to investment management. Recognizing this, since its publication, I and my pension investment staff have used the book as a training resource and have applied the processes and principles contained in it. Art is to be congratulated for again updating this book to benefit the entire pension investment industry.

W. Gordon Binns, Jr.
President
General Motors Investment
Management Corporation

Art Williams has written an extraordinary book for top level investment executives, the men and women who oversee the management of the trillions of dollars in pension, endowment, and trust wealth. He covers all the necessary technical ground that modern investment executives need to know. The reader will learn about alphas, betas, duration time-weighted returns, and many more of the quantitative devices currently used in managing investment portfolios. But more importantly, the author places all of these features of modern portfolio theory into a meaningful, practical managerial context.

The point of view of the book is not about doing investment management. It is about the selection, the supervision and management, and the retention and/or replacement of those who do investment management on behalf of the chief investment officers of corporations, foundations, universities and other institutions that have large sums invested.

The book discusses setting investment guidelines, picking managers who will follow them, and monitoring those managers to make sure they do as well as possible what you expect them to do. The book deals with the development of broad portfolio strategies and how to get them implemented properly.

It is a book I routinely suggest to students who want to learn about investment organizations and their management.

This is a book for managers, not technocrats. It is also a book that anyone who wants to be placed in charge of large pension, endowment, or trust funds should be required to read as part of their fiduciary obligations.

Dennis E. Logue
Steven Roth Professor of Management
Amos Tuck School of Business Administration
Dartmouth College

Since I joined the plan sponsor community in 1982, Arthur Williams' book *Managing Your Investment Manager* has had a permanent place on my bookshelf and a frequent place in my briefcase. In 1982 Art's book taught me the business and was almost as indispensable as a blind person's white cane. Now, after a decade of experience in the industry, I find that Art's book is no less useful than it was originally; it can always be relied on to offer fresh perspectives on contemporary issues.

The nomenclature of the investment management business is too often impenetrable. *Managing Your Investment Manager* handles this problem most gracefully; it uses, explains, and cuts through the jargon and speaks to all levels of knowledge, skillfully illuminating concepts like alpha, beta, residual standard deviation, and covered option writing. William's achievement is all the more noteworthy when one realizes that underpinning his subject matter is an almost impermeable, dense Nobel Prize winning science, which was not widely applied by the industry until 30 years after initial circulation in academic journals. *Managing Your Investment Manager*'s focus (and success) is the applied science side of the industry, helping practitioners (trustees, fiduciaries, and staff) intelligently manage and structure solid investment programs.

David A. White
Treasurer and Chief Investment Officer
The Rockefeller Foundation

PREFACE

Anyone browsing through the financial section of a book store will be impressed by the seemingly endless number of books describing ways to invest profitably. At the same time, any trustee or fund administrator who wishes to learn how to structure and operate a large pool of assets will be frustrated by the lack of information on the subject. This is truly amazing, given the staggering sums of money in public and private pension funds, the increase in fiduciary awareness engendered by ERISA, and the great impact that fund investment has on retirement income security, pension funds, the success of charitable organizations, and on personal financial wealth. A complete management system is needed to deal with this huge but frequently inadequate pool of assets and the attendant problems and opportunities. The principal components needed are a management framework for establishing goals, trained managers for implementing the goals, and an information system which provides the necessary feedback so that corrective action can be taken when actual results stray beyond predetermined limits from acceptable results.

This book has two purposes. The first purpose is to contribute to the creation and development of a management system in all three areas by presenting in a logical format the relevant issues, discussing potential solutions and the pros and cons of each, and reviewing the analytical tools for investing and for measuring investment risk and results. The book is about investing but from the viewpoint of the trustee or the fiduciary who works with investment managers rather than from the viewpoint of the investment manager buying and selling securities.

The second purpose of the book is to build a communications bridge between fund sponsors and investment managers. Unless the two groups understand the goals of the organization and its fund, the personalities involved, and the terminology of the field, it is unlikely that the goals of the organization or of the investment manager will be met.

The book is designed both to read and to be referred to. It is organized in the way the president of a corporation, union or college, or the governor of a state might look at the problem of how to operate a fund by discussing:

- What are the goals of our fund?
- Who in the organization should have the primary responsibility for the fund?
- How do we choose an investment strategy?
- How do we choose asset types?
- How do we choose investment managers?
- How do we work with our investment managers?
- How do we evaluate our investment managers?
- How do we control multiple managers?

The text of the book is followed by a mathematics refresher.

It is my hope that with more knowledge and better communication, investing can be carried out more wisely and capital allocated more efficiently, with significant, widespread benefits to all participants in the U.S. economy.

Arthur Williams III

ACKNOWLEDGEMENTS

I wish to express my sincere thanks to the many people who provided comments and insights which assisted me in writing this book. Included in alphabetical order, are: Angela Acosta, Robert Angelica, Marshall Blume, James J. Bohan, Jureg Boller, Eugene B. Burroughs, Arthur Carlson, James V. Caruso, Steven Chazzen, Heidi Church, Bonnie R. Cohen, John F. Condon, Noreen M. Conwell, William J. Crerend, Richard E. Dahab, Peter O. Dietz, Charles Ellis, Helen Emmerich, John W. English, James E. Farrell, Jr., Robert J. Farrell, Arthur J. Fenton, Robert Ferguson, Lawrence Fisher, Russell Fogler, Robert Garber, Herbert E. Gernet, Jr., Raymond L. Held, Franklin Hendler, Lisa Herman, Anthony H. Hoberman, Don L. Horwitz, Robert L. Huston, Richard Jacobson, Robert A. Jaeger, Henry James, William Kelly, John L. Kemmerer, Jr., John C. Kemmerer, John L. Kemmerer, III, Laura Levine, Sumner Levine, Martin Liebowitz, James H. Lorie, Leonard F. Mactas, James T. McComsey, Sirkka McHale, Roger Murray, Gretchen Oelhaf, Michael K. Polysius, William Price, Dorene C. Prinzo, Dimitri Raftopoulous, William J. Rahal, Kenneth J. Reifert, Philip R. Rettew, Jr., John B. Rofrano, Kathleen Rooney, Donald E. Rossi, F. Thomas Senior, Jr., Robert E. Shultz, Philip R. Sloan, John J. Targia, Irwin Tepper, Dennis Tito, Wayne Wagner, Steven J. Warner, Adrienne Wesson, Linda Westley, Hope M. Witlacil, Reverend Richard Zang, Arthur Zeikel, and Randi Zeller.

A special note of thanks is due to Robert C. Kline for assistance with the chapter on energy investments, William D. Mischell for his assistance with the chapter on pension funding, Sara Hamilton for her assistance with the chapter on investing for individuals, and M. Dan Bergman for his substantial assistance in preparing the exhibits.

CONTENTS

LIST OF EXHIBITS

CHAPTER 1

ESTABLISHING GOALS
FOR THE FUND

If you don't know where you're going, you'll probably never get there.

Even though much of the subject matter of this book relates to investing, it is really not investing with which we are most concerned. Our efforts are directed at providing a rational framework within which representatives of sponsoring organizations can deal with their funds. To do this, we will start at the very beginning by asking the question, "What are we trying to accomplish?" The answer is that we are trying to help our organization through proper management of its fund. To understand the goals of the fund it is first necessary to ask what its goals are; second, how the fund can further those goals; and, finally, how the fund can be structured to maximize the chances that goals will be met. Since the answers vary, depending on the type of organization, it is well to break down the analysis by organization types. Throughout the book, four types of organizations will be considered—corporations, labor unions, state and local governments, and charitable organizations. Personal and trust investments are considered separately in Chapter 20.

CORPORATIONS

It is traditional to state that the goal of a corporation, whether publicly or privately held, is to maximize the long-run wealth of shareholders. Although this is still the goal, it is nonetheless necessary to consider three other "constituencies": employees, government, and customers. The role of customers, though clearly important to the corporation's success, is not relevant to the subject of managing the investment manager. The significance to this subject of employees and government is, on the other hand, crucial. Employees' interests are directly related to the success of the corporation, and retirement plans are directly related to the interests of employees. Government has become greatly involved in retirement plans with the passage of ERISA (Employee Retirement Income Security Act of 1974). Because of ERISA, every act taken or even contemplated by a fund sponsor or an investment manager must be considered in light of its ERISA implications.

It therefore seems appropriate for our purposes to define the corporation's goal as maximizing the long-run wealth of shareholders while giving full recognition to the needs of employees and the presence of government regulation. It can be argued that maximizing the wealth of shareholders requires consideration of employees' needs and the omnipresence of government regulators. Although this view will not be denied, it appears that the explicit recognition of employee and government interests will enhance the corporation's chances of achieving its primary profit-making function.

Shareholders' wealth is composed of the stock price plus dividends received. Increases in the stock price and dividends are a function of growth and risk; growth is to be maximized and risk minimized. (These two factors, growth and risk, are analogous to return and risk, the two basic considerations in any investment.) Part of the fund's objective, therefore, is to increase the company's earnings and decrease their volatility. These are reasonable goals, though applying them is not easy, especially since they may conflict with the goals of giving full recognition to the needs of employees and to the presence of government regulation.

The retirement fund can have an important impact on the corporation's goal of serving the needs of employees. Every employee must consider the economic effects of becoming too old to work. Many employees look forward to a less-demanding retirement lifestyle. To the extent that a retirement plan can guarantee income so that employees will have financial security in their later years, the plan is important to the corporation goal of giving recognition to the needs of employees.

There appears to be a conflict between the goal of keeping employees content by providing them with high-cost fringe benefits and the primary corporate goal, maximizing the wealth of shareholders. This conflict is certainly real in the short run, since a dollar put into a retirement plan is a dollar less (before taxes) for dividends or reinvestment. In the long run, however, an optimal balance is possible, since the welfare of the corporation is intimately related to the productivity of the work force and the welfare of the workforce is intimately related to the success of the corporation.

While attempting to operate its retirement funds so as to maximize the wealth of shareholders, the corporation must deal with the growing presence of the federal government. An interesting paradox develops, since ERISA clearly states that retirement funds "must be operated solely for the benefit" of their participants. It also is clear that ERISA was passed partly because some companies pursued the wealth of shareholders at the expense of employee benefits. There are well-known horror stories about employees who worked for many years in the expectation of receiving a pension, but then were denied it because of a corporate merger, a plant closing, or some other unexpected event. The conflict between maximizing the wealth of shareholders and operating a plan "solely for the benefit of participants" is real, complex, and unresolved. Yet corporate management must deal with this problem in setting policies on plan benefits and investing.

The exact steps to ensure that the goals of the fund maximize long-run shareholders' wealth by contributing to the growth and stability of sales, earnings, and dividends are explored in Chapter 3. These steps depend on the financial needs of the corporation and the fund and on their ability to bear risk.

The effect of the stability and growth of the earnings for a defined benefit plan can be viewed in the context of whether the plan benefits are growing or static, although the basic outcome is similar in either case. If the benefits are static, the way to contribute to stability and growth is by seeing that the fund assets earn at least the assumed rate of return. The assumed rate of return is that interest rate, or return on investment, which would allow current assets and future contributions to grow enough to equal all future pension liabilities.

Of course, since markets decline as well as rise, it would be nice to have a cushion over and above the assets needed to meet actuarial requirements. Therefore, fund sponsors tend to favor policies producing higher returns. Also, if the cushion becomes large enough, future corporate contributions can be decreased or benefits increased.

If plan benefits are likely to increase, a corporation whose fund achieves only its assumed rate of return will suffer earnings decreases whenever benefits rise. This decrease occurs because the higher benefits will likely apply to all employees (even those about to retire) and no provision has been made for money to pay the higher benefits. Thus "unfunded past service costs" immediately appear, and they must be amortized over no more than 30 years, with an ensuing drop in earnings. Corporations expecting to increase benefits (and this seems to include almost all of them) thus have a strong incentive to achieve investment returns beyond those dictated by their actuarial assumptions.

Plans with defined contributions, such as profit-sharing plans, should have a minimal impact on the growth and stability of sales, earnings, and dividends. Plans of this type are usually adopted in lieu of some other form of compensating or encouraging the loyalty of employees. Consequently, the cost of such plans is borne by the corporation in lieu of a similar cost for another form of compensation. Further, these costs tend to be variable.

A corporation can take a number of steps to operate a retirement plan so that it gives full recognition to the needs of employees while maximizing the wealth of shareholders. A plan with assets in excess of required levels is a source of comfort to employees. It provides a greater probability that benefits will be paid and that they can be increased. Thus, both the corporation and its employees have a strong interest in seeing the plan's assets enhanced through investment gain.

The next question is, "What is the attitude toward risk that each of these parties holds?" To the corporation, an investment dollar lost is a dollar that must someday be replaced (with interest), and the reverse is true for a dollar gained from investment. To employees, a dollar lost by the fund is a dollar less security and a dollar less of potential gain in benefits. However, it is not a dollar in lost benefits. The corporation must still pay the defined benefit, and, presumably, if the corporation does not, the Pension Benefit Guaranty Corporation (PBGC) will. Thus the employee can be more tolerant of risk than is the corporation sponsoring the fund. However, where a fund is extremely underfunded, the corporation may feel that it will probably be required to surrender the maximum 30 percent of its net worth to the PBGC, and hence it can speculate with pension assets without regard to loss in the hope of making a sufficient "killing" to decrease its liability to PBGC to less than 30 percent of its net worth. In this situation the employee bears no risk and the corporation bears no incremental risk beyond 30 percent of its net worth.

To understand how a fund can be operated in such a way as to pursue the goal of maximizing the wealth of shareholders while giving full recognition to government regulation, a brief summary of the applicable laws is required.

Prior to ERISA, trust law was the major body of law applying to corporate retirement plans (though it is less than clear that national and multinational corporations paid much attention to it). Two types of trust law prevailed: legal lists and "prudent man." Under the legal-list concept, state legislation listed the criteria for allowable investments in trusts. The prudent-man doctrine indicated that a trustee "shall conduct himself faithfully and exercise a sound discretion. He is to observe how men of prudence, discretion, and intelligence manage their own affairs, not in regard to speculation, but in regard to the permanent disposition of their funds, considering the probable income, as well as the probable safety of the capital to be invested."[1]

The Employee Retirement Income Security Act of 1974 is now the dominant legislative influence on private retirement plans. Although the act is hopelessly complex in its details, its aim is elegantly simple. A corporation does not need to provide its employees with a retirement plan but, if it does, it must tell the employees in simple terms the whole truth about the plan. It must put aside sufficient money so the plan can pay the promised benefits, and the plan and its assets must be administered carefully and honestly by competent people with the sole objective of serving the interests of plan beneficiaries.

Relevant portions of the SEC Act of 1975 (Williams Amendment) describe the conditions under which the investment managers of a fund can also act as brokers for the fund and the conditions under which brokerage commissions can be utilized to pay for services to the fund and to the investment manager.

An appropriate approach to successful operation in a regulated environment is:

Be knowledgeable about the relevant law.

Be conscious of the relevant law whenever a significant decision is being made.

---

[1] Quoted from Harvey E. Bines, *The Law of Investment Management* (Boston: Warren, Gorham & Lamont, 1978), pp. 1–3.

Be conscientious in carrying out legal responsibilities.

See that the necessary legal documents are prepared, and be ready to present a legally acceptable rationale for significant decisions.

Document key decisions.

LABOR UNIONS

Jointly trusteed (Taft-Hartley) funds, as the name implies, have two sets of sponsors. Typically, a union representing a group of employees secures agreement from a group of employers to contribute a certain amount of money for each hour worked by each employee. This money is then contributed monthly to a common pool which is invested on behalf of the participants. An important distinction must be drawn between jointly trusteed and other pension funds, namely, that in a jointly trusteed fund the only assets (excluding government insurance) available to meet pension payments are those of the fund. No corporation, church group, or state or local government has guaranteed the benefits. Thus, if the assets of a jointly trusteed fund are inadequate, retirees will eventually find that their benefits cannot be met. A second distinction is that labor unions are political organizations whose members/beneficiaries elect their officers/trustees. This condition does not exist for corporations, other private organizations, or even public funds. A governor is elected by the people of the state, not just by those state employees who are covered by a fund.

These two distinctions can lead to a marked impact on the investment philosophy of jointly trusteed funds. The lack of a sponsor which guarantees benefits gives rise to the need for a conservative investment philosophy. The political nature of the organization is likely to have a varied effect. Following long periods in which the stock market has performed well, pressure is exerted on incumbents by candidates to increase return (by increasing risk). In periods when the stock market has performed poorly, the opposite will occur. Although this problem is apparent to some extent in both public and nonunion private funds, it is most evident in jointly trusteed funds.

Given this background, analysis of the goals of the organization and of jointly trusteed funds is greatly simplified. The goals of the organization are to promote the economic and physical welfare of members and their families. An important part of the members' financial and security package is their pensions. The pension fund can solve part of the members' financial needs by maintaining sufficient assets to meet benefits. A secondary but related objective is to increase fund assets at a rate greater than the fund's assumed rate of return. Like corporate employees, Taft-Hartley fund participants want to have a cushion of assets above the actuarial requirements. Further, they hope for additional asset enhancement as a source of additional benefits. However, since there is no fund sponsor to guarantee pension benefits, the fund participants are much more risk-averse than are the employees of a corporation or a public body.

STATE AND LOCAL GOVERNMENTS

The factors affecting public funds are surprisingly similar to those affecting corporate funds. In both cases the sponsoring organization provides services to "customers." To provide the services efficiently, a productive and loyal work force is needed.

The sponsor guarantees benefits to its employees, bearing the risk associated with the guarantee, in order to strengthen productivity and loyalty. Thus the goals of the two organizational types and the ways in which their funds can help meet those goals are similar. Four important distinctions should be noted. First, there are statutory restrictions (typically limiting the fund's percentage in equities) to which corporate funds are not subject. Second, many public funds are contributory, with a large percentage of their assets coming from direct employee contributions. Third, public funds are subject to much greater scrutiny than are private funds. These three factors all contribute to the tendency to establish conservative policies in operating public funds. Fourth, public funds are not subject to ERISA. However, this probably does not have a significant effect on the prudence of investments, since at some point ERISA-type legislation will probably govern public funds and in any event the standards of prudence dictated by ERISA are already having an important impact on public officials.

CHARITABLE ORGANIZATIONS

Frequently, two types of asset pools are supervised by the trustees of the endowments of charitable organizations—pension funds for employees and endowment funds which support the charitable organizations themselves. The pension funds are similar to the corporate and public funds. The endowment fund is different in that its obligation is difficult to measure. Unlike a pension fund, which is obligated to pay certain fairly predictable benefits, an endowment fund is normally obligated to support the purposes of the charitable organization. Since the importance of this support can be great, it is well to examine the goals of charitable organizations and how the endowment fund furthers those goals.

Charitable organizations seek to further specific, socially beneficial activities. Money is required to pursue almost any activity, so the maintenance and enhancement of the endowment fund's assets can spell the difference between success and failure for the charitable organization. To ensure that the endowment fund supports the goals of a charitable organization, a complete assessment must be made of the timing and magnitude of the organization's financial needs. An investment portfolio must then be established which meets those financial needs. If the organization is to maintain its level of giving at inflation-adjusted levels, it must invest in a way to achieve high real rates of return. Chapter 3 addresses this complex but vital subject.

CHAPTER 2

ASSIGNING RESPONSIBILITY
FOR OPERATING THE FUND

The simplest organization structure that will do the job is the best one.[1]

Once an understanding has been achieved of the organization's goals and how the fund can support them, a series of practical questions must be answered. Among these are:

- Who will set policies and guidelines, including the written statement of purpose and the appropriate risk/return policy?
- Who at the organization will have day-to-day responsibility for the fund?
- Who will make investment decisions?
- What other services are required, and who will provide them?
- How will fund activities be monitored?

The answers to these questions depend on the type and size of the organization, the size of the fund, the importance of the fund to the success of the organization, and the availability of experienced personnel within the organization. Therefore, each of these decisions must be made in light of the characteristics and needs of the specific organization. However, before we discuss how these decisions can be made, it will be useful to summarize the services required to operate a fund.

---

[1]Peter F. Drucker, *Management: Tasks, Responsibilities, Practices* (New York: Harper & Row, 1974), p. 601.

SERVICES REQUIRED

Services required to operate a fund are asset allocation, investment management, safekeeping (custodial), recordkeeping, monitoring, legal, and accounting services. For pension funds, actuarial services are also required.

Asset Allocation Services
The fund must decide how to allocate assets among various asset categories, such as stocks, bonds, and real estate. This decision also impacts the fund's volatility, risk of loss due to inflation, and level of income. It also serves as the practical basis for deciding the kinds of investment managers that are required.

Investment Management Services
These activities involve choosing the specific securities that will be used to achieve a fund's investment aims. They include economic analyses and decisions to purchase and sell individual securities. Chapters 8 and 9 describe the available types of investment management services.

Safekeeping (Custodial) Services
If a fund owns securities directly, rather than through a commingled fund, it is necessary to have custodial facilities for physically maintaining possession of the securities and for collecting dividends and interest, redeeming matured securities, and effecting receipts and deliveries following purchases and sales. The custodian is also in an excellent position to account for all cash and securities movements in the fund and to provide other information on the fund.

Recordkeeping Services
Among the basic records required are cash or transaction statements and valuations.

Cash or transaction statements list all transactions affecting the cash balance (contributions and withdrawals, purchases and sales, and dividends and interests), as well as any contributions or distributions "in kind." Endowment funds are frequent recipients of gifts of securities. Corporations may contribute company stock to pension plans in order to save cash, or to profit-sharing plans in order to fulfill obligations to the plans. Such gifts in kind must be properly identified and accounted for to permit correct measurements of fund performance.

Cash statements should also contain beginning and ending cash balances. These statements should be produced quarterly or monthly. Typically the statements are in chronological order by transaction, though some custodians sort alphabetically by security. The latter system makes it easier to locate transactions in or income from particular securities, but they are more difficult to use when the history of a fund is being traced. Cash statements have historically been provided on a settlement date basis by banks and on a trade date basis by brokers and investment advisers. This distinction arises because industry practice calls for a period of time (usually five business days) between the time a stock or a corporate bond is sold and the time payment and delivery are made, and custodians usually view their obligation in terms of cash settlement, whereas investment advisers typically think in terms of the time when securities are purchased and sold. Fortunately, most major custodian banks now provide cash statements on a trade date basis, also.

A valuation is a listing of each asset in the portfolio, along with its market value, as of a point in time. The cash balance on the valuation should agree with the cash balance on the cash statement.

Additional statements include summaries of contributions and withdrawals, dividends, interest, purchases and sales (either by asset category, such as cash equivalents, bonds, and stocks, or in aggregate), and administrative fees. Private retirement funds also need to track brokerage fees paid (for party-in-interest reporting) and purchases and sales by security (to report transactions under the "3 percent rule"). This information may be provided by the custodian.

Monitoring Services

To be sure a fund is operating as it should, the sponsoring organization must monitor investment results, risk policies, the effect of the investment manager's discretionary activities on the fund, and the effectiveness of the custodial process. Chapters 10 to 17 discuss these activities in detail.

Legal Services

Legal advice is necessary for every fund at its inception, and further legal advice should be available when needed. In addition, a periodic review of trust documents should be made at least every three years to ensure that the changing circumstances of the fund and the evolution of the law have not made the documents obsolete.

For discussion of the legal factors that affect them, funds can be classified into three categories: public funds, ERISA funds, and other trusts.

Public funds are established by specific legislation (usually at the state level). This legislation sets forth the purpose of the trust, the organization of the trust, the responsible parties, and the benefits to be paid. The legislation may also establish risk policy guidelines by mandating the maximum percentage in equities.

ERISA is the dominant legislation for corporate and jointly trusteed retirement funds. Plan documents must be designed to conform to the strictures of this law, one of the most basic of which is that every plan must have written documents. Beyond the establishment of the plan there are numerous requirements for legal advice in complying with the 280 pages of ERISA. As case law develops, these requirements will continue to grow.

Other trusts, which consist largely of endowments, are governed by the laws of the states in which they were established.

Certified Audits

Funds covered by ERISA and public funds must be audited by public accountants, and good business practice requires audits in any event. Such an audit typically covers a reconciliation of the beginning and ending book (cost) values of a fund, with all contributions and purchases and sales that have been made during the period under examination. The audit also spot-checks for receipt of dividends and interest.

Actuarial Services

For defined benefit pension funds, the sponsoring organization makes a "reasonable" contribution in order to provide adequate funding to meet pensioners' needs. Determining the amount of the contribution requires analyzing the age, sex, salary levels, and probability of termination/disability/death/early retirement of employees; inflation; and the return on investments available in the marketplace. Chapter 18 deals with the actuarial process.

OPERATING A FUND

Setting Policies and Guidelines
After the purposes of the sponsor's organization and the ways in which the fund can support those purposes have been reviewed by the sponsor, the next step is to decide who should set policies and guidelines for the fund. The answer is that the board of directors or the board of trustees should establish policies. Since the fund is important to the sponsor for both financial and legal reasons, the highest authority in the sponsoring organization should have the final say about the fund's policies. The source of information upon which the directors or the trustees will act is a function of the size of the organization, the importance of the fund to the success of the organization, and the availability of experienced personnel within the organization. The larger the sponsor, the greater will be the effort made by staff members as opposed to that made by officers or directors. The greater the importance of the fund to the sponsor, the greater should be the involvement of the highest levels of the organization. Finally, the greater the availability of competent personnel within the organization, the greater will be its ability to supply services internally as opposed to going outside for them.

Writing a Statement of Purpose
Even for a fund not covered by ERISA it is vital to have a written statement of purpose describing what the fund is intended to do, how the fund relates to the objectives of the organization, and how the fund's goals are to be carried out. The statement of purpose should be as specific as possible, and it should be reviewed at least annually to ensure that it is still relevant and complete. The statement of purpose should be distributed to all board members and to all people and organizations that provide services to the fund. The statement of purpose can also serve as the basis for communications with employees about the reasons for the existence of the fund and the procedures for carrying out its functions.

Establishing a Risk/Return Investment Policy
This important subject is the basis for Chapter 3, and consequently it will not be discussed here.

Assigning Responsibility for Operating the Fund
In addition to assigning the responsibility for setting policies and guidelines, a person or a group should be assigned the responsibility for operating the fund on a daily basis. Within the four organization types the choices are:

1. Corporation
   a. Board of directors
   b. Subcommittee of the board of directors
   c. President
   d. Vice president of finance or a subordinate
   e. Vice president of administration or a subordinate
   f. Vice president of personnel or a subordinate
   g. Vice president of pension investing
   h. Outside consultant
2. Jointly trusteed funds
   a. Board of trustees
   b. Subcommittee of the board
   c. Administrator
   d. Outside consultant
3. Public funds
   a. Chief executive (governor, mayor, etc.)
   b. Administrator
   c. Finance officer
   d. Pension board
   e. Outside consultant
4. Charitable organizations
   a. Board of trustees
   b. Subcommittee of the board
   c. President
   d. Vice president of finance
   e. Outside consultant

The investment aspects of a fund are sufficiently complex and unrelated to the activities of most organizations that it is desirable to have someone within the organization charged with continued, long-term responsibility. Long-term responsibility is emphasized to express concern over the situation in which a stint of overseeing fund investment managers is part of a career path for financial managers. Although such experience is useful to both the organization and the financial manager, it is highly unlikely that the organization's goals will be very well supported by the fund if the person responsible for it is transferred to a new position just as he or she is finally beginning to understand the old one. Since it usually takes several market cycles to become familiar with the investment process, it is unlikely that an organization will derive much benefit from a fund administrator who occupies his or her position for only two or three years.

A second reason for assigning responsibility for the investment aspects of a fund on a long-term basis is that boards of directors or boards of trustees are usually ineffective at carrying out the policies they have adopted. Thus it is desirable to give an individual the authority and responsibility for implementing and monitoring such policies with regard to the fund. Further, since the composition of many boards changes rather rapidly, it is desirable to provide a measure of stability to the post. Thus it is preferable to assign continuing responsibility for the fund to a person who can accept this responsibility over a long period of time. It is then entirely appropriate to rotate subordinate personnel who can use the time spent working on the fund to broaden their experience within the organization.

Choosing Assets Types and Investment Managers
To implement the investment policy, security types and investment managers must be chosen. These important subjects are discussed in Chapters 4 to 8.

Other Services
Also required are custodial, recordkeeping, monitoring, legal, and accounting services. In addition, pension funds require actuarial services. Custodial services are described in detail in Chapter 17; monitoring services are treated in Chapters 10 to 14; and actuarial services are discussed in Chapter 18. As to legal and accounting activities, since sponsors do not appear to have problems in these areas, they will not be analyzed here.

CHAPTER 3

CHOOSING AN
INVESTMENT POLICY

A unique characteristic of risk is that it exists only in the future but can be measured only in the past.

The choice of an investment policy (a risk policy) for the fund is one of the most important and perplexing problems faced by fund sponsors and fund managers. Consequently this area will be discussed at considerable length, always in the context of two premises.

1. The purpose of the fund is to support the objectives of the organization sponsoring the fund.
2. The investment policy or risk/return posture of the fund should be such as to maximize the probability that the fund will achieve its goal of supporting the organization.

This chapter presents a framework for answering the question, "How much risk can the fund take?" by looking at the definitions of risk and diversification and then asking what sources of risk confront the fund, what the historic and theoretical risk/return relationships are, how much risk a particular fund can endure, what specific risk policy decisions must be made, and how those decisions should be made.

WHAT IS RISK?

The most widely *accepted* definition of risk is the chance and extent of loss. The most widely *used* definition of risk is variability of rate of return. The more uncertainty there is about the rate of return on an instrument over some future period, the greater is the risk. Suppose a sponsor wishes to measure return on a portfolio each quarter and after a number of quarters it wants to measure the risk the portfolio has taken. It can first look at 90-day Treasury bills, which have no risk in a 90-day period. That is to say, if it buys a three-month Treasury bill, it can then know exactly what its rate of return will be over the next three months. If it buys a five-year Treasury note, the return over the quarter is less certain, since interest rates may move up or down, with a corresponding impact on the security's value. A 20-year Treasury bond has even more uncertainty than the five-year note because the effect of changes in interest rates will be greater for a 20-year than for a 5-year instrument (see Chapter 4). A 20-year *corporate bond* has greater uncertainty than a 20-year *government bond* because the corporate bond may suffer from changes in its quality (i.e., the ability of the issuer to pay interest and principal on time) as well as changes in the general level of interest rates. Common stocks have even greater risk because they do not have a fixed maturity, and consequently their prices are affected by the full force of changes in economic conditions and specific company factors. Thus the uncertainty of rate of return is a useful measurement of risk.

The amount of risk a fund has taken can be quantified by calculating the rate of return of the fund or its sectors, finding an average rate of return for the whole time period, and measuring the variability of return around the average. The exact methods for doing this include mean absolute deviation, standard deviation, and variance. These techniques are described in the mathematics refresher (see Appendix).[1]

The most annoying limitation of this measurement is that it can only be made retrospectively. That is, until the rate of return is known, the variability of that return cannot be measured. One alternative is to assume that the future will be like the past and to use past variabilities as a measure of future variabilities. There is certainly merit to this approach, though surprises await the investor who relies too heavily upon it. Another alternative is to start with a base of past variabilities and then estimate the changes caused by new factors. For instance, a company which had a certain historic variability might have more variability in the future if the company's capitalization were changed such that the

---

[1]As an alternative to measuring variability against the average, it can be measured relative to a market index, as is the case in a beta model (see Chapter 12).

debt-to-equity ratio were greatly increased. A second limitation of the variability approach is that, traditionally, most investors have not viewed unexpectedly high rates of return as risk. That is, if a stock is expected to rise 10 percent and it actually rises 15 percent, many investors have trouble considering the extra 5 percent as risk. However, under the definition of risk as uncertainty of future value, this extra profit is risk. A third criticism of the variability notion is that significant risks within a company may cancel each other out, presenting the appearance that very little risk was taken, when in fact the opposite was true. An admittedly exaggerated example might be a situation in which the president of a mining company absconded with $100 million in assets at the same time that a new mine worth $100 million to the company was discovered.

Despite the limitations of variability as a measure of risk, it is hard to find a better one. Most other approaches to risk are intuitive, and hence unmeasurable, or they involve measurements which aim at the problem, but really do not address it directly. For instance, the quality of management and its impact on stock price are important, but they cannot be measured. The equity/bond ratio is an example of a measurement which aims at the problem but does not address it. If a sponsor does not know the risk level of stocks and bonds, knowing how much of its assets are in stocks as opposed to bonds does not give it a very precise measurement of risk.

Consequently the variability approach has gained considerable acceptance among sponsors, academics, monitoring organizations, and investors.

DIVERSIFICATION

Probably the most important development in investments in the last 25 years is the exploration of the idea that certain types of risk can be eliminated through diversification. An important corollary to this idea is the principle that return can be expected to increase only as an investor increases his undiversifiable risk, not as he increases his diversifiable risk.

Diversification is the spreading of assets among a variety of securities or among securities in a variety of markets with the goal of reducing risk in a portfolio without reducing expected return. A simple example demonstrates this principle. Let us assume there is one buyer of services, namely a government wanting to purchase arms, and two arms suppliers, both of which are exactly the same in all respects. Let us further assume that the government has decided to purchase arms from only one company and the successful company has been permitted to receive a return such that its value in the marketplace will triple. Since the company which does not get the contract will have no customers, it will go out of business and its stock will go to zero. Exhibit 3–1 shows the results to the shareholders of each arms supplier's stock if initially each stock was selling for $100 per share.

Thus an investor has an expected gain from buying either stock of 50 percent, consisting of a 50 percent chance of making $200 and a 50 percent chance of losing $100. However, although the expected gain is 50 percent, the actual outcome would be a gain of $200 or a loss of the entire $100 investment, depending on which stock was bought. A smart investor would recognize the opportunity for diversification. If it purchased both stocks it would guarantee that one of them would be wiped out completely and the other would triple in value. Since the odds of either company receiving the award are equal, it would buy equal amounts of each stock. It would then have a $100 gain on a $200 investment, or a return of 50 percent, with no risk. The result would be that the investor diversified away risk without reducing its expected rate of return.

EXHIBIT 3–1
Example of the Arms Suppliers

Company	Price per Share		Gain/(Loss) to Investors
	Initial	Final	
Winner	100	300	200
Loser	100	0	(100)

The *expected* results, which are obtained by considering not only the gains and losses of each outcome but also the probability of each outcome, are:

Company	Initial Price per Share	Probability of Winning	Gain from Selecting It	Expected Gain
Winner	100	.5	200	100
Loser	100	.5	(100)	−50

$50 expected return on $100 investment = 50 percent

The existence of the principle of diversification is the first point of this section. The second point is that not all types of risk can be diversified away. For instance, a stock market investor cannot diversify away stock market risk. It can own stocks which are less risky or more risky, but as long as it owns stocks it will have stock market risk. It can deal with this risk in four ways.

First, it can spread its assets among asset categories, such as stocks, bonds, and real estate. Second, it can purchase less-risky investments, such as stocks of well-established companies instead of emerging growth stocks. Third, it can purchase assets in different markets, for instance buying non-U.S. as well as U.S. stocks. Finally, it can diversify within each market and within the chosen risk level in order to eliminate all non-market risk, as in the example of the arms suppliers. It is important to understand the difference between the first and second and the third and fourth ways to reduce risk since the former involves a proportional reduction in return, whereas the latter implies no reduction in return for a reduction of risk. This distinction is described below. Techniques for measuring these risk factors are discussed here and demonstrated in Chapters 12 and 13.

By definition, each marketplace consists of many securities, each of which is affected by at least two sources of risk. The first source is market risk, and the second is nonmarket, or specific, risk. These risks are also sometimes referred to as nondiversifiable and diversifiable risks. In other words, looking at a stock market such as that in the United States, we recognize that the rate of return for a given stock can be impacted by factors within the company, such as management, earnings, and new products, and by market factors, such as the general level of the economy, interest rates, and inflation. Further, in any given period unexpectedly favorable or unexpectedly unfavorable things can happen to either the market or the individual stock. The investor in stocks cannot escape the unexpected effects of the economy, but it can minimize unexpected effects on individual stocks by buying many different stocks. Each time it adds another stock to the portfolio it hopes to take advantage of the arms supplier effect, where the return the investor expects to make is maintained, but the risk of failing to make the return is reduced.

A convenient method for describing the diversification level of an equity portfolio is to measure its correlation with the market (see Chapter 12). This is done by making a regression analysis of the rate of return of the portfolio relative to the rate of return of the appropriate stock market index. A portfolio which is 100 percent diversified would consist of all the stocks in the marketplace and would be weighted in the same proportion as are the stocks in the marketplace. That is, a security which represents 1 percent of the value of the entire stock market would have a 1 percent holding in the portfolio, and so on for each security. With a portfolio constructed in this manner, 100 percent of the fluctuation in the portfolio can be traced to fluctuation in the market and the portfolio would be said to be 100 percent diversified, or to have an R^2 of 100. At the other extreme, if the portfolio contained only one stock, the market risk would be a much smaller percentage of the total risk and the specific risk would be a much greater percentage. For a typical stock we might find that about 30 percent of the risk in the stock is market related and 70 percent is specific. In other words, 70 percent of the fluctuations in the stock are attributable to company-related matters, whereas only 30 percent are attributable to the market. It is clear that in this case the investor whose only holding is that stock has a significant exposure to the unexpectedly favorable or unfavorable factors which might affect the stock. If the investor is very confident it has information regarding the stock which the marketplace does not have, then it may wish to put itself in a position of owning only that stock and being 70 percent dependent on its information or judgment.

Most investors, and particularly institutions, find this approach to be unsuitably risky. These investors would be willing to sacrifice the exceptional return which might come from having one excellent stock for the knowledge that they would avoid the possibility of having a disaster from one very unsuccessful stock. They might then add a second stock to the portfolio, and find out that this increases the percentage of market risk from 30 percent to, say, 50 percent. By continuing to increase the number of stocks in the portfolio, and by weighting them in the same proportion as they appear in the marketplace, the investor will find his R^2 quickly rises to the 85 to 95 percent level. If the investor feels the market is essentially efficient, or the potential gains from being "right" are not worth the risk of being "wrong," it may establish a diversification policy which aims to have 100 percent of the risk in the portfolio as market risk. In this case, the investor is willing to sacrifice the opportunity for making extra risk-adjusted return for the comfort of knowing it will never have negative risk-adjusted return. (It also increases its expected return by reducing its transaction costs to practically zero.)

There are thus three ways to look at the issue of the amount of stock market risk in a portfolio: the percentage of equities versus fixed income or cash equivalents; the volatility level of the stocks owned; and the number of stocks owned, particularly stocks in different industries. The remaining issue concerning diversification is to note that the traditional idea that higher risk leads to higher return refers to market risk and not specific risk. This certainly makes sense in the example of the arms suppliers. In that case the market consists of only two stocks, each of which is identical to the other. It makes no sense for an investor who buys either of the companies, and thus increases its specific risk relative to that of an investor who buys both, to achieve a higher expected return than the investor who buys both. In other words, if the investor could diversify away its risk, it would not deserve to be paid for assuming that risk. If anything, it seems as though there should be a penalty for the investor's failure to act in its own best interests, and in fact there is, in the sense that it has increased its risk without a commensurate increase in the expected return.

There are many cases in which investors do deserve to have a higher rate of return because they are assuming risks which cannot be diversified away. An investor owning long-term bonds will find its total rate of return more variable than that of an investor owning short-term cash equivalents. No matter which bonds are owned and in what proportions, the investor will find that over any reasonable period the bond portfolio will be more variable in returns than the cash equivalents portfolio. There being no way to avoid or diversify away this risk without also reducing the expected return, the marketplace adjusts the rate of return on the riskier securities such that, in the long run, they provide a higher return than do less-risky assets. Another example would be a portfolio invested 60 percent in an index fund and 40 percent in Treasury bills. This portfolio is inherently riskier than a portfolio invested 50 percent in an index fund and 50 percent in Treasury bills. Because stocks are more variable than Treasury bills, the investor in the more aggressive portfolio is virtually certain to have a higher level of risk. For this it can expect, in the long run, a higher rate of return.

Having considered how to measure risk and having looked at diversification, we can now turn to an analysis of the sources of risk in portfolios.

SOURCES OF RISK

There are two primary sources of economic risk to investors—depression and inflation. They are at opposite ends of the economic spectrum. In *depression*, economic activity declines and prices usually decline as well. The value of stocks, real estate, and low-quality bonds falls when the economy slows significantly. During *inflation*, prices rise and purchasing power decreases. High-quality fixed-income instruments, especially long-term bonds, suffer as interest rates rise and purchasing power of the income they produce declines.

A variety of other risks face investors. *Portfolio* risk is the extent to which assets are diversified to protect against loss in any one area. *Liquidity* or marketability risk is the potential for an investor to suffer a decline from the perceived market value of a fund or of an asset because of the necessity of liquidating all or part of the fund at a bad time.

Assuming that investments are limited to those available on the planet Earth, the broadest source of risk is *world market risk*. Such risk is impossible to avoid. If some calamity befalls the Earth, there is no possible way to avoid the risk or to hedge against it. This is an important demonstration of the principle of diversification, or more correctly, the lack of diversification.

Because there is no hedge against world market risk, we can ignore it and move on to the next broadest category of risk, *international market risk*. The risks to an investor of investing in the markets of another country are political, currency, business, and liquidity (or interest rate) risks. The *political* risk is that the foreign government will either confiscate property, as in the case of the nationalization of U.S. industry by Cuba and Chile, or pass laws unfavorable to the investor, such as laws which prevent him from removing his capital or income from the country. The *currency,* or foreign exchange, risk is that the value of the foreign country's currency will decline, thus wiping out part of the value of the investor's capital. Foreign exchange risk to an outsider is the equivalent of inflation risk to an investor within a country. The third risk, *business* risk, refers to the fact that the general level of business within a country may decline precipitously, thus causing the value of investments to decline also. The fourth risk, *liquidity* risk, refers to a potential diminution in the value of capital caused by rising interest rates resulting from a lack of liquidity in the economy.

The *national market risk* to a fund investing in its own country consists of similar types of risk: political, depression, and liquidity. Political risk from the point of view of an investor inside a country can derive from confiscatory taxation or antiproductive regulation. Although the definition of a confiscatory level of taxation is a matter of opinion, it seems reasonable to suggest that, when the government takes a larger share than the producer of revenue, the level has reached confiscatory proportions. Another definition might include double taxation of income, such as is the case with corporate dividends received by taxpayers.

Examples of antiproductive regulations include price controls, rent controls, and rate fixing in various regulated industries. This is not to deny that there is value in some of these regulations but only to point out that these exercises of government power reduce the return to investors, and hence are a risk which must be recognized.

The risk of depression is widely understood. Few, if any, countries in the world are pursuing policies which will lead to depression in the customary way. That is, there is so much emphasis on stimulating economies that a depression induced by lack of demand is unlikely to occur. Given this stimulus, it is far likelier that investors will suffer loss from an inflation-induced lack of liquidity. That is, money will be created so rapidly that inflation will reach high rates. When this occurs, paradoxically, a shortage of liquidity also occurs, since money is needed to finance very expensive inventories, plant and equipment, residences, and so on. This increases interest rates and leads to a decline in security values because of the increase in returns available from alternative investments. Thus, if Treasury bill rates go from 6 percent to 8 percent, bonds and stocks become less attractive in a risk/return sense, and consequently yields on stocks and bonds must rise and their prices decline for the market to return to equilibrium. Inflation can also lead to a depression that results from lack of government stimulus. Interestingly, in countries with progressive tax rates, such as the United States, a high rate of inflation forces up income, and therefore people move into higher tax brackets even though their functions are the same in relation to the overall economy. Government receipts automatically rise and move the budget into balance or surplus. This decreases government stimulus and can lead to a falloff in demand.

Finally, inflation leads to greater borrowing to finance current consumption and to purchase physical assets, which in turn can lead to deflation as current income is required to pay debt service from past spending.

Portfolio risk consists of how assets are diversified and distributed among risk categories (as well as how the risk categories correlate with one another) and also of *marketability risk,* the risk that the investor will have to suffer a decline from the perceived market value of the fund because of the necessity for liquidating all or part of the fund at a bad time.

Two types of risk relate to factors affecting individual securities as opposed to factors affecting the general economy or a portfolio. These are security risk and company risk. *Security risk* refers to the attitude that the investment community takes toward a particular security, such as when growth stocks are in or out of favor, and also to the marketability risk of being unable to sell the security at or near the price of the last transaction. *Company risk* refers to traditional financial and business risks.

Financial risk should be distinguished from business risk since these types of risk can occur for opposite reasons. *Business risk* refers to the lack of viability of a product or of the company's position in the market for that product. In other words, if a company's main product is not viable, as was the case for buggy whips when the automobile became popular, the company is likely to fail. On the other hand, a product may itself be quite viable, but a company may find its market position insufficient to justify continuing to produce it. *Financial risk* for a company refers to the condition in which the company has insufficient cash to pay its bills. Interestingly, this condition can occur because of too few sales or too many, since a large backlog of sales means large amounts of money tied up in inventory and accounts receivable. Financial risk can also come about because general market conditions make money unavailable at a particular time for a company of a given credit risk.

RELATIONSHIP BETWEEN RISK AND RETURN

The question of the appropriate investment policy is frequently stated as the question of how much risk the fund can endure. Implicit in this question is the view, first, that the more risk a fund endures, the higher is the return that can be expected, and second, that a fund should seek the highest return by increasing risk to the maximum acceptable point. If return decreased as risk increased, the risk policy question would make no sense, as all funds would seek to have the lowest risk and the highest return. Nonetheless, before we blindly follow the "high risk equals high return" approach we should explore the risk/return relationship in more detail. Therefore, four questions are addressed in this section of the chapter:

1. Does return go up as risk goes up?
2. If so, over what period can we be reasonably certain this will occur?
3. What is the relationship between risk and return (that is, as risk doubles, does return go up by 10 percent, 50 percent, 100 percent, etc.)?
4. How stable are risk and return for each asset type, both absolutely and relatively among assets?

Looking at the Exhibit 3–2 results for the six 10-year periods from 1926 to 1985, we see information which can be used to address these questions. In answer to questions 1 and 2, it does appear that as risk rises, so does return. Within each period, risk rises as we move along the spectrum from short-term governments to small stocks. The exception is with the relationship between long-term governments and long-term corporates. While corporate bonds have been less volatile than government bonds at times, this may be due to the higher coupon (and hence shorter duration) of corporates, or just to anomalies associated with the construction of the indexes, rather than anything fundamental to the risk/return relationship.

However, return does not fall neatly in line with risk. In fact, return does not rise uniformly for any of the 10-year periods, although it does for the full 1926–91 period. We might thus conclude that return tends to rise with risk but that this relationship need not hold even for periods as long as 10 years.

Exhibit 3–2 provides little help in answering question 3 as to the specific relationship between risk and return, at least using annual returns and standard deviations as the measurement. For the 10-year time periods shown, it is not possible to discern any such specific relationship.

As to question 4, we have some useful information. Neither risk nor return is stable for any asset type, but the relationship between risk and asset type tends to hold true in every case. That is, for each period small company stocks are riskier than stocks in general, which are riskier than long-term bonds, which are, in turn, riskier than short-term securities.

This study is rather discouraging for those sponsors and investment managers who wish to be precise in controlling their portfolios. Results

EXHIBIT 3-2

Return and Risk for Five Asset Types

10-Year Period	Short-term Governments		Long-term Governments		Long-Term Corporates		Common Stocks		Small Companies	
	Return*	Standard Deviation	Return	Standard Deviation	Return	Standard Deviation	Return	Standard Deviation	Return	Standard Deviation
1926–35	2.0	1.7	4.7	6.3	7.1	4.6	5.9	33.5	0.3	57.5
1936–45	0.2	0.2	4.5	3.3	4.0	1.5	8.4	23.9	19.2	45.5
1946–55	1.1	0.5	1.3	3.7	1.9	2.7	16.7	18.1	11.3	22.4
1956–65	2.8	0.7	1.9	6.1	2.6	5.3	11.1	16.5	15.3	25.0
1966–75	5.6	1.4	3.0	7.3	3.6	8.7	3.3	19.7	4.0	37.8
1976–85	9.0	2.9	9.0	15.5	9.8	16.2	14.3	14.2	27.8	17.7
1986–91 (6 yrs)	6.8	1.1	12.0	9.9	12.1	8.2	15.9	13.7	8.3	27.3
1926–91 (66 yrs)	3.7	3.4	4.8	8.6	5.4	8.6	10.4	20.8	12.2	35.5

*Returns are geometric (compound) annual returns.

Data courtesy R. G. Ibbotson Associates, Inc.

in the real world appear to be too unstable to permit any degree of precision in portfolio control. However, it is useful to see the results and to recognize how variable they might be. Sponsors should take this into consideration when establishing their risk/return policies.

HOW MUCH RISK CAN A FUND ENDURE?

To answer this question we must know the estimated risk/return spectrum available in the marketplace (as shown in Exhibit 3–3) and the "utility" or risk/return preferences of the fund and of the people responsible for it.

EXHIBIT 3–3

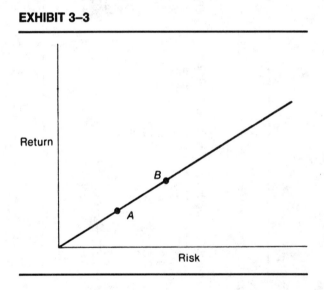

Assume Exhibit 3–3 shows the risk/return spectrum available as of a point in time for "efficient" portfolios (meaning that for any given level of risk there is no portfolio with a higher return and for any given level of return there is no portfolio with lower risk). Even for efficient portfolios it is not possible to say whether an investor should be at point *A*, point *B*, or any other point on the line. This is because each investor has a slightly different view of how much risk he can take. There is no clear-cut method for measuring the utility of an investor. However, the issues can be discussed and rational, if imprecise, policies can be developed.

There are two fundamental considerations in analyzing the fund's utility. These are:

1. How important is the success of the fund to the success of the organization?
2. What are the financial characteristics of the sponsor?[2]

A third consideration has been created by the particular provision of ERISA which enables the Pension Benefit Guaranty Corporation to attach 30 percent of a corporation's assets. This has the effect of reversing the risk policy wherein a corporation whose fund was in very bad shape would have normally taken very little risk, but now might take the opposite tack—namely, "Let's shoot the works"—because it is already suffering maximum exposure to the 30 percent attachment.

Since these factors differ in importance for each of the four major fund types, the factors will be discussed in relation to the type of fund.

Corporate Pension Plans

Since the passage of ERISA, every retirement plan has become important to the corporation, and benefit obligations must be met regardless of the financial characteristics of the sponsor. Nonetheless, it is useful to review how the factors discussed above impact the way in which a corporate fund's investment policy should be structured.

Importance of the Fund
The first consideration in determining the importance of the fund to the organization is to determine what percentage of its employees are covered by the plan and what the characteristics of those employees are (e.g., do they have special skills which would be very difficult to duplicate in the marketplace, as do airline pilots). Obviously, the higher the percentage of employees covered by the plan or the more important the types of employees covered, the more important the plan is to the success of the organization.

A second consideration in determining the fund's importance to the organization is the place of pension benefits in the hierarchy of total compensation. If, as is the case with some public utilities, a good pension is

---

[2]For endowment funds these two questions are interrelated since, if the sponsor is weak financially, the fund grows in importance, and vice versa.

given more weight in relation to current salary than would be the case in, say, the advertising industry, then the success of the fund is relatively more important to those public utilities.

It is suggested here that the more important the plan is to the organization's success, the less is the risk that can be tolerated. The greater the consequences of the fund's losing its value, the less is the risk that the fund should take.

Financial Characteristics of the Sponsor

The greater the financial strength of the corporation relative to the size of the fund, the greater is the fund's ability to bear risk. The most important measurements of the corporation's financial ability to bear risk within the fund are:

1. *Pretax income relative to the pension fund contribution.* The higher the percentage of the pretax income which flows to pension fund contributions, the more conservative the fund should be, since a risky posture might lead to large losses in the fund that would have to be made up with higher contributions, with a significant impact on the sponsor.

2. *The stability of pretax income.* The more stable the earnings of a company, the greater is its ability to bear risk. A highly cyclical company, on the other hand, may find it must increase pension fund contributions when earnings are low, again with a significant impact on the sponsor.

3. *Pretax income relative to unfunded vested liability.* The greater the liability relative to income, the more conservative the approach should be, since, again, unfavorable investment results would cause a large percentage of earnings to be diverted to elimination of the liability.

4. *Corporate assets relative to unfunded vested liability.* If the liability is eliminated through the liquidation of assets rather than paid off over time through income, the impact on the company can be measured by comparing the assets of the company to the liability of the fund. This possibility has become more significant since ERISA allows the Pension Benefit Guaranty Corporation to assume 30 percent of corporate net worth in the event of inability to meet pension obligations. If a company's assets are low relative to the fund liability, a conservative posture is implied.

Defined Contribution Profit-Sharing or 401(k) Plans

Unlike defined benefit pension plans, defined contribution plans do not serve as asset backing for contractual promises. Rather, they are pools of assets which are owned by individual employees. Whereas the investment policy of the defined benefit plan is designed to meet the risk/return profile of the sponsor, the defined contribution plan usually offers an array of investments which can be combined by the employee into a portfolio which is appropriate based on his or her own needs. These needs should include age, wealth, and attitude toward risk. Liquidity, which is important for investments held personally, is less significant for a profit-sharing plan in which the employee will not have access to funds until termination or retirement.

Age is important because younger employees are better able to withstand short- and medium-term volatility in their investments with the hope of making a higher return in the long run. They are able to do so because they have a longer time until retirement, and thus can outlast periods of economic or market decline. Also, assuming that additional investments will be made on their behalf, a decline in stock prices actually helps them buy at lower prices.

Wealthier investors are also able to take more risk than less-wealthy investors, since the former have a cushion which can be used to offset losses without leading to disastrous changes in lifestyle.

Even for investors of the same age or wealth, differences exist in willingness to take risk.

If profit-sharing plans offer a variety of asset types, investors have the tools to assemble portfolios which meet most of their needs. To the extent the sponsor is willing to supply educational information to the employee, the investment program can be even more successful.

Jointly Trusteed Funds

Importance of the Fund
This depends on the proportion of total compensation which the fund represents. For instance, a fund which provides retirement equal to 10 percent of a given employee's normal income could be viewed as less important than a fund which provides a pension of 40 percent of the same employee's nominal income. Presumably, the greater the importance of the pension benefit, the less the risk that can be tolerated, for if a risky

policy is pursued unsuccessfully, the risk is increased that the fund will not be able to pay benefits. If employees have been led to believe their pensions will be substantial, and have planned accordingly, this could have significant negative effects on them. Of course, the establishment of the Pension Benefit Guaranty Corporation has done much to reduce this risk.

Financial Characteristics of the Sponsor

Since the union itself is not providing benefits, we must look to the employer organizations which provide funding for the plan to assess the ability of the sponsor to take risk in the fund. This can be done in the manner described previously for corporations. However, since the employer organizations typically provide a specific contribution rather than guaranteeing a specific benefit, these organizations are concerned only with meeting their contributions and need not worry about the extra risk involved with guaranteeing a specific level of benefits, as is the case with corporate funds. Consequently, the financial characteristics of the employer organizations are less important in jointly trusteed funds than they are in corporate funds.

Public Funds

Importance of the Fund

Although the fund is likely to be an important benefit to employees, the importance of various public retirement plans to their respective members seems to be fairly standard. In most cases the plans are very important to the members, and this importance is especially great in the many contributory plans (the employee who is contributing to a fund is not likely to have much other savings).

Financial Characteristics of the Sponsor

In recent years this issue has taken on an importance it has not had since the days of the Great Depression. In the postwar period most people would have considered it almost unthinkable that a public fund might not be able to pay its pension benefits, but recent events have made this possibility more likely, though it is still quite remote. Factors that have led to this greater likelihood of default by public funds are the increased percentage of the work force employed by government (and thus the fewer remaining employees to support the public funds through their tax dollars), increased benefits to government employees, increased borrowing by public governments at all levels, and taxpayer revolts which could sharply reduce government tax revenues. The financial characteristics which determine a particular government's ability to meet its pension obligations are:

The percentage of the government's total revenues consumed by pension contributions.

The trend in this percentage.

The government's revenues relative to its unfunded vested liability.

The impact of inflation on the government's revenues.

Endowment funds

For endowment funds, the two measures of the ability of a fund to bear risk—that is, the importance of the fund and the financial characteristics of the sponsoring organization—are closely allied, since the charitable institution's work activities are directly supported by the endowment fund. Consequently, these two areas can be considered together for this category of fund. In measuring the importance of an endowment fund to the sponsoring organization, the questions to be asked are:

1. What percentage of the organization's income comes from the endowment fund's income?
2. Conversely, what percentage of the fund's income is required to meet this demand from the organization?
3. How large are the fund's assets relative to the organization's assets?
4. How large are the fund's assets relative to the organization's anticipated capital expenditures?
5. What impact would be felt by the organization if the fund's income increased or decreased by 10 percent? 20 percent? 50 percent? 100 percent?
6. What impact would be felt by the organization if the fund's assets increased or decreased by 10 percent? 20 percent? 50 percent? 100 percent?

The Investment Committee of the National Association of College and University Business Officers collects information on the investment

EXHIBIT 3–4
Endowment Characteristics Fiscal Year 1991
Endowment Spending Rules

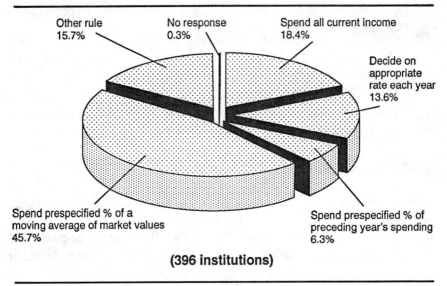

Other rule
15.7%

No response
0.3%

Spend all current income
18.4%

Decide on
appropriate
rate each year
13.6%

Spend prespecified % of a
moving average of market values
45.7%

Spend prespecified % of
preceding year's spending
6.3%

(396 institutions)

policies and results of the association's members. According to questionnaires submitted by 396 institutions, it appears that almost half of the respondents base spending on a moving average of market value. Only 18.4% of the institutions spend exactly their entire income. The survey also indicated that roughly 47 percent of the assets of private institutions were invested in equities. Exhibits 3–4 and 3–5 show spending rules and asset allocation of responding institutions.

THE UTILITY OF THE PEOPLE RESPONSIBLE FOR THE FUND

In viewing the issue of utility, or choosing an appropriate place on the risk/return spectrum, we typically think in terms of the investor, in this case the sponsoring organization. However, practical experience and knowledge of human nature dictate that we also consider the utility of the

EXHIBIT 3-5
Investment Pool Asset Allocation (%) as of June 30, 1991

Responding Institutions	Domestic Common Stock	Foreign Currency Common Stock	Domestic Fixed Income	Foreign Currency Fixed Income	Domestic Cash and Cash Equivs	Foreign Cash and Cash Equivs	Equity Real Estate
In aggregate							
Equal-weighted mean	47.1	2.4	34.5	0.8	10.1	0.0	2.2
Dollar-weighted mean	46.1	5.8	29.6	1.6	7.3	0.0	3.0
Median	48.8	0.0	33.2	0.0	7.7	0.0	0.0
By investment pool size (dollar-weighted mean)							
$25 million and under	47.3	1.3	37.2	0.4	10.0	0.0	1.8
Over $25 million to $100 million	46.3	2.4	35.8	0.8	10.0	0.0	1.9
Over $100 million to $400 million	51.7	3.5	29.0	1.0	8.4	0.0	2.9
Over $400 million	43.5	7.8	28.2	2.0	6.1	0.0	3.4
By type (dollar-weighted mean)							
Public	41.1	1.1	41.1	0.6	12.5	0.0	1.0
Private	47.4	7.1	26.5	1.8	5.9	0.0	3.6

EXHIBIT 3–5 (continued)

Responding Institutions	Mortgages	Faculty Mortgages	Venture Capital	Leveraged Buyouts	Oil and Gas	Distressed Obligations	Other
In aggregate							
Equal-weighted mean	0.4	0.3	0.6	0.2	0.3	0.2	0.9
Dollar-weighted mean	0.3	0.5	2.6	0.9	0.7	0.5	1.1
Median	0.0	0.0	0.0	0.0	0.0	0.0	0.0
By investment pool size (Dollar-weighted mean)							
$25 million and under	0.9	0.1	0.2	0.0	0.0	0.0	0.8
Over $25 million to $100 million	0.6	0.3	0.4	0.4	0.4	0.2	0.9
Over $100 million to $400 million	0.1	0.5	1.1	0.4	0.4	0.3	0.7
Over $400 million	0.3	0.5	3.9	1.3	1.0	0.6	1.4
By type (Dollar-weighted mean)							
Public	0.1	0.6	0.7	0.0	0.4	0.2	0.6
Private	0.4	0.4	3.2	1.1	0.8	0.5	1.3

Source: 1991 NACUBO Endowment Study Executive Summary. Prepared by Cambridge Associates, Inc. National Association of College and University Business Officers.

people responsible for the fund. A simple example clearly demonstrates why this should be done. Assume you are the pension director for a company which has an extraordinarily high return on sales and on equity; is not labor-intensive, and hence allocates only a small percentage of its income to the pension fund; and has been informed by the company actuary, Crystal, Ball & Co., that the fund will have a net positive cash flow for at least the next century and the fund currently has assets in excess of its vested liabilities. You are preparing an extensive memorandum indicating that the company has an enormous ability to bear risk in the fund and consequently should pursue an aggressive policy in order to achieve a very high rate of return in the long run, thus making it possible to either reduce contributions or increase benefits. Your superior, the company president, not known for mincing words, informs you he wants no possible embarrassment from pension fund investment, and "You will be removed from your position if the fund achieves a negative rate of return for any successive two-year period." Clearly, in these circumstances your perception of the fund's ability to bear risk will be changed considerably by the utility of the president and by your own utility, which may be dominated by your desire to retain your job.

Given a recognition of this phenomenon, it is interesting to consider the factors that affect the utility of the various parties to the pension fund.

> *Member of Board of Directors:* Since I'm nearing retirement age, any benefit to the company achieved from having an aggressive policy will be achieved long after I am gone. Therefore, I will tend toward a conservative policy to eliminate any problems that might disrupt my last years with the company.

> *Pension Director:* In terms of progressing within this company, the chances of helping my career by taking big risks in the fund seem to be much less than the chances of hurting my career by being unsuccessful in a high-risk policy. This leads me to be conservative. However, if I do an especially good job here, other, larger companies might hire me to oversee their funds. Perhaps I should be more aggressive.

> *Investment Manager:* If I am not at all imaginative in running this fund, the chances are I will keep the business and get my share of the estimated 8 percent per year in investment return. However, if

I take more risks, I may be able to build a name for myself and my organization and attract more new clients.

Actuary: If I am conservative in my assumptions, the company will probably not have to increase its contributions over and above my estimates, and plan participants will be highly likely to receive their benefits. On the other hand, the company may wish to reduce its current contributions in order to increase its net income, which can be done if I choose less-conservative assumptions. Perhaps my firm will be replaced if I am not aggressive enough.

Company Shareholder: I don't want the company to run afoul of ERISA or have to make excessive contributions due to poor investment results. However, the greater the return we can get on fund assets, the lower the contributions will be and hence the higher my stock price and dividends.

Although the consideration of these utility factors is potentially embarrassing ("After all, it is the sponsor and the fund for which we are presumably concerned"), nonetheless failure to consider them can be disastrous for the fund since a supposedly long-term policy may be abandoned at just the wrong time. For instance, suppose a professional analysis suggests that a fund can bear a high level of risk and therefore should be invested largely in equities, and the sponsor goes along with this recommendation even though the conservative tendencies of its officers make them very uncomfortable about the plan. If the stock market were to decline precipitously, the board of trustees might liquidate the equity portfolio near the bottom of the market and opt for short-term, fixed-income investments just when it should be doing the opposite. Conversely, a conservative fund might sell its bonds at the top of the market to move into equities that support a board of trustees's bias toward more aggressive securities.

GENERAL PHILOSOPHY

The preceding discussion of utility was intended to be fairly objective. That is, the discussion implicitly assumed that two organizations with the same characteristics would choose very similar risk policies. However, it is possible to take another step forward in the analysis of utility and to consider that investors may come to different conclusions as to the appropriate policies even when the facts are identical. Perhaps a suitable analogy is that of two people viewing the same glass of water, one of whom suggests it is half full while the other insists it is half empty. The comparable investment philosophies can be described as follows:

Philosophy 1: Maximum return for a given level of risk. The responsible parties should analyze the fund's ability to bear risk and attempt to find investments which will achieve the highest level of return consistent with this risk level.

Philosophy 2: Minimum risk for a given level of return. The responsible parties should estimate the required return the fund needs in order to meet its obligations, then find those securities which have the lowest risk consistent with this rate of return.

A sponsor actuated by philosophy 1 might analyze the historic returns and risks of various asset types, further analyze its cash flow needs, and decide the highest level of risk the fund can endure without disrupting the sponsor's earnings. Once this level of risk has been identified, securities are chosen which will have high rates of return consistent with this risk policy. Philosophy 2 is more conservative. Rather than viewing risk as the dominant force, it looks at the minimum return which is adequate for the fund's needs and on that basis attempts to find appropriate securities. Both of these philosophies are defensible. The decision as to which course to follow may reflect the general philosophy of the organization, a specific philosophy applied to the fund, or the utility of the participants.

CHAPTER 4

CHOOSING
ASSET CATEGORIES

Do what you will, the capital is at hazard.[1]

Once the sponsor has explored the question of the appropriate investment or risk policy for the fund, it must turn to the issue of what types of securities have the appropriate characteristics for the investment policy chosen. For this analysis it is helpful to divide asset types into two broad categories, marketable and less marketable, and then within each category to list asset types in order of risk, starting with the least risky. Within each broad category a natural division occurs between fixed-income investments and equity investments.

Fixed-income investments represent loans by the holder (in this case the fund) to the issuer, which is usually a corporation or a government. The issuer is required to pay a stated amount of interest and to return the principal at a stipulated time. If it does not, the holders of the fixed-income obligation can force the issuer into bankruptcy. Equity investments, on the other hand, represent ownership of the issuer. Equity investments can be issued by corporations only, since ownership in governments is not sold. Holders of equity securities are not entitled to specific income or to a return on their investment; rather, they participate in the success of the corporations through dividends and capital appreciation.

---

[1]From *Harvard College* v. *Amory* (1830), the Massachusetts court case which established the "prudent man" rule. In that case the court held that all securities have risk and that stocks are not de facto inappropriate trust investments. The quotation is from Harvey E. Bines, *The Law of Investment Management* (Boston: Warren, Gorham, & Lamont, 1978), pp. 1–32.

MARKETABLE SECURITIES

Although all assets are marketable to some extent, there are wide differences in the liquidity of various asset types. Since the characteristics of the fund will determine its need for liquidity, and hence marketability, it is useful to describe the liquidity spectrum of asset types.

Fixed Principal

Cash

Cash is the most marketable asset since it has already been turned into the medium of exchange which defines liquidity. In terms of rate of return, cash has a zero percent return and no risk is associated with that return. That is, an investor who holds cash will always have a zero percent rate of return. His only concerns are the stability of the institution in which the cash is deposited and the inflation risk which impacts all monetary assets.

Cash Equivalents

This category of assets includes all short-term securities which can be quickly converted into cash. These include U.S. Treasury bills, federal funds, certificates of deposit, and commercial paper.

U.S. Treasury Bills

The instrument with the greatest safety of principal is the short-term U.S. Treasury bill, since it is guaranteed by the U.S. government, which has a virtually unlimited ability to create funds to pay its debts. Treasury bills are offered in units of $10,000 face amount and are auctioned by the Treasury every week.

The maturities of Treasury bills range from 91 to 364 days. Treasury bills, like many other types of cash equivalents, are sold at a ''discount.'' This means the return to the holder comes, not from interest payments, but from the difference between the price paid and the face value at maturity. This rate is not the same as the true rate of return or the bond equivalent rate of return (consult Appendix 4-A for a clarification of these distinctions).

Federal Funds

These are one-day loans made between banks. Each bank is required to have a certain percentage of its deposits backed up by cash or by its own deposits at one of the Federal Reserve banks. Since some banks have deficiencies and others excesses, loans are made between banks for short periods of time.

Repurchase Agreements

Dealers in securities, especially U.S. government securities, have huge inventories and thus have huge financing requirements. Much of this financing is done through repurchase agreements, or repos. Repos are short-term arrangements under which dealers sell securities and agree to buy them back for a specified price. Since the buyer has a known cost and selling price, it can calculate its rate of interest; thus repos are in effect short-term investments. Because the securities underlying repos are very high quality, their risk is quite low.

Certificates of Deposit

These are, in effect, the savings accounts of corporations and other large investors. Banks needing funds for lending purposes will pay interest at specified rates on deposits of $100,000 or more. Subject to certain rules, the banks can make any arrangement they want as to size, interest rates paid, and maturities.

Commercial Paper

Commercial paper represents the corporate counterpart of certificates of deposit. Whereas banks attract funds by paying interest on certificates of deposit, corporations, particularly those which finance purchases by their customers, issue commercial paper. Most issuers of commercial paper sell it through dealers, though a few very large corporations are able to issue it directly.

Fixed Income

Notes

Whereas the typical maturity on a cash equivalent is one year or less, fixed-income obligations with a maturity of between 1 and 10 years at the time of issuance are called notes. Unlike cash equivalents, notes usually bear a coupon, and consequently they are really just shorter-term bonds.

U.S. Treasury Notes
The highest quality notes are those issued by the U.S. Treasury, because these notes are free from default risk.

U.S. Government Agency Notes
These notes represent an instrument of very high quality since, even though they are not directly guaranteed by the U.S. government, there is a strong presumption the federal government will not allow its agencies to go into bankruptcy.

Corporate Notes
The quality of corporate notes depends on the creditworthiness of the issuer. Creditworthiness is a function of the magnitude of assets relative to liabilities, profitability, the stability of earnings, and the degree to which earnings have been committed to pay other debts.

Bonds
Bonds are frequently divided into three categories: those secured by specific assets, such as mortgage bonds; "unsecured" bonds, which are secured by the general credit of the issuer and are more properly known as debentures; and convertible bonds, which are discussed under equity instruments. A further distinction can be drawn between bonds which are taxed and municipal, or tax-free, bonds.

Mortgage Bonds. To increase the quality rating of a bond, and thus enable the issuer to pay a lower interest rate, some bonds are secured by specific assets of a corporation. Such mortgage bonds are most commonly found in the public utility field, secured by such assets as pipelines. Although certain types of assets can be removed from the parent corporation in case of default, most people feel that if, for instance, a pipeline is of no use to the corporation transporting natural gas, it will certainly be of no use to the investor. Consequently, the risk for mortgage bonds is not a great deal lower than the risk for straight debentures.

Debentures. These bonds are sometimes called unsecured, but they are more appropriately recognized as general obligations of the issuer, and they represent a claim on all assets which are not specifically mortgaged. They are junior to tax liens and to mortgage bonds (but only with respect to the pledged assets).

Subordinated Bonds. These bonds are issued with the specific agreement that other creditors, such as banks, have higher priority in obtaining the company's assets in case of default. For surrendering part of their security, investors, of course, demand a higher rate of return on such bonds. In the junk bond binge of the late 1980s, an extraordinary variety of interest payment patterns was created. In addition to normal semiannual payment, bonds were issued as zero coupon discount bonds such that the appreciation on the bond between issue date and maturity created the desired rate of return; "payment in kind" or PIKs, wherein the interest was paid in additional bonds for a period of time; adjustable rate, in which the interest rate was changed periodically, or reset bonds, in which the coupon rate was to be changed one or more times such that the interest could be increased in order to be sure the bonds sold near par; and increasing interest rates, which provide encouragement for the borrower to pay the bonds off quickly. Other alternatives not impacting interest rates include put features, which allow the investor to force the issuer to repurchase the bonds under certain circumstances.

Mortgage-Backed or Pass-Through Securities
The mortgage market, which is enormous, has traditionally suffered from lack of liquidity and, at least with respect to residential mortgages, a unit size which was too small to interest institutional investors. It was found that mortgages could be pooled and securities issued against them, thus providing both liquidity and size to institutional investors. Included are Ginny Maes, Freddie Macs, Fanny Maes, and private pools (issued respectively by the Government National Mortgage Association, Federal Home Loan Mortgage Corporation, and Federal National Mortgage Association). Ginny Maes are obligations of the U.S. government, Fanny Maes and Freddie Macs are guaranteed by government-sponsored corporations, but are not government guaranteed, and private pools have no guarantee other than that of each mortgage borrower. These securities are frequently called pass-throughs since the payment on the mortgage passes through to the investor. As with most mortgages, the payment is made monthly and consists of both principal and interest.

Municipal, or Tax-Free, Bonds
Bonds issued by the various states, municipalities, and certain political subdivisions thereof are exempt from taxation by the federal government and by the state in which they are issued. These bonds bear relatively low

coupons because investors in high tax brackets find they have a higher after-tax return by buying, for instance, a 6 percent tax-free bond than by buying an 8 percent taxable bond. This would be true for any investor in a tax bracket greater than 25 percent. A pension or endowment fund which pays no taxes on current income would be one-third better off if it owned the taxable bond than if it owned the municipal bond.

Equity Securities

There are four types of equity securities: preferred stocks, common stocks, securities having both the privilege to buy common stock and some right to income, and those with privileges to buy (or sell) common stock without any right to income.

Preferred Stock
This category of investment can be called either fixed income or equity. In terms of priority in liquidation, preferred shareholders come after debenture holders and before common stock owners. From the point of view of the investor, preferred stock is more like a fixed-income investment than an equity investment, since, assuming the corporation is not in default, regular dividend payments are received. Further, the holder of nonconvertible preferred stock has no right to extra rewards should the corporation be particularly successful. Preferred stock is not usually a good investment for portfolios which do not pay taxes on their income, because corporations bid up the price of preferred stocks (and thus reduce the yields of such stocks) in order to take advantage of the Internal Revenue Code provision which allows corporations to deduct from their taxable income 70 percent of the income they receive through dividends from other corporations. (Since corporations pay dividends out of after-tax earnings, it would be highly unfair for the corporation holding preferred shares in another corporation to pay taxes on income from preferreds.) Because of this tax advantage, corporations bid up preferred stock prices to a point at which the yields are generally too low to be attractive to tax-exempt portfolios. Thus, virtually all tax-exempt institutions find it desirable to avoid preferred stocks.

Convertible Debentures
The least risky type of equity investment is the one which carries with it a fixed obligation to pay income and a promise to return the original

investment (in dollars) at some time in the future. This type of investment is the convertible debenture or bond. Convertible bonds carry an interest rate and a maturity date, as do other bonds, but they also have a conversion right which allows the holder to exchange them for a certain number of shares of stock during a certain period of time. In return for this privilege, which can be quite valuable if the underlying stock rises dramatically, the holder of convertible debentures sacrifices one or more of three things. First, the interest rate is usually lower than that of other debt instruments of the company. Second, the debentures are usually subordinated to other debt, so that in the event of bankruptcy other creditors have a superior claim. Third, a conversion premium is usually built into the conversion rate. For instance, a $1,000 bond might be convertible into only $900 worth of stock if the conversion took place on the date the bond was issued. The interest rate level and the amount of the premium are determined at the time of the offering, based on the supply of and demand for the issue.

Convertible Preferred Stock

Convertible preferreds, like convertible bonds, carry both a fixed return and the right to participate in the success of the corporation. Unlike convertible bonds, convertible preferreds represent an equity interest in the corporation, and therefore are junior to all bonds. Further, the right to receive dividends on convertible preferreds is not contractual, and if a corporation's board of directors feels it is not wise to pay such dividends it can choose to withhold them. (In this case the corporation cannot pay dividends on its common stock.) For the reasons given above, convertible preferreds, like straight preferreds, are typically not purchased by tax-exempt institutions.

Common Stock

This asset category represents the basic unit of ownership of the corporation. The holders of common stock are the owners of the corporation. They have rights to dividends only to the extent that such dividends have been earned by the corporation and declared by the board of directors. No fixed return accrues to the common shareholder, and in the event the corporation is liquidated, his or her right to the corporation's assets has the lowest priority. On the other hand, there is theoretically no limit to the benefit which the common shareholder can derive if the corporation is successful.

Warrants, Options, and "Rights"

These types of securities represent neither loans to the corporation nor ownership in it, but rather the privilege of buying a certain number of shares at a fixed price for a given period of time. The three types have a great deal of similarity with one another, with only nuances relating to the circumstances under which they were issued or their life span determining the designation applied to them. Warrants are typically sold in connection with offerings of debentures, and they become "detachable" from the debentures at some point after issuance. The combination of debenture and warrant provides an instrument very similar to a convertible bond. Options are issued by investors seeking to gain income or to reduce the risk of their portfolios. (Chapter 9 has a section detailing how option investing can impact portfolios.) "Rights" are issued in connection with "rights offerings." Corporations desiring to raise additional equity capital sometimes allow existing shareholders the right to purchase additional shares. For instance, a corporation whose stock is selling for 20 and which desires to add about 4 percent to its equity capital base may allow each shareholder to purchase one share at 18 for each 25 shares owned. In this case the rights would sell for approximately 8 cents each, as the holder of 25 such rights would be able to buy one share at a $2 discount (25 × $0.08 = $2). Warrants frequently do not expire for a number of years; options typically expire in three to nine months; and rights expire about two weeks after their issuance.

Futures

Whereas the outright purchase of a security involves direct and immediate ownership, an option or a warrant gives the holder the right to purchase the security at a given price within a limited period of time. A future represents a combination of the two. It is a direct purchase at a specific price, but payment is not made immediately; it is deferred until some future date.

It is possible to combine these instruments and have options on futures and futures on options.

LESS-MARKETABLE SECURITIES

The categories of less-marketable securities can include any of the security types discussed under marketable securities plus most real estate and natural resource investments.

Fixed-Income

Privately Placed Notes and Bonds

Marketable notes and bonds are offered to the public through a formal prospectus indicating that the securities have been registered with the Securities and Exchange Commission in Washington. The registration process attempts to ensure that investors are informed of all the relevant facts before they risk their money. Not surprisingly, the registration process is costly and time-consuming. This process can be avoided if the securities to be sold are offered to a limited number of sophisticated investors rather than to the public in general.

To avoid the registration process, corporations are willing to pay a higher interest rate on the bonds they sell. On the other hand, certain investors with long time horizons and large portfolios are willing to sacrifice the ability to sell their holdings in the marketplace in order to receive a higher yield on their investments. Consequently, the privately placed security has achieved a niche in the investment portfolio of many insurance companies. In recent years banks and pension funds have also increased their activity in this type of investment. Typically, private placements carry an interest rate $\frac{1}{4}$ to $\frac{1}{2}$ percent (25 to 50 basis points) above that available on public issues. They also usually provide for the repayment of substantial portions of the issue before maturity.

Mortgages

These fixed-income securities are, in a sense, privately placed mortgage bonds. That is, a borrower convinces a lender to provide funds under certain terms and conditions, one of which is that a specific piece of real estate is pledged as collateral for the loan. Unlike mortgage bonds, however, normal real estate mortgages do not have the full faith and credit of the issuer behind them, but generally only allow the lender to take possession of the collateral in case of default.

Equity Investments

Letter Stock

This type of equity, issued in the speculative market of the late 1960s, represents a method of securing equity capital without going through the SEC registration process. The purchaser of the stock signs an agreement, or "letter," indicating he has purchased it for investment and not for resale. A legend to this effect is placed on the stock certificates in order to alert the transfer agent not to effect a transfer from the holder to a second holder without being assured it is proper to do so. Letter stock developed a tainted reputation, through no fault of its own, when some mutual fund investment managers purchased letter stock at a discount from the price of the publicly traded shares, then immediately valued the letter stock at full market value in calculating the mutual fund's net asset value. This led to immediate increases in the net asset value of the funds they managed, and hence to artificial performance results.

Equity Real Estate
The ownership of land or of improvements thereon is another potential investment for tax-exempt portfolios. Such investments can be made directly or through commingled funds. Some caution must be exercised in the direct ownership of income-producing real estate to avoid the "unrelated business taxable income" provisions of the Internal Revenue Code. These provisions suggest it is appropriate for a tax-exempt fund to invest money and pay no taxes on its income, but that it is not appropriate for such a fund to operate a business in competition with taxable organizations. UBTI is also created through "debt financing," that is, income which is created by financial leverage, or borrowing, such as through a mortgage or in a brokerage margin account.

Natural Resources and Royalties
It is possible for funds to invest in natural resources such as oil and gas.

Royalties. Rights to receive royalties from patents, copyrights, or oil and gas production can also be sold to investors. These rights can be sold directly or, in the case of oil and gas, through trusts. A royalty trust is created by an energy production company which gives or sells interests in its properties to a trust. These interests can be related to the gross revenue or net profits of the properties. They can also be preexisting rights to royalties which were purchased by or granted to the production company. Chapter 6, "Alternative Investments—Energy," provides further information on how energy investments can be structured.

NON-U.S. INVESTMENTS

Six arguments can be made in favor of diversification outside the investor's own country.

First, there are opportunities abroad which are not available in the United States. For instance, diamonds, gold, certain metals, and, increasingly, oil and gas are either nonexistent in the United States or more abundant overseas. Second, there are numerous fine companies outside the United States, many of which deserve consideration by U.S. investors. Third, the long-term economic outlook for the United States may be less attractive than it was in the past. This may be because of a diminishing supply of energy and other natural resources, or a lower level of capital investment.

Fourth, investments can be made outside one's country to avoid severe economic or political disaster in the sponsor's own country. Fifth, investments denominated in foreign currencies provide a hedge against inflation. Given a high level of inflation in the sponsor's country, domestic stock and bond investments may suffer severe losses of purchasing power. To the extent that other countries have lower inflation rates, their currencies will tend to be much stronger than that of the sponsor's country. Of course, this process can work to the detriment of the sponsor as well as to its benefit. The sixth argument in favor of foreign diversification is that it permits a given level of return to be earned with less risk. This can be seen from the example in Exhibit 4–1. In this case it is assumed that investments can be made in two countries, in both of which an identical rate of return can be earned (10 percent) and an identical variability of return exists (±5 percent). On the surface it would seem to make no difference to the investor in which country it places its funds, since both countries have the same return and risk. The key question is, "Are the markets of the two countries highly correlated, or do they move independently?" If the two markets are perfectly and positively correlated (i.e., they move exactly together), it makes no difference in which country the investor places its assets. In this case the returns in both countries would be the same in each period. The ideal situation, however, would be one in which the two markets had positive expected returns but were negatively correlated (i.e., they tended to move in opposite directions). In this case, when one market is declining, the other would be rising, and the fund could achieve average (+10 percent) results by investing half its assets in each of the two countries. Average

Exhibit 4–1

Condition 1: Perfect positive correlation (identical results)

	Year 1	Year 2	Year 3	Cumulative (not compounded)
Country A	10%	5%	15%	30%
Country B	10	5	15	30
Investor	10	5	15	30

Investor return = 10 percent each year with risk of ±5 percent

Condition 2: Perfect negative correlation (opposite results)

	Year 1	Year 2	Year 3	Cumulative (not compounded)
Country A	10%	5%	15%	30%
Country B	10	15	5	30
Investor	10	10	10	30

Investor return = 10 percent each year with risk of ±0 percent

results would also be achieved when the two markets reversed their roles. Consequently, the return would be very stable around the average return expected, and it would be very high relative to risk. Examples of this phenomenon are shown in Exhibit 4–1 under the assumption that each market returns 5 percent, 10 percent, or 15 percent in each year (i.e., an average return of 10 percent ±5 percent) and 50 percent of the available funds are placed in each market at the beginning of the period.

There are two common arguments against investing outside the United States. The first is that U.S. pension funds are investing on behalf of workers in the United States and, since pension funds are a major source of the capital which is required to stimulate the growth of jobs, this money should be kept here. The second argument is that non-U.S. investments have currency risk as well as investment risk. Since the liabilities of most pension funds are denominated in dollars, the assets should also be denominated in dollars. Although both of these arguments have merit, it is likely that the continued globalization of investments will attract U.S. investors of most types.

As to the appropriate amount to invest in non-U.S. assets, there is no set of rules which can be followed. However, it is instructive to compare the values of assets outside the United States with those of assets inside the United States in order to gain an idea of the general

Exhibit 4–2
Total Market Capitalization

	1981		1991	
	$ Billion	Percent of Total	$ Billion	Percent of Total
Austria	1.6	0.1%	16.6	0.3%
Belgium	7.8	0.3%	39.9	0.7%
Denmark	4.4	0.2%	28.8	0.5%
Finland	(not incl.)		9.0	0.2%
France	37.5	1.7%	199.8	3.4%
Germany	62.5	2.8%	224.7	3.8%
Italy	24.0	1.1%	75.7	1.3%
Netherlands	20.0	0.9%	100.5	1.7%
Norway	2.3	0.1%	14.2	0.2%
Spain	16.7	0.7%	69.7	1.2%
Sweden	17.0	0.8%	51.7	0.9%
Switzerland	40.8	1.8%	115.3	1.9%
U.K.	176.8	7.9%	622.7	10.5%
EUROPE	411.4	18.4%	1,568.6	26.5%
Australia	57.8	2.6%	93.3	1.6%
Hong Kong	42.3	1.9%	66.3	1.1%
Japan	402.7	18.1%	1,688.4	28.5%
New Zealand	(not incl.)		100.5	1.7%
Singapore/Malaysia	34.8	1.6%	42.8	0.7%
EUROPE, AUSTRALIA, FAR EAST	949.0	42.6%	3,559.9	60.0%
Canada	104.1	4.7%	153.4	2.6%
Mexico	9.6	0.4%	(not incl.)	
South Africa Gold	22.2	1.0%	9.4	0.2%
U.S.	1,145.4	51.4%	2,206.6	37.2%
WORLD	2,230.3	100.0%	5929.3	100.0%

Source: Morgan Stanley/Capital International

proportions of the various securities markets. This information is provided in Exhibit 4–2.

Non-U.S. Fixed-Income Securities

Investment in non-U.S. bonds usually is in government-guaranteed instruments. This is because most U.S. investors prefer to limit credit risk, especially in markets where they may be unfamiliar with corporate or

Exhibit 4–2 (*continued*)
Market Capitalization vs. Gross Domestic Product

	1991	
	Cap Weighted	*GDP Weighted*
Austria	0.3%	1.1%
Belgium/Luxembourg	0.7%	1.3%
Denmark	0.5%	0.9%
Finland	0.2%	0.7%
France	3.4%	8.4%
Germany	3.8%	9.9%
Italy	1.3%	6.3%
Netherlands	1.7%	1.9%
Norway	0.2%	0.7%
Spain	1.2%	3.3%
Sweden	0.9%	1.3%
Switzerland	1.9%	1.5%
U.K.	10.5%	6.8%
EUROPE	26.5%	44.1%
Australia	1.6%	1.8%
Hong Kong	1.1%	0.4%
Japan	28.5%	17.6%
New Zealand	1.7%	0.2%
Singapore/Malaysia	0.7%	0.2%
EUROPE, AUSTRALIA, FAR EAST	60.0%	64.3%
Canada	2.6%	3.2%
Mexico	(not incl.)	(not incl.)
South Africa Gold	0.2%	—
U.S.	37.2%	32.7%
WORLD	100.0%	100.0%

Source: Morgan Stanley/Capital International, Boston International

bank issuers. Also, in most countries, financing for private borrowers is conducted primarily through banks, thus limiting the supply of corporate paper.

The principal source of risk in non-U.S. bonds is credit risk. Investors who limit their activities to the major countries, with developed industrial bases and a history of debt repayment, should have little credit risk. The primary risk then becomes currency risk. This risk can be dealt with in a number of ways. The sponsor can ignore currency, expecting long-run fluctuations to balance themselves out. It can hedge all or a portion of the risk, either by hedging each position or by taking a portfolio approach and hedging the major risks. This can be done by thinking of currencies as a separate asset category and having long or short currency positions in order to reduce volatility. This approach is similar to the one described as "optimization" in Chapter 7, "Creating Portfolios." Finally, it can adopt a reactive approach, and hedge after a certain loss has been incurred.

GUARANTEED INVESTMENT CONTRACTS

Guaranteed investment contracts (GICs) are insurance policies which provide an investment return with some insurance benefit. They are normally general obligations of the insurance company and as such are broadly analogous to unsecured promises of any organization, although some insurers offer GICs backed by dedicated pools of assets and an additional guaranty by the insurance company.

GICs have grown dramatically in recent years, primarily because of their popularity in profit-sharing plans. This popularity arises from four factors: perceived safety, benefit responsiveness, book value accounting, and the respectable rate of return over Treasury investments.

Safety is perceived to be high because insurance companies, as regulated entities, are required to back their obligations with assets. Historically, insurance company failure has been rare, and state insurance guarantee funds provide additional, though limited, backup.

Benefit responsiveness is the contract provision which permits the holder to receive funds at book value upon death, disability, retirement, or, under specified conditions, for reallocation to other investment options within the plan. GICs which are not benefit-responsive are very hard to distinguish from debentures, and thus have few distinctions from privately placed notes.

Book value accounting allows GICs to be carried at cost plus accrued interest, although the Financial Accounting Standards Board is reviewing this practice. However, since benefit-responsive GICs have cash flows at book value, a strong case can be made that book value is market value.

The greater *return* achieved is normally a spread of 50 to 100 basis points above that of U.S. Treasury obligations of the same maturity. The return is even more attractive if it is noted that, due to benefit responsiveness, the holder has options, under certain circumstances, to remove funds at book value plus accrued interest. If the yield curve is in its normal upward sloping position, the yield spread versus instruments of similar maturity would frequently be several hundred basis points.

Types of GICs and GIC-Related Products

There are a variety of options for GIC contracts, including whether they are simple (paying interest annually) or compound (where interest is reinvested until maturity date), and whether the holder participates in returns earned by a portfolio above a floor rate. In addition, there are two important expansions of the GIC concept. *BICs* are bank investment contracts. They are similar to GICs, but are offered by banks rather than by insurance companies. *Synthetic GICs* are fixed-income investments which have a "book value wrapper." With the book value wrapper, a financial institution or other guarantor promises to redeem assets at book value. For a fee, a guarantor takes market risk (but not default risk) during the term of the contract. The risk to the guarantor is relatively limited since the approach calls for liquidity to be provided outside the contract. Also, under normal circumstances, the upward slope of the yield curve makes investments worth more as time goes on. For example, if 5-year rates are 8 percent and 4-year rates are 7.5 percent, a 5-year 8 percent bond will be worth more than par in a year, as it will carry an 8 percent coupon versus the market rate of 7.5 percent. This profit is earned by the guarantor when early withdrawals are made.

Analyzing GICs

It is a daunting task to analyze the credit of insurance companies. Four rating agencies provide public ratings—Moody's, Standard & Poor's, Duff & Phelps, and A. M. Best. For a fee, Townsend and Schupp and Weiss Research provide ratings to their clients. However, the asset structure and liability structure of insurance companies are frequently so large, diverse, and complex that it is extremely difficult for outsiders to develop an intimate knowledge of the cash flow characteristics of the company. Extensive analytical data are reported to the public annually, with a lag of several months, and much more limited information is provided quarterly.

Further, the potential for disintermediation, or a "run on the bank," makes much of the analysis irrelevant. If policyholders rush to withdraw their funds, there is little that even the soundest insurers can do to prevent a crisis.

Despite the difficulty of analyzing insurance companies, there are some characteristics which are of concern. On the asset side, liquidity, diversification, and quality of assets are important, as is the level of reserves (equity) as a percentage of assets.

As to liabilities, diversification of policy types and geographic coverage are important. Also, the greater the ability of the policyholder to remove assets on short notice, the greater the potential for disintermediation. Whereas historically it has been viewed as an advantage if policies have liquidity features, it may be that in the future sponsors will want to eliminate liquidity features in policies so that disintermediation by other policyholders will not occur.

In bankruptcy, insurance company assets are claimed by priority established by state law. For instance, in New York State there are eight priority classes in a liquidation proceeding.

Class one covers costs of liquidation, class two employee wages, and class three outside goods and services supplied recently. Insurance policies are class four priority. Classes five through seven cover claims of governments, general creditors, and those covering surplus contribution notes. All other claims are included in class eight.

Realistically, even though insurance policies have a high priority in liquidation, unless there are subordinated bondholders or equity owners below the policyholder in the capital structure, the security of the policy is limited. With mutual insurance companies, there is no equity ownership below policyholders, since policyholders own the company.

Almost all states have insurance guarantee funds. However, these are designed more to assist individuals purchasing policies directly than fund sponsors purchasing policies on behalf of their employees. While the guarantee is theoretically the same, the politics of how money is split in a liquidation or rehabilitation can lead to important differences in settlements.

Most GICs are purchased through some form of competitive bid. This can be very attractive, since it provides the opportunity for the fund to achieve the highest rate level at a point in time. It is disconcerting, however, to recognize that the insurance carriers which are most in need of funds, possibly because of their own financial problems, may be the ones which make the highest bids.

Several insurance carriers failed in the early 1990s, with First Executive Life and Mutual Benefit Life being prominent examples. First Executive failed because its heavy concentration of high-yield (junk) bonds caused investors to cash in policies when the junk bond market declined in 1990. Mutual Benefit had suspected losses in real estate and highly leveraged loans which, again, caused investors to withdraw funds.

Issues in Constructing a Blended Rate GIC Portfolio

GICs in profit-sharing or 401(k) plans are normally combined in blended rate pools. A continuous, single pool of contracts is established and each investor has a pro rata share of interest income and principal. When a participant withdraws assets, he or she receives book value plus accrued interest. These pools are like money market funds in that principal is fixed and the interest rate varies. Because the contracts are purchased over a number of months or years, the rate on the pool will lag market rates, being lower during periods of rising rates and higher during periods of declining rates.

In combining GICs into a portfolio, issues to be considered include need for liquidity, quality level, diversification, the shape of the yield curve, and implementation issues.

The liquidity needs of the fund must be calculated to be sure that adequate funds are available for benefit payments. Liquidity can be achieved by controlling maturity, using simple interest contracts which pay interest annually, and by special arrangement with insurance carriers. Quality should be specified as to both minimum and average desired. Diversification is important as to both quality of issuer and maturity.

If the yield curve slopes sharply upward, the fund receives a larger premium for longer term investments, providing compensation for loss of flexibility due to the longer commitment.

Implementation issues include whether the sponsor invests directly or hires a consultant or manager, and how frequently to bid. More frequent bidding provides greater liquidity and diversification against interest rate fluctuations.

Likely Trends in GICs

Pure GIC funds may well decline in popularity for two important reasons. To the extent that book value accounting becomes less permissible, sponsors will feel freer to look at a broader variety of instruments in the "new stable asset funds." Second, the need to diversify credit risk will put further pressure on sponsors to move beyond the limited offerings of insurance companies.

FUTURES

Futures will undoubtedly play an increasing role as vehicles for investors who traditionally have limited themselves to securities.

Futures are publicly traded, standardized contracts which obligate the seller to provide the buyer with physical delivery of a commodity, or with payments which approximate the value of a defined asset or asset class, on a specific date in the future. They are similar to, but distinct from, forward contracts, which are direct purchases or sales of an asset, but with the settlement date postponed past the normal one to seven days. Whereas forward contracts are negotiated individually, futures are uniform, like shares of stock in a company. They provide uniform definition of the commodity, contract size, and terms of settlement, as well as a marketplace for trading. Futures also have a system for ensuring financial performance, through margin requirements, both initial and variation, and a well-developed clearing procedure.

Futures are not traded by outright purchase or sale, but rather by posting of margin as a good faith deposit against the liability assumed. For instance, an investor wishing to purchase $1 million of S&P 500 index futures does not pay $1 million for the futures. Rather, by purchasing the future, it has contracted to buy, and pay for in the future, a certain number of S&P 500 contracts, the cost of which was $1 million at the time of the purchase. So that the seller can be confident that the purchaser will be able to meet its obligation, a clearing mechanism has been established. The futures exchange and its members guarantee the contract, as does the investor's broker.

To give the broker confidence that the investor will meet its obligation, the broker requires the investor to maintain cash or government securities as margin against the obligation. The deposit for "initial margin," which might represent 20 percent of the contract, is increased or decreased daily as the size of the future liability (the price of the S&P 500 contract) falls or rises. This daily "variation margin" must be posted in additional cash or collateral by the investor, in what is called "marks to the market." Margin requirements are set by the relevant futures exchange, and can be increased or decreased depending on the exchange's analysis of the risks in a particular contract.

An investor which is not trading on margin would allocate $1 million for the purchase of $1 million of S&P 500 futures. This deposit is made either with a broker or bank, frequently in the form of Treasury bills, and earns interest. In addition, put and call options on futures are also available on some contracts.

Futures can be categorized a number of ways: hard (such as copper or gold), or soft (agricultural), or financial (stocks, bonds, and currencies); asset substitutes (financial) or liquefied physical assets (hard and soft). They can also be classified by whether they permit physical delivery, like agricultural commodities, or just cash settlement, as with the S&P 500.

Futures are employed by producers and users of physical commodities to protect against price swings. A farmer can sell wheat before the wheat is harvested in order to "lock in" a selling price. A baker can purchase wheat months before needing it in order to "lock in" a purchase cost. In this case futures are being used as a means of transferring risk, similar to the purchase of an insurance policy. For a price, the hedger assigns and the party on the other side of the transaction (frequently a speculator) assumes risk of price fluctuation.

Futures can be used by institutional investors in three ways: as a substitute for an asset class, to remove the risk of an asset class (hedging), or as a profit center.

Substitute

An investor wishing to own U.S. equities can buy S&P 500 futures instead of investing in all 500 stocks or purchasing an index fund. This might reduce transaction costs, reduce administrative expense, or, if futures are purchased at a discount, enhance profit. If the investor can manage its cash position to outperform Treasury bills, it can add incremental profit to the return earned on the futures.

Hedging

An investor wanting exposure to non-U.S. companies but not exposure to non-U.S. currencies can purchase stocks and sell the related currencies. If an investor wants to have the benefits of being long certain stocks in a market without having stock market exposure, it can purchase the stocks and short-stock market futures.

Hedging currency risk is difficult to do precisely, since movement in the underlying portfolio, or receipt of interest or dividends, changes the value of the asset being hedged and thus leads to some imbalances in the hedge.

Profit Center

Futures can also be purchased or sold for profit, either individually or in portfolios. Investment decisions can be made for fundamental or technical reasons, and holding periods can be for hours, days, or months.

The rationale for investing in futures is that they represent a significant component of wealth, and that the returns on futures have a low correlation with the returns on other asset categories, thus providing the function of reducing portfolio volatility. Further, since the world is becoming increasingly integrated financially, all assets have a relationship with others, rather than being independent factors. For instance, changes in interest rates impact the price of oil as well as stock and bond prices. Agricultural prices impact inflation and, thus, interest rates and stock prices. Economic growth leads to changes in interest rates and commodity prices.

Finally, certain futures managers have achieved returns which are above those seen in securities, in some case with surprisingly low volatility.

ISSUES WITH USING FUTURES AS A PROFIT CENTER

Investors wishing to use futures as a profit center should consider the following issues: if futures have a positive expected return, are futures inherently speculative, and how do futures impact the return/risk profile of their portfolios.

In addition, implementation issues include whether to use a passive or active strategy, manager styles for active strategies, compensation to managers, complexity, and limiting risk.

Expected Rate of Return

It does not appear that futures (with the exception of stock, bond, and money market futures) have a positive expected rate of return. That is, they are a zero sum game, with the amount won by winners equaling the amount lost by losers (before transactions costs). There is no reason why corn, copper, or Deutsche marks should be worth more next year than they are this year, although in periods of high inflation physical commodities might have a high nominal return (i.e., ignoring inflation). In contrast, bond futures represent fixed-income instruments which accrue interest; stock index futures represent holdings in common stocks; and companies retain earnings and pay dividends from earnings, leading in both cases to positive expected returns. An analogy in real estate is that apartment buildings have an expected rate of return, from rent, but raw land does not. Thus, use of futures implies positive impact by the portfolio manager, rather than a passive return from holding an asset class.

Are Futures Speculative?

Since futures do not have a positive expected return, a significant issue is raised as to whether they are inherently speculative when used as a profit center. As a class, futures would appear to be speculative (again excluding stock, bond, and money market futures), since the only way a profit can be earned is by taking it from the party on the other side of the transaction.

Impact on Return/Risk Profile

Futures, individually and collectively, do not appear to have a high correlation with traditional investments such as stocks, bonds, and cash. Therefore, to the extent a rate of return can be achieved, this return is likely to be uncorrelated with returns of other assets in a portfolio, and hence will reduce the overall volatility of the portfolio.

Implementation Issues

Sponsors wishing to invest in futures are likely to choose an active strategy. There are as yet no index funds investing in futures, although it is possible to create them and someone may do so before long. However, index funds would not be likely to have a positive expected return.

Manager style can be determined by the type and number of contracts traded, volatility characteristics (margin leverage, maximum "drawdown" or loss from any previous high, and portfolio composition), and the extent to which the investment process is driven by fundamental versus technical factors.

Compensation structures require careful analysis. Sources of compensation include fees, percentage of profits, commissions on transactions, and interest income, if the manager receives all or a portion of the interest income on collateral posted for margin.

Fees can be quite high in futures trading because of two factors: The successful managers are able to name a high price, both in fees and percentage of profit, for their services. Further, futures trading is an activity highly dependent on up-to-the-minute sources of information and analysis of that information. Therefore, successful futures traders frequently have large overhead comprised of round-the-clock trading facilities, expensive communications networks, and highly paid analytical staffs.

Futures invested through commingled accounts, known as commodities pools, are subject to intense regulation and disclosure, both before and after the initial investment. The latter arises because futures are not traded by outright purchases or sales, but rather by posting of margin as good faith deposits against the liability assumed. For instance, an investor wishing to purchase $1 million of S&P 500 index futures does not pay $1 million for the futures. Rather, it has contracted to purchase $1 million of S&P 500 stocks at some point in the future. So that the seller can be confident that the purchaser will be able to meet its obligation, a clearing mechanism has been established. The futures exchange and its members guarantee the contract, as does the investor's broker. To give the broker confidence that the investor will meet its obligation, the broker requires the investor to maintain cash or government securities as a margin against the future obligation. This margin, which might represent 20 percent of the contract, is increased or decreased daily as the size of the future liability (the price of the S&P 500 contract) falls or rises. An investor that is not trading on a leveraged basis would allocate $1 million for the purchase of $1 million of S&P 500 futures. In some cases, this deposit is made with the manager, which may keep a portion of the interest earned on the amount not required to be deposited as margin.

The documents associated with futures investment can be both complex and tiresome, suggesting that professional assistance is required prior to investment.

Investors should also give strong consideration to risk minimization. Futures traders who trade for noninstitutional investors frequently use leverage, that is, they invest more than 100 percent of the assets under their management. Further, some traders concentrate in order to maximize gains. Sponsors should have full understanding of the risks being taken by the manager.

Limits to risk can take two forms—written guidelines, which contractually limit the activities of the manager, and use of limited partnerships. With partnerships it is possible to lose at most 100 percent of the investment. While this sounds onerous, with a separately managed account and the use of leverage, it is possible to lose more than 100 percent.

ADDITIONAL COMMENTS ON HEDGING CURRENCY RISK

In hedging currency risk, the investor is not making a short sale of currency futures, since a short sale implies selling something that is not owned. Rather, the investor is decomposing the risk associated with non-U.S. investments into two components—stock market risk and specific risk associated with individual stocks, on the one hand, and currency risk on the other. The investor is selling a risk which it owns (through ownership of stocks denominated and traded in non-U.S. currencies) and thus is not shorting, at least not in an economic sense. Mechanically, the transaction has the appearance of a short sale. In contrast, the seller of U.S. stocks described above is selling short, since the stock market risk in the stock portfolio is not identical to the stock market risk in the future.

APPENDIX 4-A

RATE OF RETURN CALCULATIONS FOR FIXED-INCOME SECURITIES

A. Return on bond carrying coupon paid once per year.
   Price: 100.   Coupon: 6 percent.   Maturity: One year.
   Return: 6/100 = 6 percent.
B. Return on instrument with 6 percent discount (no coupon).
   Price: 94.   Coupon: None.   Maturity: One year.
   Return: (100 − 94)/94 = 6.38 percent.

C. Return on bond paying semiannual coupon (the normal case).
   Price: 100. Coupon: 6 percent. Maturity: One year.
   Return: Value of first coupon + Value of second coupon +
   Six months' interest on first coupon = 3% + 3% +
   3%(0.03) = 6.09 (assuming 6 percent reinvestment rate).
D. Bond equivalent return given true annual rate.
   Annual rate = 6.0 percent.
   Semiannual (bond equivalent) return = ((square root of
   1.06) − 1) × 2 = 0.02956 × 2 = 5.91 percent.
   Proof: Square root of 5.91 = 2.956
   2.956 + 2.956 + 2.956(0.02956)
   = 6.0 percent.
E. Bond equivalent return of 6 percent discount instrument.
   Price: 94. Coupon: None. Maturity: One year.
   1. Find true annual rate as in B above (6.383).
   2. Take square root of 1 + true rate expressed as decimal.
   3. Subtract 1.
   4. Double and multiply by 100.
   Carrying out 1 through 4:
   True rate = 100/94 − 1 = 0.0638
   Square root of 1 + true rate = square root of 1.0638 = 1.03142
   Subtract 1 = 0.03142
   Multiply by 2 = 0.06284
   Bond equivalent rate = 6.284
   Proof: Square root of 6.284 = 3.142
   3.142 + 3.142 + 3.142(0.03142) = 6.38

A and B show returns assuming annual compounding. D and E show returns on a bond-equivalent basis, that is, with semiannual compounding. Note that the bond yield (C) understates the true annual return.

F. Terminal wealth: The amount an investor has at the end of a specific period. Terminal wealth depends on the initial amount, the timing and the amount of income, and the rate achieved on reinvested income (assumes no interim contributions and withdrawals).

G. Return (also called realized compound yield): The compound annual return on the beginning value which will provide the investor with a specific terminal wealth (assuming no interim contributions and withdrawals).

For calculations of return when portfolios have contributions and withdrawals, see Chapter 10.

APPENDIX 4-B1

WORLD INVESTABLE CAPITAL MARKET
December 31, 1990

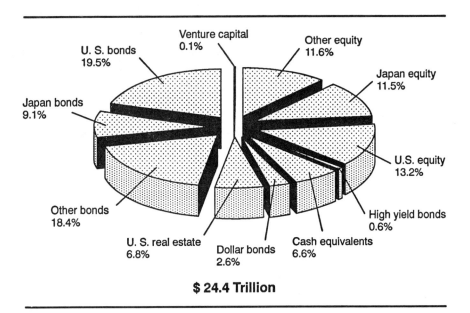

Venture capital
0.1%

Other equity
11.6%

U. S. bonds
19.5%

Japan equity
11.5%

Japan bonds
9.1%

U.S. equity
13.2%

Other bonds
18.4%

High yield bonds
0.6%

U. S. real estate
6.8%

Dollar bonds
2.6%

Cash equivalents
6.6%

$ 24.4 Trillion

1980 total approximately $11 trillion.
Source: Brinson Partners, Inc.; Ibbotson & Siegel.

APPENDIX 4-B2

U. S. INVESTABLE CAPITAL MARKET
December 31, 1990

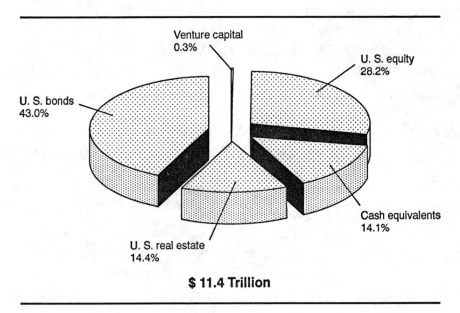

Venture capital 0.3%

U. S. equity 28.2%

U. S. bonds 43.0%

Cash equivalents 14.1%

U. S. real estate 14.4%

$ 11.4 Trillion

Source: Brinson Partners, Inc.

CHAPTER 5

ALTERNATIVE INVESTMENTS

A fiduciary shall "diversify plan assets to minimize the risk of large losses, unless under the circumstances it is clearly prudent not to do so."
ERISA

Alternative or nontraditional investments include all investments except marketable stocks and bonds. Covered in this chapter are real estate, venture capital, leveraged buyouts, timberland, raw land, farm land, leased property, and short selling. Energy is discussed in the following chapter. These investment types are treated separately from stocks and bonds because most institutions and investors manage or invest in stocks and bonds, but only in recent years has significant interest developed in other areas (a major exception being the long-standing real estate activities of insurance companies). While these special investments differ from each other in many respects, they do share some common characteristics, including lack of liquidity, lack of historical analysis and data, and difficulty of tracking performance and comparing performance results. Finally, all serve the purpose of providing diversification to the more traditionally structured portfolio.

Since many of these investments are offered via limited partnerships, this chapter also contains a section on factors to consider when investing through this investment structure.

BACKGROUND

Some investors believe that all asset classes of similar risk will have similar returns. Therefore, alternative investments are not worth the effort, risk, transaction costs, and illiquidity they entail. While this suggestion has merit, at least four reasons exist why investors might find investment in alternatives to be worthwhile. Because of the principle of diversification (see page 18), assets which have the same expected returns but whose returns are uncorrelated can be combined into a portfolio which has the same expected return but a lower volatility level than either of the assets. In this case, the investor has a lower risk for a given level of return or a higher return for a given level of risk. Second, most investors who have dealt in the stock and bond markets find them to be extremely efficient. That is, as new information becomes available, it is rapidly absorbed by the marketplace, with little opportunity for an individual investor to make profits at the expense of other, less-informed competitors. However, the alternative asset area is different in that, due to the uniqueness of the individual investments and lack of a centralized marketplace, the markets are much less efficient. While this detracts from liquidity, it also presents the potential for profit-making opportunity.

Third, the price of alternative investments tends to move based on economic factors rather than emotional ones to a greater extent than is true for securities. Thus, whereas the value of a stock might change 25 to 50 percent in the course of a year or two bull and bear market cycle, the value of buildings and other alternative investments tends to move significantly less.

Admittedly, there are times when it is difficult to sell real estate and other alternative investments principally due to the absence of financing or the high level of interest rates available to prospective investors, but nonetheless prices appear to be more stable than for stock market equities. An exception might be high-technology venture capital investments, whose prices tend to reflect the prevailing emotion in the new issue stock market.

Finally, an investor or its investment manager frequently can have a positive impact on the economics of the investment through hard work, creativity, and intelligence. Whereas an investor cannot do anything to make a stock or bond more valuable, it can, for instance, plant new shrubs in front of an office building to try to make the building more attractive to new tenants.

Alternative investments are sometimes called risky and illiquid. This may or may not be true in each individual case. A distinction must be drawn between risk and liquidity. Risk is frequently thought of as the volatility of rate of return. A more traditional notion is one of results deviating significantly from expectation or the chance of losing one's capital. Liquidity, on the other hand, is the ability to buy or sell at or near the fair market value. In securities, the definition of liquidity is the ability to sell at or near the last sale but alternative investments are not fungible (i.e., are unique) so the idea of a "last sale" is not relevant. For alternative investments, a more appropriate definition is the time required to sell at fair market value. Most alternative investments are illiquid, but if enough time is available before cash is needed, they can be liquidated at a reasonable representation of their market value. Risk varies considerably. The owner of a well-leased commercial office building may run very little risk of selling the building at a loss. On the other hand, an investor in a new company may well lose its entire investment.

Risk also depends on whether the investor is an owner or a creditor. Participation in many asset types can be obtained with an equity or a fixed-income structure. Real estate provides the best example, where equity participation can be achieved through ownership of property, while a fixed-income investment very similar to a corporate bond can be made by lending money to the purchaser or owner of a property. Depending on the investor's position and asset and income coverage, the level of risk can be dramatically different.

Unrelated Business Taxable Income

In general, otherwise tax-exempt organizations are taxed on income which is unrelated to the purposes for which the organization received its tax exemption. The purpose of this tax is to place competing organizations on an equal footing in terms of taxation. Thus, schools are not taxed on tuition income, but would be taxed if they owned manufacturing or retail businesses unrelated to their specific educational goal. Pension funds and foundations are not taxed on income from their investments, but would be taxed if they engaged in businesses. The tax is not punitive, but is similar to that on taxable businesses. Expenses relevant to the creation of the unrelated income are deductible in arriving at the amount of income subject to tax.

Two special areas of the law on unrelated business taxable income are of interest to fund sponsors. Property unrelated to the activity for which the organization received its tax exemption, which was acquired with borrowed money, that is, is debt-financed, normally triggers a tax. For example, if an investment or business property is purchased subject to a 75 percent mortgage, 75 percent of the income is subject to tax, less the deduction for 75 percent of the related expenses. Similarly, the same ratio of capital gain would be subject to tax, as well. However, special rules apply to debt incurred by qualified retirement plans to finance real estate investments. The UBTI rules do not apply unless the acquisition price is not fixed at the date of acquisition; the amount of indebtedness is dependent upon future revenues, income, or profits; the property is leased by the retirement trust back to the seller; the property is acquired from a person related to the plan or the seller provides nonrecourse financing for the transaction; and the debt is subordinated to other indebtedness on the property or bears interest at a rate significantly less than the market rate.

Securities lending also is an area which potentially can be taxable if certain conditions are not met. If security lending fees are to be treated as passive income, the borrower must provide collateral which is "marked to the market," that is, revalued, each business day; the tax-exempt organization must be permitted to terminate the loan on notice of at most five business days; and, upon termination, the tax-exempt organization must receive securities identical to those loaned. If these three conditions are met, securities lending is considered an investment rather than a business activity.

Unrelated business income is not illegal or immoral; it is merely taxable. Therefore, a sponsor might be willing to engage in business activities, and pay the appropriate taxes, rather than forsake an exceptional opportunity. However, the notion of a tax-exempt organization paying taxes is unappealing to most trustees and their constituents, so any organization considering such a move should look not only at the economics but also the political ramifications of engaging in taxable activities.

Investment versus Business Practices and Ethics

Most professional investors in the securities industry adopt a fiduciary posture with respect to their clients. These professionals recognize that they have expertise significantly beyond that of most of their clients and feel an obligation to act fairly with respect to those clients. However, in the business world in general, different standards prevail. Each party is motivated to achieve the highest level of long-run profit it can, rather than necessarily seeking a fair deal, or providing full disclosure to the person on the other side of the transaction. When dealing with alternative investments, sponsors should assume they are operating in a business rather than a fiduciary climate. Accordingly, they should seek professional advice, be sure they thoroughly understand the obligations of each party to a transaction, and recognize that the people with whom they are dealing do not necessarily feel an obligation to disclose unfavorable aspects of the transaction.

REAL ESTATE

The size of the U. S. investable real estate market is enormous. As of the end of 1990, real estate investments totaled about $1.6 trillion. This compares to about $3.2 trillion in U. S. stocks, according to Brinson Partners, Inc. (see Appendix 4-B2 on p. 66). Given this huge size, it is somewhat surprising that investors have not taken a larger position in real estate. This may be because of illiquidity, tax benefits which fall to real estate investors but are of no value to tax-exempt investors, administrative problems of owning real estate, and the highly publicized (and perhaps highly exaggerated) boom and bust nature of real estate.

Real estate provides a wide range of possible risk postures for investors. On the one hand, it is possible to own mortgages on very high quality buildings leased to high quality tenants, and on the other, to borrow money to purchase raw land in an area miles from the nearest road. However, while the choice of investments may theoretically be unlimited, as a practical matter it is difficult for passive investors to find the appropriate vehicles representing the broad spectrum of risk possibilities. Thus, practically speaking, investors must decide among a much narrower range of alternatives.

The real estate market has witnessed a significant change in recent years. Whereas, in the past, individual investors and small developers were the typical buyers of properties, with long-term financing from banks, insurance companies, and savings institutions, current buyers include domestic and foreign pension funds and real estate partnerships. These groups are much more stable investors as they typically have long time horizons, and often make investments for cash. The historical owners of real estate now find it difficult to purchase real estate because of negative leverage. Leverage is negative when interest rates are higher than the capitalization rate, the latter being the pretax operating profits of a real estate investment divided by the price to be paid. For instance, if interest rates are 10 percent and the capitalization rate is 11 percent, an investment with no down payment will have a positive cash flow. If the rates are reversed, an investment with no down payment will have a negative cash flow. The higher interest rates are relative to the capitalization rate, the greater the down payment required to establish a breakeven cash flow. Thus, with negative leverage individuals are no longer as able to control a large building with small amounts of equity. Similarly, developers can no longer build a building and count their profit as the equity, with a mortgage providing an amount equal to the total cash cost of construction and land. While this condition of negative leverage has hurt entrepreneurial developers, it has led to real estate being held in stronger hands.

Direct Investment or Commingled Funds

Equity or fixed-income investments can be made directly, in joint ventures or partnerships, or through open-end or closed-end commingled funds. Each of these investments has certain characteristics which may be important to the investor. Direct investment provides the investor with the greatest ability to control its portfolio, as it can review each purchase before it is made, make decisions about management of the property, and decide upon the appropriate time and terms at which to sell. Direct investment can be made with the sponsor alone making decisions or through the counsel of an investment advisor, who can be hired on either a discretionary or nondiscretionary basis to advise the fund. The disadvantage is that the selection of properties may be limited to small investments, since the constraint represented by portfolio size may limit the investment to relatively small units. Also, it may be difficult to diversify the portfolio properly due to the small size of the fund.

Commingled Funds

Commingled funds provide the simplest method of operation. As with securities mutual funds, investors pool their assets and permit a professional manager to select and manage the investments. Due to the larger size of the commingled portfolio, it is possible for the manager to choose among investments which might be too large for the individual clients.

Open-end funds are those which provide the ability to add or remove cash during the life of the fund. Closed-end funds have a single offering period, after which the investors have no opportunity to buy additional shares or remove their funds until the prearranged liquidation date. While the open-end principle is appealing in many respects, a disadvantage exists in that real estate investments are individually unique and illiquid. This means it is difficult to value the investments and hence know what is the fair price at which new investors can join or existing shareholders can leave the fund. Real estate investments are almost always valued by an independent appraiser (though some people question this independence since the appraiser is hired by the sponsor of the fund), but real estate appraisal is very much an art rather than a science. Also, the manager of an open-end fund will have difficulty in planning his acquisition strategy, since he will not know if the fund will have net purchases or sales in future periods. Open-end funds normally have an advantage, however, in that purchases of property can be made on a continuing basis over a number of years. This is important because it is extremely difficult for any investor to know whether prices are relatively high or low at any point in time. Consequently, purchases made over a number of years will help avoid risks associated with any specific year and, in effect, provide another source of diversification, in addition to type of property, size, age, location, and terms of leases, the more traditional factors considered in diversification. However, sponsors of medium-sized and larger pension funds can achieve diversification similar to that available to open-end funds by investing in a number of closed-end funds.

Undeveloped Land

Undeveloped land is a speculative investment. It does not produce income and, unlike a stock which pays no dividend, there is no underlying earnings process operating to build up value. Further, real estate taxes and administrative fees lead to negative cash flow so the investment absorbs cash rather than generating it. Thus, undeveloped land would normally not be an appropriate investment for a prudent, tax-exempt investor. This is not to say there are no economic opportunities in land, but rather that the nature of this investment usually does not lend itself to investment by fiduciaries on behalf of third parties.

Agricultural Land

Unlike undeveloped land, agricultural property does provide income. Therefore, it does not at first seem speculative. However, three factors serve to make agricultural investments difficult for pension and other tax-free funds. First, the cash return as a percent of the value of the investment tends to be quite small, as investors and farmers have bid up the price of farmland to the point where cash returns are low. Second, for a one-crop, one-location investment, risks are extremely high for any given season, as the influences of weather, pests, and supply and demand can greatly impact current results. Finally, farming is a complex, capital-intensive business which requires experienced and conscientious management, typically beyond that available within most fund sponsor and investment organizations. As such, farming is more of a business than an investment, and is not readily adaptable to the needs of passive, tax-exempt investors.

Timberland

Since most pension funds have very long time horizons, they are well suited to owning illiquid investments. Yet, since pension funds should not speculate, they are not well suited for investments which do not produce income or otherwise generate increases in asset values. Timberland is an interesting investment because, while it may not create immediate income, the natural growth of trees provides a constantly increasing value to the investment. However, considerable uncertainty exists with respect to the price of timber and the cost of cutting it at some future date. Further, management of timber forests requires expertise. Thus, although there are certain attractions to this type of investment, there are a number of drawbacks and complexities which must be faced.

Real Estate Administration

As with other nontraditional investments, the lack of market indexes, difficulties of valuation, and absence of comparative samples make measurement of a real estate portfolio difficult. Further, whereas it is simple for a pension fund to purchase hundreds of millions of dollars of securities, it is agonizingly difficult to purchase even a thousand dollars' worth of real estate. This, combined with the need to insure, pay taxes, collect rents, and otherwise manage the investment, adds to the administrative burden of owning real estate.

Two developments may prove to be significant to pension fund real estate investors. In order to assist those investors who are interested in real estate, the Pension Real Estate Association was formed in

1982. Its goal is to inform and educate real estate managers, fund sponsors, and other interested people regarding investment in real estate from the point of view of a major institutional investor. Second, a real estate total return index has been formed by Frank Russell Company in cooperation with a number of major institutional investors. This index shows the return earned by various types of properties in several geographic markets.

Deal Structures

In addition to real estate equities, investors have the opportunity to own mortgages or hybrid investments. The hybrids include convertible mortgages (which can be converted into ownership of property) and participating mortgages (which allow the lender to receive a percentage of increases in the property's revenue). Several examples of possible deal structures are listed below.

Joint Venture
A developer sells a 75 percent interest in an office building to a pension fund, keeping the remaining 25 percent. The developer grants a 10 percent preferred return to the pension fund, meaning that, before the developer receives any revenue, the pension fund must receive 10 percent. (However, if the building does not generate enough revenue to provide a 10 percent return to the pension fund, the developer is not obligated to make up the difference.) The preference could apply year by year, or could be cumulative. Once the building is earning a 10 percent return, all profits go to the developer until he is receiving a 10 percent return on his 25 percent investment. After that, profits are split 75 percent to the pension fund and 25 percent to the developer, as are capital gains upon sale of the building.

Participating Convertible Mortgage
An investor purchases a building, with 90 percent of the purchase price supplied by a pension fund which holds a participating convertible mortgage. The investor's return in the early years is limited since all the building's income in the early years is required to pay interest on the mortgage. As the building's cash flow increases, the owner of the building can receive 10 percent of the income as long as the interest on the mortgage is paid first. Since the mortgage is participating, the pension

fund receives an increasing amount of income if the building's cash flow is adequate to more than meet the interest obligation of the mortgage and pay the 10 percent return to the owner. The mortgage is convertible into 90 percent of the equity of the property; thus, if the building is sold at profit, the pension fund will receive 90 percent of the capital gains.

Outright Purchase
Pension fund purchases 100 percent of the building. To minimize management problems, it engages a real estate management firm to manage the building.

There can be any number of combinations of financing arrangements depending upon the investment in question.

VENTURE CAPITAL

For our purposes, venture capital will be defined as the investment in new or unproven companies whose shares are not publicly traded. Venture capital investors can make direct investments or join with other investors in commingled portfolios (typically in the form of limited partnerships). They must also consider the industry emphasis they feel is appropriate. In recent years, high-technology electronics have proved to be by far the most successful area. This is because of the tremendous change in technology combined with the large number of commercial uses for this technology. Other areas of the economy have not produced nearly such spectacular results, indicating that perhaps venture capital investment is most successful when dramatic technological change is occurring. Biotechnology may be the next area of great innovation.

The venture capital industry is a tight-knit fraternity, requiring participants to have not only funds but also access to new investments, and the ability to assist new companies in becoming successful. Entrepreneurs, recognizing this, tend to gravitate toward the most experienced venture capitalists. This suggests that investors should stay with the more knowledgeable and successful groups, rather than deal with new entrants who might not only lack experience, but also might be seeing only those new companies which have been turned down by the more-experienced venture firms.

Company Growth Cycle

New companies go through cycles consisting of product development, introduction of a new product to the market, penetration of the market, rapid growth, and mature growth (see Exhibit 5–1). Venture capital is a source of funds up to the rapid growth phase. Venture capitalists find it convenient to characterize their investments based upon the company's stage of development to help determine the amount of risk involved. *Start-up* financing is provided to companies which are developing a new product. As the product is introduced into the market and penetration begins, additional financing would be considered *early stage*. Finally, when the product has demonstrated success and the company is increasing its production capability, financing would be provided for an *expansion phase*. The exhibit also shows the sales and profitability status of companies in the respective stages of development, and during the period when venture capital financing is required.

Venture Capital Performance

Investors reviewing historical results in the venture capital area will undoubtedly find past rates of return to be extremely impressive. However, in this process it is useful to consider two factors. One is that venture capital is a highly fragmented industry, and it is difficult to consider the investment record of all participants. It appears that of the four major segments—small business investment companies, corporations, individuals, and institutional investors—the first three have had a marginal record, but the institutional firms have fared much better. When considering historical performance figures in any field, it is well to keep in mind that only firms with good track records are still in business, and the ones with bad records are gone. It is also advisable to consider the relationship between the success of the venture field and the state of the financing markets. When large amounts of cash are available for financing new ventures, the price of new ventures is high (the percentage of the company purchased per dollar of investment is low) and returns to investors tend to be low. Further, to the extent that public and institutional investors are rushing into initial public offerings (IPOs), venture capitalists can cash in their investments at very attractive prices. However, if this market is dull, it may be much more difficult for even the most successful investment to be turned into cash.

EXHIBIT 5–1
Venture capital financing and company growth stage

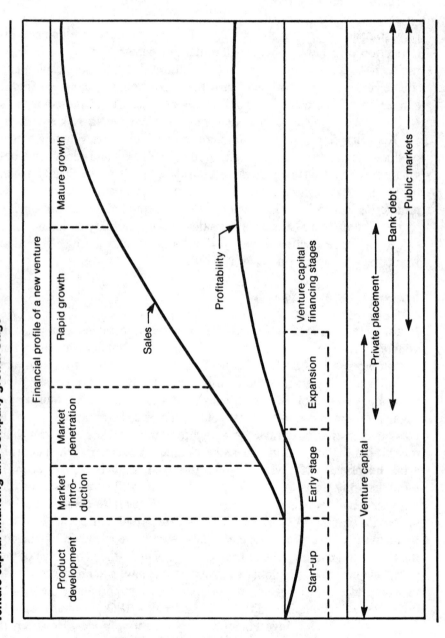

Source: Merrill Lynch Venture Capital Co.

An example of the importance of the initial public offering market can be seen by viewing the "hot" new issue market in 1983. Whereas in 1982, 33 venture-backed companies went public and raised about $602 million, during 1983, 143 companies went public and raised $3,238 million, an increase of over 300 percent in numbers of companies and more than 400 percent in dollars raised versus the year 1982.

Also, during the full year 1983, approximately $12.6 billion was raised from initial public offerings, while approximately the same amount was raised cumulatively during the 12 years previous to 1983!

Not surprisingly, returns to investors slumped following 1983, as prices which had been pushed to high levels fell back to more normal levels.

Measuring Rates of Return in Venture Capital

A definitional problem exists in measuring the rates of return on venture capital and, to a lesser extent, on other nontraditional investments, because of the venture capital manager's use of pooled vehicles and investments where payment is made in stages. The investor can view its allocation to venture capital as starting at three different times: when it segregates funds to start a venture capital program, when it funds a pool, and when the venture manager invests in a company. Suppose, for instance, the fund sponsor decides to invest $10 million in venture capital. The fund makes this investment through a partnership rather than using individual investments in order to achieve diversification and because the pension fund is not part of the venture capital fraternity and is not offered many of the more attractive investments. The venture capitalist, after raising a pool of assets, takes several years to invest the funds. Suppose, after five years, the sponsor's share of the portfolio is valued at $20 million. By one measure, the portfolio will have doubled, or achieved about a 15 percent annually compounded rate of return. However, assume the fund took about a year to find the partnerships it wanted to invest in. The fund sponsor might suggest that the venture fund actually made about 20 percent per year since the fund doubled in four years. But the venture capitalist would likely have taken several years to invest the proceeds of the partnership offering. Assume the venture capitalist on average took two years to invest the funds of the partnership. He might then argue that the money was invested an average of three years, and thus the annual rate of return on the fund, which doubled in three years, was 26 percent.

It is not clear that one or the other of these methods is correct, but it seems a bit unfair for the venture capitalist to claim the high return since he could not have made the investments he made had he not known capital was available to call upon whenever he needed it. Thus, it is stretching logic somewhat to suggest that only the actual capital employed should be counted toward calculating the rate of return. In any event, it is important for investors to recognize that it takes time to assemble venture capital programs, and everyone associated with an investment should be clear as to the assumptions behind any past performance record.

A related subject is the valuation process for venture capital investments. In order to measure rates of return, it is necessary to have accurate beginning and ending valuations and, to calculate time-weighted returns, valuations at any point when additional money is contributed or invested. Since no public market exists for venture investments, a set of conventions is frequently relied upon. Investments are valued at the lower of cost or market until a subsequent transaction is made between arm's-length parties. For example, if a private placement is done in which the fund participates at $10 per share and the company appears to be succeeding, the investment will be carried at $10 per share. However, if the corporation fails or enters a period of difficulty significantly beyond that contemplated, the investment would be written down. If, at a subsequent date, another investor purchases shares at a higher price, say $15 per share, the assumed market value of the shares is increased to $15 per share. If the investment appears to be succeeding but no subsequent transaction is made, the investment is still carried at $10 per share.

In valuing companies it is logical to compare them to publicly traded issues of a similar type. In this regard, it is important to recognize that securities which are not registered under the securities laws cannot be freely bought and sold, and thus should be discounted 20 to 40 percent from the value which would be carried by publicly traded securities of an identical company.

Restricted or Control Securities

Generally, securities acquired in a transaction not involving a public offering are considered to be restricted; stock acquired in such a transaction is sometimes called "letter" stock. For example, securities acquired in a private placement from the issuer, or from someone who directly or indirectly controls the management of the issuer, are restricted. Similarly, unregistered securities acquired through employee stock options, or stock purchase plans, are restricted unless the issuer has registered the securities for sale.

Control securities are those owned by a person who directly or indirectly controls the management and activities of the company issuing the securities. Senior officers, directors, and certain large shareholders of a company are usually considered to be control persons even with respect to stock they purchased in the open market.

Securities and Exchange Commission Rule 144 permits the sale of restricted or control securities only if current information about the company that issued the securities is readily available to the public and the financial community. Further, restricted securities are subject to a two-year holding period. Finally, Rule 144 restricts the amount of securities that may be sold during any three-month period. Legal counsel is highly desirable for anyone contemplating the sale of such securities.

A related rule, Rule 145, governs the sale of securities received in mergers and consolidations. Such sales are generally permitted if the issuer has registered them prior to distribution.

LEVERAGED BUYOUTS

Leveraged or management buyouts are high-risk, high-return investments which involve existing rather than new companies or businesses. In a leveraged buyout, typically the investor group, in cooperation with most or all of existing management, purchases the stock or assets of a company by using a small amount of equity and a large amount of borrowed money. Depending upon the nature of the transaction, there can be a number of securities involved, each with a different risk, income, and capital appreciation opportunity. A simple example (see Exhibit 5-2) might be a company which is purchased for $100 million by forming a new company with $10 million of equity and $90 million of borrowed funds or other senior securities. The equity is supplied by management and an investor group, and by institutional investors who are required to purchase notes or preferred stock as well as equity. The $90 million might consist of $50 million of floating-rate bank loans secured by (or at least supported by) inventories, accounts receivable, and fixed assets.

The bank debt might carry an interest rate of 150–200 basis points above prime. A group of pension funds might provide funds in the form of subordinated notes, carrying interest at a fixed rate equal to 200 basis points over the interest rate of a comparable maturity Treasury note at the time the deal is struck. Finally, an additional class of securities, in the form of preferred stock, might be sold to insurance companies with a dividend yield 200 basis points under a Treasury note of the same maturity. Since these insurance companies pay taxes as corporations, only 30 percent of the preferred dividend is taxable to them. Therefore, they are willing to accept a lower yield than would the purchasers of the subordinated notes who have less risk. (Partly mitigating this risk is the fact that, as in the example below, the preferred stockholders invest only 60 percent as much as the note holders, but are allowed to purchase the same amount of common stock.) From the investee corporation's point of view, the lack of deductibility of the preferred stock dividend is not a serious negative since LBOs of this variety are operated for cash generation rather than income generation, and hence frequently pay little or no taxes. The subordinated note and preferred stockholders would each, in conjunction with these purchases, also purchase stock equal to 45 percent of the initial capitalization. Management and the investor group which structures the investment and finds investors supplies the remaining $1 million.

If the company continues to operate successfully, it will gradually retire the debt and preferred stock. At that time, even if the company has not increased in value, all the investors will have made significant returns. If the company has grown and prospered, the potential return is even greater.

For example, if the company is sold in seven years for an amount equal to the purchase price, even with only the bank debt having been retired, the returns to each investor group will be as shown in Exhibit 5–3.

The outcome of LBO investments is very uncertain. In addition to normal business risks, the high level of debt makes the investment even more risky. Thus, it is appropriate that the purchased company have the characteristics desired in leveraged buyouts. First, it should have a small debt load so cash from operations can be used to pay off the newly created debt. Second, the business should be stable, rather than highly volatile, so financial disaster does not strike during a recession. It should not be technology-driven, so products are not made obsolete by those of competitors. The management should be experienced and have a proven

EXHIBIT 5–2
Sources and Terms of LBO Financing

Percent of Total Financing	Source and Type	Interest or Dividend Rate	Percent of Ownership	
50	Commercial bank loans	Prime + 150–200 basis points	—	
20	Pension funds— subordinated note	Fixed rate at 200 basis points over Treasuries	40	
10	Insurance companies— preferred stock	Dividend yield 200 basis points under Treasuries	40	
9	Pension funds— common stock		9	
9	Insurance companies— common stock		9	
2	Management and financing agent— common stock		2	20
100 percent			100 percent	

record of success. Further, if the company has excess assets, such as inventory or accounts receivable, which can be shrunk to pay off debt, or somewhat inefficient operations, so profits can be increased, the probability of success will be enhanced. This is especially true since the goal is to pay down the debt to a manageable level as soon as possible, and all available sources of cash must be tapped. Finally, to the extent that the purchase price can be assigned to specific depreciable assets, thus giving them a high tax cost, substantial depreciation charges can be taken against income, reducing taxes and further increasing cash flow.

EXHIBIT 5–3
Annual Rate of Return over Seven Years

Holder of	Sale at Purchase Price	Double Purchase Price
Subordinated note + Common stock	18.2	26.5
Preferred stock + Common stock	18.6	29.4
Common stock	29.2	48.6

LEASED PERSONAL PROPERTY

As corporations continue to streamline their balance sheets and attempt to utilize all their assets at maximum efficiency, it is increasingly common for them to lease property. This can occur upon the initial acquisition of the asset, or in a sale leaseback, in which the owner sells the property to an investor and agrees to lease it back on specified terms. This type of investment is primarily a financing arrangement rather than an investment in personal property by the sponsor. Thus, it is more logically looked at as a private placement of debt than as an investment in a nontraditional asset. Given the nature of the equipment or other personal property which serves as collateral for the loan, investors should look to the credit of the borrower rather than the value of the collateral for their return.

SHORT SELLING

Short selling involves borrowing an asset and selling it. In the normal case, the short seller anticipates that the asset will decline in price. If the asset does decline, the short seller can purchase the asset and repay the loan by delivering the borrowed asset to the lender.

Mechanics

Take a case where a stock is selling for 50. The short seller borrows 100 shares of the stock from a brokerage firm which holds shares of the stock on behalf of itself or its clients, and sells them. One hundred shares sold at 50 yields proceeds of $5,000. If the stock declines to, say, 40, the short seller can purchase 100 shares ("cover" its short) at a cost of $4,000. The short seller can relieve its obligation to the lender by returning 100 shares. With the sale proceeds of $5,000 and a purchase cost of $4,000, the short seller has made a profit of $1,000.

As with all transactions, the investor must have the financial wherewithal to conduct it. With a normal purchase, this ability is demonstrated by paying in full for the asset purchased. With a short sale, an open liability exists until the borrowed shares are repaid. Thus, the investor must post margin to prove that it can make good on its commitment to repay the securities borrowed.

The lender of the shares is entitled to any distribution on them. Thus, if the shares pay a dividend during the period when the short position is open, the short seller must pay the lender the amount of the dividend.

Since a credit balance results from the proceeds of the short sale, institutional investors are able to secure a portion of the interest which the short seller's broker earns on the short sale proceeds. This rebate might be 75 percent of the broker call loan rate, the rate at which brokers borrow from banks (in which case it would approximate the Treasury bill rate).

Risks of Short Selling

Since asset prices can rise as well as fall, short sellers run the normal risk of being wrong in their judgment. The purchaser of an asset makes money when the price of the asset rises and loses money when the price of the asset falls. A short seller makes money when the price falls and loses money when it rises. However, there are four additional risks to short sellers, other than those from normal price fluctuations. These risks derive from unlimited potential loss, short squeezes, price acceleration, and custodial failure.

The purchaser of a stock can lose only his or her investment, but can make an unlimited profit. A short seller, in contrast, can only make 100 percent on investment (if the asset sold short falls to zero), but can lose an unlimited amount. This asymmetry is the most important distinction between long investment and short selling.

The short seller's loan of securities is repayable on demand. Since the short seller does not have the shares it borrowed (since they were sold), the short seller may have to go into the marketplace to repurchase them. If the number of shares sold by the short seller is large relative to the stock's trading volume, it may be difficult to repurchase shares without driving their price up. If the short seller does not deliver the shares, the lending broker has the right to "buy them in," meaning it goes into the marketplace and repurchases them for the account of the short seller. Any loss is the obligation of the short seller.

This problem is compounded by the fact that the ability of the short seller to borrow shares is importantly a function of the aggregate number of shares sold short. Further, this short position is publicly announced each month for all stocks, thus giving traders an opportunity to *squeeze* shorts by purchasing shares and running the price up until short sellers are forced to cover.

The problem of *acceleration* arises from the peculiar impact of price moves on the equity of a short seller. If an investor purchases a stock and the price declines 50 percent, the investor loses 50 percent of its investment. In order for the investor to lose all of its equity, the stock must still decline by 100 percent. For a short seller, if a stock rises 50 percent, 50 percent of the short seller's equity is lost. However, at that point, if the stock rises a further 33 percent, the short seller loses 100 percent of its equity.

Margin regulations require that the short seller post additional cash or collateral as the stock rises and the short seller's equity erodes.

Exhibit 5–4 titled Arithmetic of Short Selling shows how this acceleration works at various levels of stock price movements.

Investors who own assets and keep these assets at custodians run little risk if the custodian fails. A trustee will be appointed to reorganize the custodian, and, after a delay, the investor will receive its assets, assuming it has records which substantiate its position. With a short seller, the short position is likely to be carried at a broker rather than a bank. Although brokers are highly regulated, they are not viewed as being as strong custodians as are the major trust banks. More importantly, if the broker fails, the short seller does not have securities at the broker. Rather it has a credit balance and a loan, both of which are held in a margin account. While this does not automatically lead to a loss, it raises the risk to the short seller.

Uses of Short Selling

Short selling can be used in three ways—to hedge risks, as a profit center, and, for taxable investors, to postpone a capital gain.

In certain hedging or arbitrage strategies, a portfolio of undervalued stocks is purchased and a portfolio of overvalued stocks is sold short. If the two portfolios are carefully constructed, stock market risk of the long portfolio cancels out the stock market risk of the short portfolio, leaving the investor with only the gains or losses from stock selection.

When employed as a profit center, an investor looks for overvalued assets and hopes to profit by their decline in price. This is analogous to the investor which purchases stocks.

Exhibit 5-4
Arithmetic of Short Selling

	Cash	Securities Borrowed and Hence Owned	Equity in Account	Securities Owed as % of Equity (% invested)	Equity as % of Market Value of Shorts
Deposit $100 with broker	100	0	100	0%	100%
Sell short $100 of stocks	200	(100)	100	100%	150%
If stocks fall 20%	200	(80)	120	67%	67%
If stocks rise 20%	200	(120)	80	150%	50%
If stocks rise 33⅓%	200	(133)	67	200%	43%
If stocks rise 40%	200	(140)	60	233%	33%
If stocks rise 50%	200	(150)	50	300%	0%
If stocks rise 100%	200	(200)	0	Infinity	

Long investor
If stocks decline 100%, all equity is gone.
If stocks decline 50%, half of equity is gone.
After stocks decline 50%, they need to decline 100% for all equity to be gone.

Short investor
If stocks rise 100%, all equity is gone.
If stocks rise 50%, half of original equity is gone but equity in account has gone from 100% to 33%.
After stocks rise 50%, they need to rise only 33% for all the original equity to be gone.
This phenomenon is called "acceleration."

When a sponsor adds a short seller to its portfolio of managers, it creates a hedge for the portfolio. To the extent that long managers and short managers can both produce profits, they can both add value to a portfolio. Since the pattern of returns will be very different from the two types of managers, the effect on the portfolio will be to dampen volatility.

A taxable investor with a large gain in a stock can protect against loss in the stock by selling it short "against the box." Instead of selling the actual shares owned, the investor borrows a similar number of shares of the same stock and sells these shares. This transaction does not constitute a sale, and thus is not taxable. While the two positions are held, both gain and loss potential are removed. This will, however, lead to loss of interest on the money tied up, unless the investor is able to secure a rebate from the lender of the shares.

INVESTING THROUGH LIMITED PARTNERSHIPS

Partnerships are not an investment, but rather a structure for making investments. Most investments are made either in separate accounts or through funds which commingle the assets of a number of investors. Partnerships are pooled vehicles like commingled funds, but by contract terms and practice are usually quite different. Some partnerships are businesses which trade in securities or futures, while others invest passively in securities and take on the character of mutual funds. Still others own illiquid securities, like venture capital or leveraged buyout investments, or physical assets, like real estate or oil and gas. Because the partnership usually has limited withdrawal rights, the general partner has extremely broad discretion over the fund, and disclosure may be limited, a thorough analysis is necessary prior to investing in partnerships. This analysis should be directed in seven areas—investment activity, general diligence, fees and expenses, withdrawal rights, legal issues, accounting and tax matters, and conflicts of interest.

Investment activity: The sponsor should attempt to determine the sources of return in the partnership; sources of risk, including leverage, concentration, and short selling; who in the organization contributes to the sources of return; how is risk controlled; and what common factors exist which could lead to a large number of investments declining in value at one time.

General diligence: Checks should be made of the amount and trend in assets under management; who is the custodian for the partnership's assets; and the existence of a backup plan if the general partner is one person and is injured, disabled, or becomes inactive. It is also advisable to make reference checks, and know about any existing positions which the investor will be buying into. Finally, the manager should be visited in its offices to see if its resources are commensurate with its investment process and client base.

Fees and expenses: Compensation or reinvestment to the general partner can be in three forms: expenses paid, fees, and percentage of profits (also called incentive fees).

Partnerships vary greatly as to which expenses are borne by the partnership and which by the general partner or management company. The larger the fee to the management company, the more expenses it should bear. If the general partnership is engaged in only one business and has only one pool of assets, it is not uncommon for this pool of assets to bear all expenses of running the partnership. In this case, any fees or incentives paid to the general partner are pure compensation and should be analyzed as such.

Issues concerning incentive fees are the percentage of profits paid to the general partner; the percent of loss, if any; presence of a hurdle or minimum rate under which no incentive is paid; or a preferred return which allocates a disproportionate share of the profits to the general partner after the investor has received a certain return, or a loss carry-forward such that time periods which have losses are aggregated with periods of gains, to allow the investor to recapture lost capital before paying an incentive fee. Finally, does the incentive apply to all assets or are there separate incentives for groups of assets such that an investor could have a loss overall but the manager receive an incentive on those investments which were successful? As to expenses, the sponsor might want to investigate possible limits on the ability to charge expenses to the partnership; salaries to general partners; any markup on costs charged to the partnership, including interest expense; commissions on transactions placed through affiliates; and whether soft dollars (directed commissions) are allocated for research, office expenses, or marketing.

Also of interest is the arrangement with respect to indemnification of the general partner by the partnership. For instance, if the general partner engaged in illegal activities, would the partnership be liable for legal costs and penalties?

Withdrawal rights: The sponsor should investigate how often withdrawals are permitted, whether withdrawal applies to all money or just initial capital or profits, whether there are special rights or limitations during the early phase of the partnership's life, and whether the lock-up period is realistic relative to the type of investment or is related to the manager's desire to control assets. It is also important to know how long after the withdrawal period are funds paid out (e.g., are they withheld pending audit), to what extent reserves can be held back, and whether interest is paid on reserves.

Withdrawal also could be triggered by events, either legal or related to the general partner. Legal events include notice that the general partner is indicted or that it is a target of a grand jury investigation.

Incapacity of general partners or principals includes death, incapacitation, resignation, inactivity, or withdrawal of certain sums of money. As to the latter, it is desirable to know how much money the general partner has invested in the partnership and whether investors will be given prior written notice of withdrawals by the general partner before the limited partner has to issue its own withdrawal notice.

Conflicts of interest: Potential conflicts include investments by the general partner outside the partnership, and commissions or fees earned by the general partner from the partnership. A conflict may also exist with respect to the general partner's time and attention, which might be devoted wholly to the partnership or to other investment or noninvestment areas.

Legal issues: Investors should carefully review the three documents governing the investment. The *private placement memorandum* discloses the nature of the investment, risks, and background of the general partner; the *partnership agreement* is the binding agreement between the investor and the partnership; and the *subscription agreement* provides representations by the investor which are relied upon by the general partner, to be sure the investor is legally permitted to make the investment.

An inquiry can also be made of any regulatory violations by the general partner, any relevant lawsuits, and any side letters between the general partner and a limited partner.

Accounting and tax matters: The sponsor should review the financial statements of the partnership, as well as the letters from the general partner to investors. The partnership should have an annual audit by a public accountant; it is rare, if ever, that it is advisable to proceed if no audit is available. Tax issues should be addressed, especially for tax-exempt entities which are subject to tax on unrelated business taxable income. The extent of potential liability for taxes, as well as the partnership's ability to provide necessary records, is important.

AVOIDING DISASTERS

While every investor, beneficiary, and court of law recognizes that there are risks to investing, no one is particularly happy to look back at a portfolio and find it has lost money. When the loss exceeds a modest percent and approaches a total loss, the unhappiness can change to anger. Thus, it is worthwhile to consider how disaster might be avoided.

Fund sponsors attempting to diversify portfolios into areas other than stocks and bonds may quickly find themselves operating beyond their knowledge level. While this is understandably a source of concern, especially when the investments are illiquid, nonetheless it is possible to invest rationally, if several rules are followed:

1. Deal only with reputable people with established expertise in their fields.
2. Analyze the structure of the investment to be sure the fund is adequately rewarded for the risk to be taken. This means being sure the fund does not take all the risk while the promoter takes the lion's share of the profits.
3. Diversify broadly. While it is possible a single oil well may turn out to be uneconomical, it is unlikely an established operator drilling sensibly chosen prospects will drill all dry holes.

In most cases it is advisable to invest in a manner which provides liability limited to the amount of the investment. This means choosing corporate or limited partnership structures, and not general partnerships or joint ventures.

Insurance can also be used in cases where noninvestment risks are large. Finally, the investor should consider nonlegal implications of the investment, especially where there are social ramifications. While most people feel it is desirable for pension funds to invest in housing, few of these supporters will be in evidence when the fund is evicting tenants for failure to pay rent.

If these factors are kept in mind, it is entirely possible for fund sponsors to invest successfully in alternative investments.

CHAPTER 6

ALTERNATIVE INVESTMENTS—ENERGY

The oil business, as you know, is liable to sudden and violent fluctuations.
John D. Rockefeller

Given the enormous capital needs of the oil and gas industry, it is surprising that more direct investment by pension funds in energy has not taken place. This may be due to the fact that the large oil companies have tapped institutional funds via the stock and bond markets, and energy investments were historically viewed by many investors as tax shelters, thus not appropriate for tax-exempt institutions. It is likely that, in the future, these factors will seem less important, and pension funds will increase their direct investments in energy.

Direct investments, as opposed to investment in stocks or bonds of oil companies, can be categorized in terms of two objectives: discovery of assets and income. Discovery activities are categorized by the degree of risk involved, which in turn is usually a function of the proximity of the well to structures which have produced hydrocarbons in previously drilled wells. The most risky discovery activity is called "wildcatting," followed by development and offset drilling. *Wildcatting* is drilling on acreage in which there is no previous history of discovery. *Development drilling* is exploration in the general area of previous successes, or more precisely on a site within one spacing unit from a well capable of production from the same horizon as the development well. A *spacing unit* is the minimum permissible area between wells, as established by the relevant governmental authority; the *horizon* is the horizontal zone beneath the surface. (A given well, if drilled deep enough, may find hydrocarbons at different zones or levels.) *Offset drilling* is drilling in the same geologic formation in which another well is currently producing. These terms are not defined precisely and investors must confirm that their idea of a development well is the same as that of the promoter who wishes to secure the investor's financial support, to be sure the program is appropriate for the investor's need and the investor is adequately compensated for the risk being taken.

Passive income investments, in which someone else has explored for and operated the wells, can be made through purchase of working interests in producing properties or through purchases of royalty interests on producing properties. If the investor purchases a working interest it is, in effect, a partner in the property. As such, it shares in revenues, expenses, and the ensuing profits or losses.

Royalties are a portion of the revenue stream produced by a well. A *landowner royalty* accrues to the owner of the mineral rights in the land. (Mineral rights are distinguished from the surface rights which entitle the holder to use the surface of the land.) *Overriding royalties* are shares in the revenue stream, distinct from the landowner royalties, which are sold or awarded to people by the promoter, operator, or anyone who owns part of the working interest. These royalties, or overrides, permit the holder to participate in revenues without incurring any costs. In smaller oil companies, an overriding royalty may be granted to a geologist or well operator whose extra efforts can be vital to the success of an exploration or production program. Also, the owner of a lease can sell the lease to an operator or another promoter while retaining an overriding royalty on any production from the lease. The number of overriding interests on a well can be unlimited, and since each holder of a royalty is entitled to receive revenue without sharing in costs, the investor must be careful that its interest, called the *net revenue interest,* is not so overburdened with overrides that the hydrocarbons in the ground cannot be economically produced or, more likely, that the risk of finding and producing it is not proportional to the reward.

Since overriding royalties are granted by a lessee rather than the owner of the property, they last only as long as the lease is valid. In comparison, landowner royalties run in perpetuity, since they run with the land rather than with the lease on that land.

Investment in producing properties is less risky than exploration, but still not without risk. Oil and gas properties can vary greatly in their life cycles. Virtually all production declines over time, such that each year's production after the first year or two is less than that of the previous year. This production function can decline rapidly over a few years, or slowly over decades. The shape of this function (longevity of the wells) is an important determinant of the value of the property or lease. Further, individual wells are subject to a variety of interruptions due to factors such as the changing mix of oil and gas, encroachment by water, and errors in estimates of the size of the reservoir, so considerable risk is entailed in individual wells regardless of estimates made in advance, or even of past operating history.

Oil and Gas Deal Structures

Once the investor decides how it wants to participate in the energy area, it must then turn to the structure of the investment. As with most investments, the deal can be analyzed partly in terms of "who invests what, who does what, and who gets what." This is especially important in oil and gas investments where the deal structures are myriad. Passive investors typically do not participate in the management of the enterprise, so the question becomes what share of the revenues or profits does the promoter get relative to the amount he or she invests, and what other income, if any, the promoter derives from the relationship.

The promoter can receive a disproportional share of the profits of the activity in at least four structures: reversionary interest, promoted interest, carried interest, and functional allocation.

In a *reversionary interest* (also called a *back in*), the investor receives all or most cash flow up to a certain point, such as the point where his investment is paid back, either with or without some preestablished rate of return, after which a share, or an increased share, of profits reverts to the promoter. In the *promoted interest,* the operator invests along with the investor, but receives a disproportionate share of the profits relative to his investment. Under a *carried interest* structure, the operator gets a free or carried participation in the program without any investment.

In a *functional allocation,* cost sharing parallels tax treatment and is less applicable now due to changes in tax laws. The investor typically paid intangible costs of drilling, that is, those costs, such as for drilling the well, which result in no depreciable asset, and thus are expensed for tax purposes. The promoter paid the cost of leasing the property for drilling and for tangible costs which are capitalized for tax purposes, such as for the pipe and equipment for completing the well. This structure was common in tax shelters, since the tax-paying investor was anxious to pay costs which could be expensed for tax purposes in the current year, rather than owning capital assets which had to be depreciated over a number of years.

While there are no truly standard deal structures, it may be helpful to consider a frequently discussed sharing arrangement, the so-called third for a quarter structure. After performing a geologic analysis, the organizer leases land. The promoter then approaches three investors and offers them each one fourth of the profits from the well in return for their each putting up one third of the cost. Thus, the organizer supplies lease and geologic information and the investors supply capital, with each taking 25 percent of the profits. More precisely, in this arrangement, also called "a quarter carry to the casing point" or more fully "a third for a quarter carry to the casing point," the investors pay all costs up to the point at which the well is drilled, but before the metal casing pipe is installed. After that, the investor and the promoter work straight up or heads up, meaning they share proportionally in costs and revenues. Usually, the quarter carry to the casing point arrangement applies only to the first well in a prospect, or group of wells to be drilled in one area. In addition, however, there is usually some sort of management fee, perhaps equal to 10 percent of the AFE (authority for expenditures, or amount spent to drill the first well), or some profit on the land. Thus, in the third for a quarter structure, the promoter, in return for its analytical and organizational costs, receives a "free look at the bottom of the hole" of the first well before the decision to set casing and complete the well. This structure is widely used among oil industry participants in transactions with each other.

Deal structures can be modified endlessly and carried out in combination with each other to provide structures which can suit almost any need, and confuse all but the most experienced. No investor should hesitate in the slightest to have all terms defined precisely, as even the most sophisticated industry participants sometimes use terminology differently.

Investors should be aware that the deal structure, in addition to impacting the way profits are distributed, may also impact the incentive of the operator. In a functional allocation, where the investor pays costs of finding the well and the operator pays costs of completing it, the operator may seek wells which have very high return despite the high risk. It may also decide not to complete wells which have small but positive expected returns, since it bears the cost of completion.

In a carried interest arrangement, where the operator pays no costs, it may not be as selective in the wells it completes as it might be if it were spending its own money. In deals with a reversionary interest, the operator may have little incentive to manage a well which is profitable, but has little chance of exceeding the investor's investment.

As a further caution, investors are well served if the sharing arrangement is based on a package of wells, called a drilling program, rather than on individual wells, so the operator's ability to maximize its own interest is more restricted. For instance, it is desirable to have the payout based on the entire program, so the good wells will carry the marginal and dry ones. This would prevent the promoter from having an incentive to look after only the most productive wells rather than all the wells, thus creating the most return for the investor.

Choosing a Partner

The oil industry is sufficiently complex that very few sponsors can operate without an experienced partner. Further, if the fund is tax-exempt and wishes to avoid unrelated business taxable income, it must be a passive investor. Choice of the partner is crucial. It is important that the partner be knowledgeable, financially able to meet its commitments, and have an investment objective similar to that of the investing fund. Clearly, tax benefits are not the goal of pension funds. Large oil companies may be interested in building up their reserve positions as opposed to developing near-term income, whereas a pension fund may or may not share that objective. On the other hand, a pension fund may wish to own oil reserves as an inflation hedge, but have no desire for income due to its cash flow structure. An operating partner might be more interested in maximizing current cash return. While any of these goals can be desirable from the point of view of a specific investor, it is vital that the fund and the operator have objectives which are similar and well articulated in advance.

Analyzing Investment Returns from Oil and Gas

Three measurements are commonly used in reviewing oil and gas deals: payout, internal rate of return, and return on investment. *Payout* is the number of years until the investor has received back its initial investment after all expenses and fees before income tax. Payout is an important concept since many deal structures involve changing revenue, or profit sharing, after the deal has "paid out," that is, the investor has received his money back. *Internal rate of return* is the interest or discount rate which makes the present value of the income stream, again after expenses and fees, equal to the investment. This calculation can be made before or after income taxes are deducted. *Return on investment* is the ratio of cash received to cash investment, both before considering income taxes.

The prospective returns from an investment are very much a function of the projection of future income. One of the key assumptions in oil and gas investing is the estimate of escalation, or increases in prices for oil and gas. While no insight will be provided here as to how to make these projections accurately, several things can be noted. First, there is no law which requires that prices go up; gravity operates on oil prices as it does on those of other commodities and securities. Second, the price of hydrocarbons, while certainly related to inflation, need not track inflation—oil prices could act very much differently from the overall inflation rate during even reasonably long periods of time. Finally, the cost of finding and delivering petroleum products may act much differently from the price itself. While the two are likely to move in the same direction, they might do so at much different rates. All these factors must be considered when analyzing projections of the costs and revenues of an oil drilling program.

Note of Caution on Reserve Estimates

Estimates can be made of the amount or value of energy in the ground, for instance, in evaluating the fair price to pay for producing properties. These reserves are classified as proven, probable, and possible. However, the value of energy reserves must be considered in the light of the imprecision associated with making estimates of the volume and producibility of hydrocarbons, as well as in the uncertainty as to future prices for them and the cost of their extraction.

Use of Consultants

Investors would be well served to employ independent consultants who are paid by the investor, and respond to the investor's needs. Consultants can be useful in judging the capabilities of the promoter or operator, the likelihood of a venture's success, and the fairness of the allocation of revenues and costs.

APPENDIX 6-A

EXAMPLE OF SHARING ARRANGEMENT IN AN OIL AND GAS INVESTMENT

It may be helpful to think of the process through which an oil and gas transaction might take place. The following example was supplied by Robert L. Huston of Energy Advisors, Inc., a New York City energy consulting firm.

King, a landowner, owns the minerals underlying his Texas ranch property as well as the surface land itself. Hunt, an oil operator, negotiates a lease for five years with King which enables Hunt to enter King's property, drill for, and produce oil and gas.

Hunt invites other investors to join him in drilling a well on King's land which is subject to the oil and gas lease. Three investors join Hunt, and each has a 25 percent leasehold interest. These fractional or percentage interests are called *working interests*, and well drilling costs are shared by these four working interest owners. Should oil or gas be discovered, Hunt and his partners will receive their share of working interest revenues in this same 25 percent ratio, and they will also pay all costs to operate the well.

In negotiating the original lease, King retains a royalty interest in any oil or gas found on his land; this is called *landowner royalty*. Typically, a landowner royalty reserves one eighth of the minerals, so King will receive 12½ percent of the gross proceeds of any oil or gas sales at the wellhead. Well operating costs are not deducted from gross income in calculating King's 12½ percent royalty income.

In addition to the mineral royalty retained in the lease with Hunt, Mr. King will receive a cash bonus for signing the lease. This lease bonus will be supplemented by annual lease rental payments to King until a well is drilled on the leased property. These payments are called *delay rentals*.

Summarizing the transaction, well drilling costs of $1 million are shared as follows:

	Percent	Dollars
Mr. King	0	0
Mr. Hunt	25%	250,000
Mr. Finder	25%	250,000
Seeking company	25%	250,000
Looking company	25%	250,000
	100%	$1,000,000

The well is successful, and oil and gas gross revenues of $200,000 are received in the first year. Costs are $35,000 to operate the well, paid by the working interest owners. Revenues and costs are shared as follows:

	Percent of Gross Revenue	Dollar Amount of Gross Revenue	Less Operating Costs	Net Dollar Revenue Interest	Percent Working Interest Income
Mr. King	12.5	$ 25,000	0	$ 25,000	0
Mr. Hunt	21.875	43,750	$ 8,750	35,000	25
Mr. Finder	21.875	43,750	8,750	35,000	25
Seeking company	21.875	43,750	8,750	35,000	25
Looking company	21.875	43,750	8,750	35,000	25
	100%	$200,000	$35,000	$165,000	100%

Once production is established it is not unusual for Hunt or another working interest owner to sell a portion of his respective property. For example, Hunt might sell 20 percent of his 25 percent share of the working interest, or 5 percent of the total working interest, to raise cash for further drilling. This is simply a transfer of a piece of the working interest with income rights and expense obligation exactly like the other working interest owners.

Another common transaction in the industry is for a working interest owner to create from his interest an *override* or *overriding royalty* which is not truly royalty, and not like the other working interests. An override created from a working interest is free of well operating costs, but is not like a landowner royalty in legal terms. This is because the override stems from the leasehold interest rather than the original land-owner interest.

Mr. Buyer acquires a fractional interest in the gross revenue from a property when he purchases from Mr. Hunt an override in the amount of 20 percent of Hunt's 25 percent working interest. This fraction of the working interest equates to 4.375 percent of the gross property interests, or 8/8 as it is expressed in oil jargon. Similar to King's landowner royalty, Buyer's override entitles him to receive a percentage of the gross revenues without deducting well operating costs.

Example:

	Percent Gross Revenues	Percent Operating Costs
King	12.5	0
Buyer	4.375	0
Hunt	17.5	25
Finder	21.875	25
Seeking company	21.875	25
Looking company	21.875	25
	100%	100%

APPENDIX 6-B

QUICK RUN THROUGH AN OIL FIELD:
A GUIDE TO OIL FIELD TERMINOLOGY

The following discussion may assist investors who are not familiar with the terminology of the oil and gas exploration industry.

Geologists search for geologic structures or prospects where hydrocarbons are trapped in the earth's crust. Search is made by gravimetric methods (measuring changes in the earth's gravity), magnetic methods (measuring the earth's magnetic field), and seismic methods (measuring the type of rock based upon its sound or shock wave transmission capabilities), with seismic being by far the most important. Once an area is found which appears desirable, the landman arranges leases by paying a cash bonus to the landowner, and promising a share of the future revenue in the form of the landowner's royalty. The bonus can be almost any amount from zero to tens of thousands of dollars per acre, depending upon the history of the land, and the current state of the oil market. Landowner's royalties were historically ⅛ of revenues, but in highly productive areas they can run from 3/16 to 30 percent. If, as is the case with much promising land (prospective acreage), a lease already exists, the landman negotiates with the lease holder rather than the landowner.

After drilling rights are obtained, a drilling site is chosen and a permit secured from the state or federal government. A drilling contractor is then employed who will drill the well for a charge based upon a fixed price contract (turnkey), a charge per foot (footage), or a daily rate. The drilling contractor will use a rotary drilling rig (which drills by rotating horizontally) or, if the well is especially shallow, a cable tool rig (where a chisellike tool is continuously lifted and dropped to cut into the soil and rock below). Material cut by the rotary rig is removed by drilling mud, which is pumped into the hole and back out; material chipped loose by the cable tool rig is removed with a bailer, a long tube-shaped bucket which is lowered into the hole and bails out the hole. After the well is drilled, a decision must be made as to whether or not to complete the well. Samples, taken from the drilling mud, bailer, or cores (larger samples), are examined for the characteristics associated with the probability of recovering oil and gas. These are the presence of oil, gas, and water, as well as the porosity and permeability of the formation.

A formation or drill stem test can be made by lowering a tool into the well and recovering material directly from the foundation. This material can be inspected for oil and gas.

The well can also be logged to try to determine the characteristics of the formation by lowering instruments into the well bore and measuring the reaction of the well to gamma rays, neutrons, or electrical charges. For instance, since oil and gas have high resistivity to electricity, and salt water has low resistivity, valuable information about the potential for oil and gas production from the formation can be determined by passing an electric current through it and measuring the electrical resistance of the sand or rock.

Geologists are interested in the amount of oil which might be contained within the formation as well as the ease with which the rock will yield the oil. *Porosity* represents the amount of pore space available to contain fluid within the rock. *Permeability* (measured in millidarcies) is a measure of the ability of the oil to flow from within the rock. Contrary to popular perception, oil wells are not subsurface swimming pools filled with highly liquid oil. Rather, oil and gas exist in tiny pockets within oil-bearing sands and rock. Porosity measures the extent to which the rock is like a sponge on one extreme, or like a dense piece of granite on the other. Permeability measures the ease with which the oil trapped inside the sponge can be released. Oil shale, by way of explanation, is highly porous rock which is highly impermeable. That is, it contains great amounts of oil, but the oil does not flow easily from the rock.

After analysis of all available information, a decision is made as to whether or not to case the well. *Casing* is steel pipe run inside the well to protect against cave-ins and to isolate and seal the formation. After casing, the well is cemented by pumping cement down through the casing and forcing it up the outside of the casing between the casing and the rock or dirt formation. The well is then perforated by using jetlike explosives to shoot holes in the casing at the point where the oil-bearing formation exists. Tubing, another series of pipe, is then run inside the casing to recover oil or gas. At this point, if significant pressure exists below the surface, oil or gas may flow naturally. Frequently, however, additional stimulation is required and the well is fractured by forcing water or chemicals into the well bore and out through the perforation into the formation. And, of course, the familiar pump jack, which pumps oil from the well, can also be used to bring oil to the surface.

The natural forces which drive hydrocarbons from the well include gas, water, and gravity. These forces can be assisted by secondary recovery methods which include flooding the well with water or injecting gas or steam. In secondary recovery, either wells originally producing (or meant to produce) oil or gas are converted, or new wells are drilled, such that these wells can be used to force water, gas, or steam into the ground to drive the oil and gas up through the remaining wells.

CHAPTER 7

CREATING PORTFOLIOS

[A good portfolio] is a balanced whole, providing the investor with protections and opportunities with respect to a wide range of contingencies.
Harry Markowitz, Portfolio Selection

Portfolios are created by combining asset categories in a way that is appropriate, given the investment policy of the fund. Keeping in mind the sponsor's attitude toward risk, diversification, and utility, the sponsor must address five policy decisions. These are:

Which asset categories?
In what proportions?
How risky should each asset category be?
How diversified should each one be?
How much latitude should there be to change each of these policies?

The questions of which assets and in what proportions are *strategic policy decisions*. Changes in proportions on an interim basis are called *tactical policy decisions*.

These questions can be asked regarding two major areas: countries and asset types. A sponsor must consider which countries to invest in, what proportions to invest in each country, how aggressive or conservative the assets in each country should be, and how well diversified those assets should be (i.e., to what extent the approach will emphasize securities selection as opposed to just mirroring the market).

Similarly, these questions can be raised regarding asset types: which asset types (stocks, bonds, etc.), what percentage in each asset category, how aggressive each category should be (i.e., should the fund own risky stocks or conservative stocks), and how diversified each asset type should be. Finally, the sponsor must decide to what extent the investment manager will be allowed or encouraged to change these decisions. For instance, policy might require 60 percent of assets on average to be designated for equities but the investment manager could be allowed to vary this percentage between 0 percent and 100 percent, depending on its market outlook. On the other hand, it would also be possible to say the 60/40 asset mix should be maintained for each quarter.

SPECIFIC DECISIONS CONCERNING COUNTRIES

Deciding which countries to invest in can be based on a number of factors. The size of the securities market is one. The larger the market, the more investment opportunity there is within the country. Also, according to capital market theory, an investor should apportion its assets according to market valuation, although it is less clear that this applies among countries than within countries. A second factor is gross domestic product, the measure of the value produced by the economy as opposed to the value of all stocks. Another possibility is to consider the historic or projected growth rate of each country's economy or stock market in order to anticipate those countries which will have superior growth rates in the future. An investor who is concerned with the low level of capital reinvestment in the United States relative to that of other countries may wish to choose countries based on the reinvestment rate. It is also possible to use a "bottom up" as opposed to a "top down" approach. In other words, the investor may wish to participate in some particular industry or company and to develop an international position in this manner. Finally, the previous experience of the sponsor or the investment manager may provide a basis for choosing countries. For example, a corporation which has a subsidiary in Germany may find it easier to invest in that country than in others.

Decisions on what proportions to invest in different countries can be made on the same bases as decisions on which countries to invest in. That is, the decisions can be based on the size of the market or economy in each country, the economy's growth rate, the reinvestment rate, a choice of particular industries or companies, or the comfort level derived from previous experience.

The choice of risk level and diversification level of each asset category reflects the sponsor's willingness to earn the return of the market as opposed to relying on the success of a manager in securities selection. Relying heavily on the manager's ability in this area makes it possible for the fund to have especially good results while introducing the risk that it will have especially bad results. In practice, sponsors are likely to end up with one of two positions. Either the fund will be structured quantitatively, and hence the diversification level will tend to be rather high, or the sponsor will rely on an investment manager to structure the fund, in which case the manager will likely opt for an active approach and a lesser diversification level.

In addition to knowing the basic investment policies of the fund, the investment manager must know to what extent it has discretion to vary the policies set forth by the sponsor.

SPECIFIC DECISIONS CONCERNING ASSET TYPES

The five policy decisions—which ones, what proportions, what risk level, what diversification level, and how much discretion to give the manager to change these policies—must be decided for the various security types. As to "which ones," Chapter 4 contains a broad list of security types. Exhibit 3–2 shows approximate risk/return relationships for some of these assets. Thus it is possible to get a general idea of the relative risk of each asset type. It should be noted that the actual level of risk may vary considerably from period to period, though it is likely that the ordering of asset risks will remain the same. It is inconceivable, for instance, that stocks would be less risky than short-term securities for any significant period of time.

The second question, what proportion in each asset, is intertwined with the question of what risk level to choose since a given level of risk could be achieved by having, say, 60 percent in conservative stocks and 40 percent in aggressive bonds, or 50 percent in aggressive stocks and 50 percent in conservative bonds.

Twelve ways have been identified to make asset allocation decisions, depending on who makes them and the methodology used. The latter can be further categorized into analytical and fund-specific approaches. The appendix at the end of the chapter provides examples of how to use several of these methods.

WHO IS THE DECISION MAKER?

Committee decision: An investment committee can use its intuition, experience, and analytical input to decide on the asset allocation for the fund. Just as it could use its judgment to choose a manager, it can use judgment to allocate assets.

Investment manager makes all investment decisions: Sponsors can hire an investment manager who will make all decisions about asset allocation. This includes policy (strategic) as well as tactical asset allocation. For example, a balanced fund manager managing all the assets of the fund will decide which asset categories are to be used, what proportions, the risk level of each asset category, and diversification levels, and will further decide how and to what extent to change these factors.

Investment manager makes asset allocation decisions: It is possible for the sponsor to have managers that are managing individual stock and bond portfolios and still have an investment manager that manages the overall asset allocation. This asset allocation manager might have two functions: to see that the portfolio is fully invested at all times at the asset allocation level required, and to invest cash balances which appear in the underlying accounts in the long-term asset for which the portfolio is designed. This service might be desirable for a fund concerned with two problems, asset drift and suboptimal use of cash. If a fund wishes to be 60 percent in stocks and 40 percent in bonds, the natural movement of markets will lead to a different asset allocation. Over the long run, equities should outperform bonds, leading the fund to be more than 60 percent in equities, and thus riskier than intended. Over shorter periods of time, natural cycles within stocks and bonds can also change this allocation.

The second reason for having this management arrangement is to ensure that cash is fully invested at all times. Most equity managers will not keep portfolios 100 percent invested. Rather, it is common for portfolios to be 90 or 95 percent invested, with the balance in cash. Under normal market circumstances, cash underperforms both bonds and stocks, leading to a "cash drag" on the portfolio.

In both cases, this investment fine tuning will likely be carried out with the use of stock and bond futures, and thus will not impact the underlying portfolios or managers. It can also be implemented with index funds.

Consultants advise: A consultant can be used to make asset allocations decisions, both policy and tactical. This consultant may have no direct securities or futures activities, but can direct the movement of assets among managers. As with the asset allocation overlay, it is possible to do this with either futures or index funds.

Consultants can also be helpful to sponsors wishing to work either directly or through investment managers, since the consultants may have experience, software, and data that are difficult for the sponsor to duplicate at a reasonable cost.

To the extent that a pension plan sponsor wishes to integrate its asset allocations with its liability projections, it will be necessary to work with experts in both investments and actuarial science.

ANALYTICAL METHODS

Relative value: Asset allocation decisions can be made based on the relative value of asset classes. A methodology of calculating expected returns for stocks and bonds can be used at any time to measure the relative value of each. The sponsor can then allocate assets according to the area which is most undervalued, and to the extent that the area is undervalued.

Simulation: The sponsor can forecast future asset values in its fund, and probabilities of achieving them, through simulation. For instance, we know the probability of achieving heads on the flip of a coin is 0.5 but since each flip can be either heads or tails, it is possible to have 10 heads in a row. If a computer is used to randomly "flip" the coin for 1,000 series of 10 flips each, we can see how many times out of 1,000 would yield 10 straight heads. This technique can be applied to portfolios by assuming certain estimates about the rates of return on stocks, bonds, and other assets, the variabilities of those returns, and the degree to which the assets are correlated (have similar movement in similar time periods). The historical data supplied by Ibbotson Associates can be used to estimate future data. A sponsor can then simulate the chances of meeting certain financial goals of the fund for different asset mixes. The asset mix with the most appealing probabilities is then chosen.

Although this approach can be very useful, it is essential to recognize the importance of choosing the correct assumptions, the impact of changing inflation rates, and the need to consider liabilities as well as assets.

Optimization: Using the same techniques used in simulation, an investor can create an "efficient frontier" of portfolios which have a range of risk/return characteristics. Each portfolio on the frontier has more return and more risk than the portfolio to its left (see Exhibit 7–1). These portfolios are "efficient" because for each level of return there is no portfolio which is less risky, and for each level of risk there is no portfolio which has more return. The appendix at the end of this chapter has an example of a series of portfolios created by optimization.

Both simulation and optimization are best performed using real (inflation-adjusted) returns. Otherwise, distortions due to inflation may

EXHIBIT 7–1
Efficient Frontier Graph, 15 Years 1977–1991

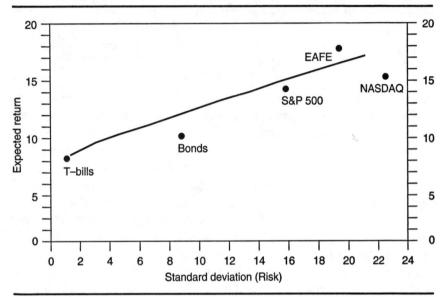

impact results, and numbers projected into the future take on the appearance of such vast wealth that almost any investment policy appears to lead to a bonanza.

FUND-SPECIFIC METHODS

There are five ways that sponsors can choose asset allocation policies based on their internal needs.

Income needed: A fund's assets can be allocated so as to produce the estimated amount of income needed to meet the organization's cash requirements. Either current or future needs can be considered. The latter is significantly more difficult because it requires a forecast of future cash flow from investments and, particularly, dividend payments on common stocks.

For sponsors whose funds have cash needs that can be measured with precision, it is possible to establish a portfolio that will generate cash when it is needed. In a process called *dedication,* a portfolio of bonds is chosen which will have coupon payments and redemptions at precisely the time and in the amounts required to meet the cash needs of the sponsor. Chapter 9 describes this and other fixed-income management control techniques.

Minimum required total return: Looking beyond income, the sponsor can consider not just cash income received but also capital gains achieved or expected to be achieved, thus expanding the idea from income only to a total return. (See example at the end of this chapter.)

Maximum affordable contribution: Funds such as pension funds with established liabilities can be operated with the goal of maintaining a contribution level which is below a certain range, in order to cap the maximum financial drain on the corporation. (See example at the end of this chapter.)

Maximum decline in assets: The fund can also be run to minimize the possibility of a loss exceeding a certain level. (See example at the end of this chapter.)

Comparative: It is possible to look to other funds to see what they do. See Exhibit 7–2. To the extent that the sponsoring organizations are similar, similar investment policies may be appropriate. For instance, if a company has a greater ability to bear risk than do other companies, it could establish a policy which is aggressive compared to those pursued by the other companies. The appendix at the end of this chapter contains an example of use of the comparative method.

An investor might use a number of approaches, then work to integrate them into a single policy. Then approval would be requested from the board of directors or board of trustees and the policy would be communicated to the investment managers. Periodic reviews would be made to see whether the managers were following the policy and whether the policy was adequately serving the needs of the sponsor.

APPENDIX

Optimization

The sponsor decides upon the asset categories with which it is comfortable, choosing cash equivalents, long-term bonds, U.S. stocks, non-U.S. stocks, and real estate. In order to have historical information to use in its optimizer, it chooses as proxies for these asset categories Treasury bills, Treasury bonds, S&P 500, EAFE index, and the Ibbotson series for real estate.

EXHIBIT 7–2
Percent Asset Allocation of Retirement Plans (as of 12/31/91)

	Corporate Plans Over $100M	Corporate Plans Under $100M	Taft-Hartley	Local Government	Endowment	Foundation
Equities						
5	77.0	68.5	59.8	63.5	79.5	68.6
25	63.5	61.9	50.1	53.0	66.2	63.3
50	57.4	53.7	46.0	47.6	53.6	58.2
75	48.1	47.5	38.2	36.3	43.4	49.5
95	24.1	30.7	27.3	24.6	30.3	35.3
Bonds						
5	45.4	56.1	64.9	67.3	58.3	55.1
25	37.0	44.9	48.8	55.5	44.5	41.5
50	30.0	35.8	44.7	45.6	38.7	34.9
75	23.3	28.8	33.1	35.8	30.4	30.5
95	11.2	19.7	16.0	19.9	10.5	24.9
Cash Eq						
5	16.9	18.9	17.5	16.1	20.4	15.4
25	8.6	9.0	10.1	7.8	10.3	7.3
50	6.3	5.5	6.9	5.8	5.3	4.0
75	3.8	2.9	4.1	3.2	1.8	2.6
95	1.6	1.0	1.6	0.6	0.2	1.6

Source: SEI Corporation

Running the simulation, the resulting "efficient frontier" shows low-risk portfolios composed solely of real estate and high-risk portfolios composed solely of EAFE stocks. In optimization, the extremes are set by the lowest risk portfolio, which tends to be the asset with the lowest risk, and the highest return asset, which with a 100 percent allocation is always the highest return portfolio. However, the middle portfolios are also composed almost exclusively of real estate and EAFE, a combination which could not easily be accepted as the basis for all of the fund's investments.

Upon examination, it seems that real estate is valued by appraisal rather than at market, so the volatility of real estate is shown on a different basis and at a lower level. Further, the boom in Japanese equities in the late 1980s, which dominated the EAFE index return, is viewed as an aberration. Therefore, real estate volatility was increased to a point halfway between that of bonds and stock, under the premise that real estate has characteristics of both bonds, in that rental payments are like bond coupons, and equities, in that income tends to grow with inflation. Likewise, EAFE equities return was reduced to 1 percentage point above that of U.S. equities under the assumption that non-U.S. economies might grow faster than the U.S. economy, but only slightly so.

This simulation produced a more balanced portfolio, but one outcome was bothersome. Bonds were never chosen for any of the portfolios. This, it was learned, was for two reasons. Bond returns were only slightly higher than T-bill returns, and bonds were more volatile. Further, bond returns are somewhat correlated with stock returns. Since stock returns were so much higher than bond returns, the optimizer preferred to have a bit of stocks (for their high returns) and a bit of T bills (for their lack of volatility and lack of correlation with equities) rather than having any bonds.

This was not comforting to the sponsor, which feared that a steep recession or depression might be very harsh on equities. In this environment, long-term, high-quality bonds would prosper. Therefore, the sponsor added an arbitrary 20 percent in long-term Treasury bonds to the portfolio.

Upon further analysis, the sponsor decided that it was more interested in inflation-adjusted (real) results than in nominal results, so it re-ran the simulations with inflation-adjusted numbers. These were calculated by subtracting the Producers Price Index for each time period from the return of each asset for that same time period. Standard deviations of the resulting real returns were calculated, as were correlations.

Then, the sponsor, being hesitant to make such an important decision based solely on historical results, decided to forecast returns. This it did by starting with the current rates on bills and bonds, and using the implied return from looking at the earnings yield on stocks and factoring in a modest growth rate on stocks. Real estate returns were estimated at halfway between stocks and bonds.

As a further check, the sponsor decided to run the process backward. It chose the asset allocations with which its investment committee felt comfortable to see the risk/return characteristics of that portfolio. It did the same thing with its current asset allocation and with the allocations of several of its peer companies. With all the results in hand, the committee then chose an allocation.

The sponsor, a corporate pension fund, after talking to its actuary, decided it would be best to try to integrate its asset projections with its liability projections. It then worked with the actuary to see how changes in asset levels interacted with changes in liabilities, and the impact on future contributions.

MINIMUM REQUIRED RETURN

A sponsor thinks stocks will return more than bonds, and thus wants to have the maximum percent in stocks. However, it also wants to have an acceptable chance of making at least the minimum required return over a time horizon.

It made a five-year projection of the cash requirements for the fund and concluded that a 7.5 percent per year compound return (43.6 percent cumulative) was required to meet the fund's future needs. Based on the Ibbotson Associates results (Exhibit 7–3B, five-year periods), the sponsor noted that the stock market did not reach this objective almost 30 percent of the time. That is, almost 30 percent of the time the stock market has total returns of less than 43.6 percent (actually 44.7 percent) over five years. A 30 percent chance of not achieving the minimum required return was regarded as excessive, so it was considered inappropriate to invest the fund 100 percent in equities. It was deemed acceptable, however, for the fund to miss the objective 20 percent of the time. Therefore, the fund was invested 87 percent in bonds, earning 8 percent per year and maturing in five years (46.9 percent cumulative for five years) and 13 percent in stocks returning 20.4 percent cumulative (stocks earned less than 20.4 percent in only 20 percent of the five-year periods), for an appreciation of 43.6 percent to $143 = (146.9 \times 0.87) + (120.4 \times 0.13)$. In this case the fund would achieve or exceed its objective 80 percent of the time based on the 1926–1991 results. The formula to calculate these percentages is shown below:

Fraction in stocks × Dollars in stocks at the end of period for each dollar invested

+ Fraction in bonds × Dollars in bonds at the end of the period for each dollar invested

= Desired return

If the amount in stocks equals X and the amount in bonds equals $1 - X$,

EXHIBIT 7–3
Historical Stock Market Results 1926–91

A. The five best results and the five worst periods

	Three-Year Period		Five-Year Period		Ten-Year Period	
	Year Ended	*Best Result*	*Year Ended*	*Best Result*	*Year Ended*	*Best Result*
	1935	30.9	1954	23.9	1958	20.1
	1928	30.1	1955	23.9	1959	19.4
	1956	28.9	1936	22.5	1956	18.4
	1945	27.2	1958	22.3	1991	17.6
	1955	25.7	1989	20.4	1951	17.3
	Average	28.6	Average	22.6	Average	18.56
	$1 grows to	$2.12	$1 grows to	$2.77	$1 grows to	$5.44

	Three-Year Period		Five-Year Period		Ten-Year Period	
	Year Ended	*Worst Result*	*Year Ended*	*Worst Result*	*Year Ended*	*Worst Result*
	1931	(27.0)	1932	(12.5)	1938	(0.9)
	1932	(26.9)	1933	(11.2)	1939	(0.1)
	1974	(9.3)	1934	(9.9)	1937	0.0
	1941	(7.4)	1941	(7.5)	1974	1.2
	1933	(7.1)	1931	(5.1)	1940	1.8
	Average	(15.53)	Average	(9.25)	Average	0.42
	$1 grows to	$0.60	$1 grows to	$0.62	$1 grows to	$1.04

B. Decile distribution

	Three-Year Period		Five-Year period		Ten-Year Period	
Decile	*Annual*	*Cumulative*	*Annual*	*Cumulative*	*Annual*	*Cumulative*
Best	30.9	124.1	23.9	192.2	20.1	522.4
2	24.6	93.4	19.4	142.4	17.1	385.7
3	18.4	66.0	15.4	104.5	16.2	347.5
4	16.4	57.7	14.3	95.0	13.9	268.3
5	12.7	43.2	12.8	82.6	11.1	185.6
6	10.2	34.0	10.2	62.2	9.3	142.8
7	7.8	25.1	7.7	44.7	7.8	112.0
8	5.2	16.4	3.8	20.4	6.5	87.1
9	(1.4)	(4.0)	(0.2)	(1.0)	3.3	38.0
Worst	(27.0)	(61.0)	(12.5)	(48.6)	(0.9)	(8.5)

All returns are annual percent returns, compounded.

$$(X)\ (1.204) + (1 - X)(1.469) = 1.436$$
$$1.204X + 1.469 - 1.469X = 1.436$$
$$1.204X - 1.469X = 1.436 - 1.469$$
$$-0.265X = -0.033$$
$$X = 0.033/0.265$$
$$X = 0.13$$
$$1 - X = 0.87$$
$$\text{So, } X = 13 \text{ percent stocks and } 1 - X = 87 \text{ percent bonds}$$

Proof: $0.13 \times 1.204 = 0.157$
$0.87 \times 1.469 = 1.278$
$0.157 + 1.278 = 1.435$

MAXIMUM AFFORDABLE CONTRIBUTION

Suppose the corporation decides the most it can afford to add to its planned contribution to the fund is $1 million per year, or $5 million over a five-year time horizon. Suppose further that the fund has $25 million, so that the $5 million deficiency represents a 20 percent loss. The fund can then make an estimate of the highest percentage in equities which would permit attainment of the goal of having at most a 20 percent loss over a five-year period. To phrase the issue another way, what percentage invested in stocks, with the remainder in Treasury bills, would have a high probability of exceeding 80 percent of the current value? It is possible to use a number of definitions of "high probability"—the average five-year return, the bottom 20 percent of five-year returns, the bottom 10 percent, and so on. In this case, we will use the average of the five worst five-year periods measured in the years 1926–91. As shown in Exhibit 7–3A, this is −9.25 percent.

That is, an investor who started with $1 in each of the five worst five-year periods would have ended up with 61.7 percent of his original investment. We can apply the formula shown above to find the applicable percentage in equities by substituting for the amount in "bonds" the amount we will have in Treasury bonds. Assume bonds earn 8 percent per year or 46.9 percent for five years.

If the amount in stocks equals x and the amount in bonds equals $1 - x$,

$$(x)(0.617) + (1 - x)(1.469) = 0.8$$
$$0.617x + 1.469 - 1.469x = 0.8$$
$$0.617x - 1.469x = 0.8 - 1.469$$
$$x = 0.785 \text{ or } 78.5 \text{ percent stocks}$$
$$1 - x = 0.215 \text{ or } 21.5 \text{ percent bonds}$$

Proof: $0.785 \times 0.617 = 0.484$
$$0.215 \times 1.469 = 0.316$$
$$0.484 + 0.316 = 0.80$$

We then can conclude that, based on the assumption that Treasury bonds will yield 8 percent and stocks will do no worse than the average of the worst five five-year periods in the years 1926–91 (a loss of 38.3 percent to 61.7 percent of the original investment), a portfolio of 78.5 percent equities and 21.5 percent Treasury bonds will be worth at least 80 percent of its current value five years from now. This permits the corporation to keep its contribution within the maximum affordable limits.

MAXIMUM DECLINE IN ASSETS

The sponsor can view historical returns and risk levels (particularly the latter) and see the extremes of the results which may occur. For instance, looking at the historical rates of return for the years 1926–91 (Exhibit 7–3), the worst three-year period in the U.S. stock market left investors with about 39 percent of the assets they possessed at the beginning of the period (a loss of 27 percent per year). The sponsor can look at its fund's position and judge the psychological and financial impact this would have on the sponsor. Suppose, for example, the sponsor felt the most it could withstand in a three-year period without severe repercussions from board members or without endangering its operating success would be a 30 percent drop in assets. This would indicate, using the above formula, that the sponsor should not have more than 64.3 percent in equities, assuming the balance is in riskless assets earning 8 percent per year.

There are limitations to these techniques, however. First, it is assumed that stocks owned by the sponsor are as risky as the overall market, and that the manager gains or loses nothing from stock selection. More importantly, this method can be used only when the minimum return can be achieved by investment in low-risk or riskless assets such as bonds or Treasury bills. This can be shown by the following example. Assume the sponsor views results in terms of the worst case or some form of "adjusted" worst case. For instance, in the worst five-year period in the stock market during the years 1926–91 an investor lost 48.7 percent of his assets. The average loss of the worst five five-year periods is 38.3 percent, indicating that 61.7 percent remain. Assume that five-year bonds earn 8 percent per year, so that over a five-year period they would return $46.90 for each $100 invested. An investor could ask what percentage in equities will allow it to meet its objective of a 50 percent gain in fund assets over five years, assuming stock market results are no worse than the average of the five worst five-year periods in the years 1926–91. We would like to apply the formula from the previous example, but this is not possible, since the five-year bond rate is less than the objective rate and we are expecting a loss on stocks. Consequently, no combination of stocks and bonds will achieve the objective rate of 50 percent gain over five years.

COMPARATIVE METHOD

XYZ is a manufacturing firm serving a number of highly competitive industries. It was established 50 years ago, is growing about in line with the gross national product, and is labor-intensive. When comparing its financial characteristics, as described on pages 29 and 30, to those of other corporations, it discovered that:

1. A high percentage of its pretax income was flowing to pension fund contributions. Thus, if the fund pursued an aggressive policy and the results were poor, the corporation would be significantly impacted by the increased contributions that would be required to make up the deficiency in funding. This indicated that a conservative risk posture was appropriate.

2. The corporation's pretax income was not stable. If a serious recession hit the economy, the corporation's profits might be in a cyclical trough at the same time that the stock market declined seriously. Thus, if an aggressive policy were pursued, the corporation might have to increase its contribution when its earnings were low. This suggested that a conservative policy was appropriate.

3. The corporation's pretax income was high compared to the unfunded vested liability. The pension plan was well funded. Thus, profits would be less seriously impacted if a funding deficiency arose than would have been the case if a large liability existed. This indicated that an aggressive policy was possible.

4. The corporation's assets were low relative to the size of the unfunded vested liability. This indicated a relatively low ability to bear risk. For instance, if the company had to liquidate its assets to pay pension benefits, the company's basic operations might be severely impacted.

Based on this information, the corporation decided it was somewhat below average in its ability to bear risk. It then reviewed the activities of other sponsors (Exhibit 7–2) and found that the median corporate plan under $100 million had 53.7 percent of its assets in common stocks and the 75th percentile had 47.5 percent. It decided it wanted to be halfway between the median and the 75th percentile and thus chose 50 percent in equities. Approval for this policy was sought and received from the board of directors, and the policy was communicated to the investment managers in writing.

This procedure could be extended to include other relevant characteristics. For instance, it would be possible to compare the age level of the company's employees with that of other companies' employees. A company with a relatively old work force should invest conservatively since its fund may lack sufficient time to endure short-term stock market aberrations while waiting for long-term superior rates of return.

The comparative approach is helpful and has a fiduciary appeal. That is, if the fund administrators are doing the same thing as everyone else, with some adaptation to their own circumstances, it is hard to fault. On the other hand, it is possible that each organization's circumstances are different and, to quote an old Wall Street saying, "The majority is always in the wrong." Thus a more analytical approach has appeal, as well.

Any methods based on historical information are subject to the criticism, "But things are different now." It seems to many observers that the last 60 years had almost every conceivable set of good and bad conditions, so future results are highly unlikely to fall outside the extremes of those years. The strongest argument to suggest things are now different is an analysis of interest rates. Whereas in the past Treasury bills averaged a return of about 2½ percent and stocks a return of 9 percent, it now appears Treasury bills are closer to 7 percent, so stocks should be much higher. Those finding this analysis appealing can base their simulations on ''real'' (inflation-adjusted) returns rather than actual returns to eliminate the inflation component of high interest rates.

In addition to prescribing the basic policy toward risk described by the percent in equities, the sponsor must also consider the impact on portfolio risk of the risk level of the individual asset categories, such as equities. Logically, the risk level of equities would be established as an investment policy. However, this usually is excessively restrictive to the investment manager. Thus the sponsor typically must allow the manager to choose the equity risk policy with the sponsor adjusting the percent in equities to achieve the desired overall policy.

The preceding analysis assumes the portfolio owned was completely diversified, that is, no attempt was made at stock selection. Obviously, to the extent the portfolio is not diversified, there is further risk. Through unsuccessful stock selection the investment manager who has followed the sponsor's directions as to percentage in equities and as to the risk level of the equities owned may still achieve a lower return than expected. Thus, in an actively managed portfolio it is necessary to consider further variations in the rate of return from securities selection and their impact on the portfolio.

In addition to setting policies regarding the asset types to be owned, the proportions in these asset types, the risk level, and the diversification level, the sponsor must establish policy regarding the extent to which the investment manager will be permitted to vary those policies. A fund may average 50 percent in equities by going between 0 percent and 100 percent or 49 percent and 51 percent. A similar situation exists with regard to the risk levels of the securities owned. Finally, changing the diversification level can have an important impact on the fund's results. Sponsors with many investment managers may find it appropriate to reduce the managers' flexibility in changing policy decisions for two reasons. First, sponsors with many managers usually hire each manager for a specific purpose; if a manager changes that purpose, this partly defeats the objective for which the manager was hired. Second, as the managers change policies, their actions may offset one another. As one manager is increasing the fund's percentage in equities, another manager may be decreasing it, the only result to the fund being that its transaction costs have increased. Thus, the policy toward changing objectives should receive direct consideration from the sponsor.

CHAPTER 8

CHOOSING POLICIES FOR INVESTMENT MANAGERS

Managing money is an easy business. There are only two rules.
Rule 1: Don't lose money.
Rule 2: Don't forget Rule 1.

After deciding on investment policies and asset categories, the fund sponsor must turn to the question of who will make the actual investment decisions—that is, who will be the investment manager. A number of decisions must be made, including whether the fund should be managed internally or externally; how much discretion the investment manager should have; whether the assets should be invested directly in securities or indirectly through pooled or commingled funds; whether the style employed should be active or passive, and if active, then what active style should be employed; and how many managers are needed. Each of these decisions may be interrelated with other decisions discussed in this or other chapters. This complicates the process of answering the many questions the sponsor faces, but by analyzing each of these matters separately, a framework of decision is provided for the sponsor. In addition, the appendix includes a questionnaire to assist sponsors in screening prospective investment managers.

INTERNAL VERSUS EXTERNAL INVESTMENT MANAGEMENT

This area has been touched on in the Chapter 2 discussion of assigning responsibility for operating the fund, but additional comments are desirable. Although some people suggest that a monkey throwing darts can achieve as high a return as the most knowledgeable investment manager, there appears to be no trend whatsoever toward the use of this method of investment. Rather, the trend is quite the opposite, with sponsors desiring more and more sophistication from their investment managers. Because of this trend, most organizations are unlikely to feel that they have the level of capability needed to manage large investment portfolios of varying asset types. Clearly, such expertise can be hired or developed by very large sponsors, and in fact a number of large sponsors are doing this. In considering whether to use internal staff or external managers, sponsors should address the following questions:

1. What are the advantages of internal versus external investment management?
2. What expertise does investment management require?
3. Does this expertise exist within the organization?
4. If not, do budgetary considerations permit hiring people with the necessary qualifications?
5. Can senior officials of the organization properly supervise the activities of an investment manager?
6. Is the organization willing to expend the time and effort required to manage investment funds?
7. Is the organization willing to accept the risk associated with this function?

The Advantages of Internal versus External Investment Management

The principal advantages of internal management are that it gives the sponsor far more control over investment policies and over the individual securities held, that the people making investment decisions will be more familiar with the sponsor's needs, and that the sponsor can develop a better insight into the problems faced by outside investment managers. The advantages of external management are that the outside manager typically has far more resources, that it may have special capabilities such as in dealing with private placements or mortgage investments, that it may be able to demand lower commission costs from brokers and dealers, and that for bond investing it may be able to get better prices by combining smaller blocks of bonds into more marketable larger blocks. Although the outside manager has less time to spend on a particular fund than would an insider, it develops insight and perspective from viewing many sponsors with different needs. If the truth were known, it would probably be found that the real reason behind most moves from external to internal investment management is performance, or more precisely, the feeling that "We can do as well as those guys."

The Expertise Required for Investment Management

The investment manager working within the organization will need knowledge of the two major decision areas, namely how to allocate assets among sectors and which securities to buy within sectors. That is, he or she will need to decide what allocations to make among stocks, bonds, liquid assets, and other investments, and will also need to decide which stocks to buy, which bonds to buy, and so on. The importance of the allocation question, and hence the significance of the manager's expertise in this area, rests to a large extent on the sponsor's position with respect to setting an overall risk policy. If the sponsor establishes firm guidelines as to the percentage of the portfolio which should go into each asset sector, then the manager's activities can be concentrated in security selection. Conversely, if the sponsor has only general guidelines, then the investment manager must choose as well as implement the fund's investment policy. The type of expertise required to make intelligent allocations among investment vehicles is knowledge of economics, particularly monetary economics, and experience with stock and bond market levels over at least two market cycles. (Of course, familiarity with the sponsor and its fund is vital.)

The knowledge required to invest in equities includes much of the experience indicated above plus a familiarity with individual industries and companies. Investment in fixed-income securities requires a strong knowledge of monetary economics as well as experience with a large number of bonds and bond issuers. If the manager is to invest in real estate, he or she must have a thorough knowledge of the evaluation process for investing in mortgages and real estate equities as well as a network of contacts which will provide a source of investments. Such a network is necessary for both real estate and private placements, which are characterized by less-liquid markets than are public investments.

An important factor with which the investment manager must concern itself is lead/lag relationships, which can frustrate even knowledgeable investors. The market discounting function usually causes information to be reflected in securities prices before most investors recognize that this has happened. Consequently, in reflecting on any piece of information, the investor must always remember that "This may be important, but if it is already recognized by the market, then it may be too late to act on it."

Does Investment Management Expertise Exist within the Organization?

The vast majority of foundations, public organizations, and labor unions will not have sufficient in-house expertise to manage portfolios unless people have been hired expressly for this purpose. Corporations, on the other hand, will tend to have more of the required experience because of their frequent need for investing excess cash in securities and also because of their sale of securities to finance their own activities. A corporation's investment expertise will depend partly on the extent to which its activities involve buying and selling securities and partly on the extent to which it makes investment decisions itself, as opposed to relying on outside investment organizations. A further consideration is the extent to which the corporation is diversified. Highly diversified companies are in a sense a portfolio which senior officials must manage. If management is accustomed to evaluating merger and acquisition candidates, it may find planning a securities portfolio to be within the realm of the company's abilities.

Are the Costs of Hiring In-House Investment Managers Justifiable?

The budgetary considerations are quite straightforward, involving only the cost of using an internal investment staff versus the cost of using outside managers. The cost of outside investment management is typically based on the size of the account and on whether the relationship involves management only or management plus custody and recordkeeping. Let us assume the sponsor intends to undertake only investment management activities and will leave custody to a bank. The cost of outside management is usually about one half of 1 percent for accounts in the $1 million to $5 million area, with a reduction in the fee to as low as $1/10$ percent for amounts over $100 million. Investment advisers usually charge more than banks, and banks which are performing custody work usually charge a fairly modest incremental fee for providing management in addition to custody. This charge may be only one or two tenths of 1 percent. Thus, the difference in cost between internal and external investment management will be largely dependent on whether the alternative to in-house investment management is the bank providing custody or some other organization. On a $10 million portfolio the investment management fee might be $25,000 to $50,000 per year, and for a $50 million fund with three managers the fee might be $100,000 to $200,000 per year.

Although an in-house staff of any size, from one person part-time to a cast of hundreds, is conceivable, an effective organization should have at least one person concentrating on each major asset category and an overall investor/manager who would be responsible for asset allocation, liaison with the rest of the sponsor organization, and administration of the investment management group. That is, an in-house group which is managing stocks and bonds should have three professionals, and in addition it should have clerical and administrative support from two clerical people.

Minimum estimates for salary might be $200,000 for the department head, $150,000 for an experienced investment manager for one asset sector, $125,000 for a somewhat less experienced person for the other asset sector, $50,000 for a senior clerical person, and $30,000 for a junior person. The salary budget of $555,000 per year should be doubled to about $1.1 million to provide a total budget which would include subscription services, office space, travel, computer, communications, and other typical expenses. However, brokerage commissions, custodial fees, and accounting and auditing expenses are not included. On the basis of these estimates and considering only cost, a fund below $200 million in size would probably not justify the expense of internal investment management (½ percent of $200 million = $1 million) and a fund of over $400 million probably does justify it. The above analysis assumes that the entire portfolio is managed internally. In the more common case, the sponsor decides to manage part of the portfolio internally and to leave the balance to outside managers. If a sponsor decides to manage one third of its assets internally, the fund would have to be about three times as large, or over $1 billion, to justify internal management on a cost basis. Since some sponsors view having an internal staff as an important advantage in understanding the activities of outside managers, they may be willing to have higher operating expenses in order to gain the added insight provided by internal management. Since the costs of both external and internal management vary greatly, each sponsor should calculate its actual outside costs and compare them to its estimated internal costs in order to find the break-even point.

Can the Organization Supervise an Investment Manager?

The supervisory requirements placed on senior officials are much the same whether the fund is managed internally or externally. In either case, the control systems discussed in subsequent chapters will be adequate for these purposes. It should also be noted that in either case controlling an investment process is different from controlling other areas of the sponsor's activities and consequently does not fall within the direct experience of most senior management personnel.

Is the Organization Willing to Manage Funds?

This question can be asked by an outsider but it can really be answered only by the sponsor. There will certainly be much "discussion" within the organization before a board of directors or a board of trustees will agree to internal management. This decision will relate to the perceived risks and benefits of internal versus external management, including the risk of embarrassment.

Is the Organization Willing to Accept the Risk of Fund Management?

In reality there is probably very little difference in risk to the organization between internal and external management. That is, if the manager does well and the fund prospers, the organization will benefit, regardless of who was responsible for the success. Similarly, if the manager is unsuccessful, the organization will suffer commensurately. The risk to the individuals within the organization is a different matter. Many officials will feel that a mistake made by an outside investment manager is the investment manager's fault, whereas bad results obtained by an internally managed fund might reflect on the personnel who decided to use internal management, a practice contrary to that of most sponsors. Moreover, most sponsors find it easier to remove an account from an outside manager who is operating unsuccessfully than to disband an equally unsuccessful internal staff. ERISA tends to support the notion that it is less risky for the sponsor to have an outside manager by saying that under certain conditions a sponsor can escape liability for the acts or omissions of its investment manager by choosing outside managers.[1]

In summary, the advantages of internal management to the sponsor are greater control over the policies pursued and the securities purchased, greater familiarity of the investment manager with the goals and characteristics of the organization, and greater ability of the investment manager to devote time to the sponsor's portfolio. The disadvantages are a lack of the perspective gained by viewing many different customers and their portfolios and, presumably, a much lower level of resources available to the investment manager. The cost of internal management is normally greater than that of external management for small funds (about $400 million or less) and less than that of external management for large funds.

Sponsors wishing to begin internal management might consider the following approach. Rather than moving a large piece of a diversified portfolio in-house immediately, a sponsor may divert the annual contributions, the income, or the annual contributions plus income on investments to the in-house pool. Further, the sponsor might start with a reasonably passive bond portfolio as the first step toward investing. In this way relatively small amounts of money will be invested in the less risky assets, and consequently the sponsor can begin an internal operation without taking undue risk.

INVESTMENT MANAGER'S DEGREE OF DISCRETION

It is possible for the sponsor to have an investment manager but to give it only part of the responsibility for investing. The degree of discretion is a function of the organization's willingness to become involved in the investment process and of the extent to which it has defined its investment policies (see Chapter 3). The degree of discretion ranges from allowing the managers to have the most control to allowing them to have the least control.

---

[1] These conditions are that the outside investment manager must be "qualified" (meaning that it is a bank, an insurance company, or a registered investment adviser, as defined), that the manager must acknowledge in writing that it is a fiduciary, that the sponsor must have been prudent in hiring the manager, and that the sponsor must have been prudent in continuing the use of the manager (see ERISA, Sec. 405).

1. The manager makes all decisions.
2. The sponsor provides either general guidelines as to percentage in equities, such as "Do not exceed 60 percent in equities," or specific guidelines, such as "The equity/fixed income ratio will be maintained as close to 60/40 as possible."
3. The sponsor provides either general or specific guidelines as to the risk level (beta) of the equity portfolio.
4. The sponsor provides either general or specific guidelines as to the quality of stocks or bonds.
5. The sponsor reviews all recommendations prior to their execution.

Most funds are now managed with separate managers for different asset types, and thus the primary source of risk can be quantified in advance. Thus, it has become common to allow the manager complete investment discretion with its investment style.

Discretionary management enables the manager to implement its strategy and take advantage of block purchases and sales as occasions arise. However, the policy of limiting discretion of the investment manager has three advantages. First, the sponsor retains control over what investments are held. Second, there is a greater opportunity for the sponsor to understand the manager and for the manager to get to know the sponsor. Third, the manager is required to think out and articulate its reasons for making a suggestion, rather than potentially "shooting from the hip." Of course, the policy of reviewing all recommendations prior to their execution partly defeats the purpose of having an investment manager. It makes no sense to have an investment manager if the sponsor or the committee of trustees rejects a large percentage of the investment manager's suggestions. Also, many investment managers indicate that the time lost in obtaining approval for recommendations causes the fund to lose part of the benefit of the recommendations. Some managers have even gone so far as to provide documentation that discretionary accounts tend to have better results than do nondiscretionary accounts. If the manager is a large organization, this may be true since the nondiscretionary account will be among the last to buy and sell all the time. Some skeptics, on the other hand, contend that this is all rationalization on the part of the manager who wants to avoid the extra paperwork and effort required by nondiscretionary accounts.

A less dramatic example of limiting the manager's discretion occurs when the sponsor requires that all purchase recommendations be reviewed in advance but gives the manager authority to act on sale recommendations without prior approval. The logic here is that it is advisable to act promptly to prevent a loss but it is not necessary to act hastily to achieve a potential gain.

As a practical matter, the policy of reviewing all transactions prior to their execution imposes a discipline on the manager to think of the long term rather than the short term, since the manager will know that by the time a transaction is approved and the order executed any short-term trading benefits will be lost. The success of the nondiscretionary approach will be largely contingent on the degree to which the manager's recommendations are accepted. If they are accepted as a matter of course, the manager will feel confident in his or her role and can act freely to apply his or her best judgment on behalf of the fund. If the manager is frequently overruled, he or she will be frustrated. In that event it is unlikely that a successful relationship between the manager and the sponsor will be achieved. Every investment manager who has nondiscretionary accounts can provide instances in which a perfectly valid recommendation was turned down because a trustee had a brother-in-law who lost money in a similar stock.

As a final point, a method of operation that is guaranteed to lead to a poor relationship between the sponsor and the investment manager is one in which an investment committee reviewing all recommendations not only turns down the manager's proposals but also makes proposals of its own. This not only reduces the value of the manager, it turns the manager into a research assistant who is expected to be a "jack-of-all-stocks." If in fact the trustees do not wish to accept the manager's choice of a given purchase, they should ask the manager to make an alternative suggestion rather than provide choices of their own. If the trustees find themselves rejecting an uncomfortably large percentage of the investment manager's recommendations, it might be feasible to have the manager make two purchase recommendations rather than one in order to give the trustees an opportunity to pick one and thus reduce the embarrassment to both parties. If too many recommendations are rejected, the sponsor should consider using a new adviser or managing the fund internally.

DIRECT VERSUS INDIRECT INVESTMENT FUND OWNERSHIP

Sponsors that are willing to relinquish discretionary control over purchase and sale decisions on individual stocks can own securities either directly or through participations in commingled (pooled) funds. Both banks and mutual fund management organizations provide pooled funds in which sponsors can invest. The advantages of a pooled fund are ease of administration, high diversification, and low cost, at least for small amounts of money. The disadvantages are the sponsor's inability to adapt the investments of the commingled fund to its own objectives and the sponsor's inability to control the risk posture of the commingled fund.

Advantages of Commingled Funds

Ease of Administration

From an administrative point of view, the holder of a commingled fund owns only one security. It need not be concerned with collecting dividends and maintaining custodial records. Since commingled funds almost never issue certificates, it need not worry about custodial problems or the physical transfer of securities. The investor's interest is represented by electronic bookkeeping entries only.

Diversification

Since a pooled fund combines the assets of many contributors, it can achieve a high degree of diversification by purchasing a large number of securities. Theoretically a small portfolio could achieve a similar level of diversification, but transactions and administrative and management costs usually discourage the holding of large numbers of securities. Both sound investment practice and ERISA require that portfolios be diversified. The implications of high and low levels of diversification are described in Chapter 3.

Cost

Just as it is easier for the fund to own participations in a commingled portfolio, so it is easier for the investment manager to combine the assets of many sponsors into one fund. It need not provide separate management for the sponsor, nor need it provide individual custodial and extensive recordkeeping facilities. Consequently, it is able to charge lower fees to the fund sponsors, particularly for small portfolios.

Disadvantages of Commingled Funds

Unadaptable to Sponsor Needs

Since a pooled fund represents the assets of many sponsors, it is impossible to adapt the portfolio to the needs of each sponsor. Consequently, the sponsor must choose a pooled fund which most appropriately fits its needs and then accept the decisions of the investment manager as to what securities the pooled fund will hold. This limitation can be partly avoided by investing in commingled funds with different objectives, so that the resulting portfolio reflects the sponsor's objectives.

Sponsor Unable to Control Risk

A sponsor who wishes to achieve a specified risk level must constantly monitor the risk policies of the commingled fund in which it invests. For instance, if a sponsor wishes to be 50 percent in equities and 50 percent in bonds, it may invest in two commingled funds, one equity oriented and the other fixed-income oriented. If the manager of the equity-oriented fund decides the market is going down, it may cut back the fund's position in equities to 50 percent. The sponsor might then find it had not invested 50/50 but that it owned 50 percent bonds, 25 percent equities, and 25 percent cash equivalents. Of course, the manager of the equity-oriented fund may be right in its opinion on the market, but the sponsor's asset allocation objective will be frustrated.

Active Management through Mutual Funds

Typically, fund sponsors hire investment managers and the managers actively manage securities. Some very large funds and aggressive ones frequently add or replace investment management organizations. However, another alternative is available for sponsors who wish to be active, yet do not wish to evaluate individual securities. Sponsors can use specialized commingled funds as their primary investment vehicle, and allocate money among these funds. For instance, a sponsor might have views as to the relative benefit of stocks versus bonds, or of growth stocks relative to value stocks. It could thus pick commingled or mutual funds which reflect these objectives. If stocks became more attractive relative to bonds, money could easily be pulled out of the bond fund and placed in an equity fund. Similarly, if growth stocks become more attractive relative to value stocks, funds could be switched from the growth stock fund to the value stock fund. As pooled funds become even more specialized, emphasizing certain industries as well as investment styles, the sponsor could even control its investments among energy, consumer, or cyclical stocks, or even the oil, computer, or drug industries. The fact that pension, profit-sharing, and endowment funds do not pay taxes facilitates this type of management, whereas taxable portfolios might find it more advantageous to switch securities on an individual basis so that tax consequences of each transaction can be considered.

The Single-Sponsor Commingled Fund

When a corporation has many subsidiaries, and particularly when those subsidiaries were acquired, the corporation will tend to have a great number of pension plans. This can create havoc with the investment process since even the smallest pension plans deserve the best efforts of investment managers. In addition, these plans may have very different characteristics or the employees covered by them may be in different age groups or salary classifications. It thus becomes impossible to establish an overall investment policy which is appropriate for all of the plans. To cope with such situations, some large sponsors have established their own commingled funds. In the simplest form there would be two such funds, one for equities and the other for bond investments. A plan whose needs might allow high short-run variability in the hope of high long-run return might be 90 percent in the equity fund and 10 percent in the fixed-income fund. Another plan within the same corporation might have different goals which could be met by having 10 percent in equities and 90 percent in bonds. Carried to an extreme, this approach could provide for a private placement fund, a mortgage fund, and so on. It is also possible to have more than one manager within each asset category, such as a growth stock manager and an income stock manager. The only disadvantage of the separate commingled fund structure is that it does not facilitate having a manager which times the market by moving from stocks to bonds. If desired, this could be accomplished by hiring a manager which does market timing, either directly or by using a futures overlay.

ACTIVE VERSUS PASSIVE INVESTMENT MANAGEMENT

The next decision the sponsor must make before choosing investment managers is whether to adopt an active or passive approach.

Rationale for Passive Management

The idea has been presented that it is un-American to invest passively. It is true that George Washington and Daniel Boone probably would not have been comfortable achieving average results rather than trying to conquer new worlds. However, the problems faced by pioneers were different from those faced by managers in a highly developed world.

It is undeniable that, on average, investors who actively manage their accounts will underperform the average passive holders of securities. Active investors, in total, have transactions costs and pay fees. Passive investors do not. Stocks perform the same regardless of who owns them, so the precost return of both is the same. Therefore, active investors on average underperform their passive counterparts.

While some investors can outperform others, not everyone can beat the market. Increasingly, professional investors are well trained. They all went to good schools and studied the same textbooks. They all receive the same information or misinformation, including the conventional wisdom of the day. Also, they subscribe to the same information services, talk to the same analysts, and read the same newspapers. With the same training and same information received at the same time, it is hard for them to outsmart each other.

Further, there is a cost in trying, as well as a risk of failing to one degree or another versus the chosen benchmark.

With large sums of money moving rapidly as information is discovered, securities prices are efficiently (accurately) priced.

These factors have converted a large body of sponsors to passive management.

Passive versus Indexing

Most investors who think of themselves as investing passively actually index. They attempt to achieve the returns of a benchmark or index by replicating to one degree or another the securities in the index. This means that they change the securities in their portfolio whenever the creator of the index changes the index's composition. Apparently, this is done with the knowledge that transactions costs will reduce future returns, but with the conviction that it is better to track the benchmark than to risk underperforming it.

An index fund is a portfolio just like any other portfolio. Looking under the facade, it looks less like a magical representation of an asset class than a broad but very specific portfolio. The returns on that portfolio will, in any single time period, be equal to the returns on each asset in the portfolio times the weight each asset represents of the total portfolio. Further, the index fund has characteristics, which can have varying results in different time periods. For instance, an equity index fund has a certain proportion in oil stocks. To the extent that oil stocks perform better than the market as a whole in a certain period, the index fund will tend to outperform portfolios which have less concentration in oil and will tend to underperform portfolios with a greater concentration in oil. Rather than being magical, the results are arithmetical.

In addition, it is not just the factors making up the index that can outperform or underperform the market. Even the index portfolio itself can become a factor, with investors favoring it, as they did in the latter 1980s, or disfavoring it, as they did in the late 1970s and early 1980s.

HOW MANY INVESTMENT MANAGERS?

If a passive strategy is adopted, it probably makes sense to choose no more than one manager for each asset category (stocks, bonds, etc.). If active management is preferred, or if only part of the portfolio is to be managed passively, a decision must be made as to the number of managers. The alternatives for this decision can be outlined as follows:

1. Should all of the funds be managed by one manager?
2. If more than one manager is chosen, should the managers be generalists investing in both stocks and bonds, or should they be specialists by asset category?
3. Should more than one manager be chosen for an asset category, and if so, on what basis?

Using more than one manager has these advantages: diversification, the potential ability to achieve the best efforts of a number of specialists, and the increased resources available to the sponsor in the way of investment or other ideas. On the other hand, there are certain problems associated with having more than one manager. These problems include higher cost (since almost all managers charge on a declining fee scale basis), greater administrative burden on the fund sponsor, and, most important, increased responsibility for the sponsor, which must then decide how to allocate money among managers. This burden is greatest when the managers are asset category specialists, since then the decision as to asset allocation falls entirely on the sponsor. That is, if one manager controls equities and the other controls bonds, the sponsor makes the asset allocation decision by establishing the amount that each manager has to invest. Even worse, the sponsor may be reluctant to change the allocation policy because it is cumbersome or embarrassing to move assets from one manager to another. Thus, having a single manager eases the sponsor's administrative burdens, reduces its costs, and enables it to rely more heavily on the manager in making decisions as to the appropriate asset allocations. On the other hand, using multiple managers increases diversification, permits the sponsor to choose specialists, and gives the sponsor greater control over asset allocation.

Within a given asset category, such as equities, it is possible to have more than one manager. The typical reason for doing so is to increase diversification (that is, to decrease the chances that the fund will be harmed if a manager has particularly bad investment results) and to balance styles (a concept related to diversification). In the former case, the sponsor may decide that it is desirable to have a growth philosophy in the portfolio but that more than one manager of growth stocks will be chosen in order to diversify the results. Conversely, it may be considered desirable to have a portfolio which reflects the market as a whole in terms of proportions of growth stocks, income stocks, and value stocks, and the sponsor may try to achieve high risk-adjusted rates of return by choosing the best growth manager, the best income manager, and the best value manager. There is considerable merit to the idea of having a number of investment managers with different styles. If this method of diversification is to be successful, however, it is critical for the sponsor to choose a manager which excels at the style it wants rather than trying to alter a manager's style to suit the sponsor's need.

DUE DILIGENCE IN CHOOSING MANAGERS

When analyzing prospective managers, efforts should be directed in five areas—investment activity, general diligence, fees, legal issues, and conflicts of interest.

Investment Activity

The sponsor should attempt to understand the factors determining the manager's return, such as by concentration in companies of certain capitalization size or industry group, sources of risk, including from concentration in a limited number of issues and the risk of the issues owned, who in the organization contributes to the sources of return, how deep is management, how is risk controlled, and what common factors exist which could lead to a large number of investments declining at one time.

General Diligence

Checks should be made of the amount and trend in assets under management, and of the number of employees. It is also advisable to make reference checks from existing clients, former clients, and others. The manager should be visited in its offices to see if its resources are commensurate with its investment process and client base. Sponsors may also want to inquire into policies of equity managers on proxy voting, as proxies are considered part of the asset represented by common stock holdings.

Fees

The level of fees should be reasonable in light of the nature of the activity and any limitation in assets which the manager imposes on itself in order to prevent performance from being diluted by excessive growth in assets under management. Unfortunately, comparison with other managers is the primary method of determining the reasonableness of fees. If performance or incentive fees are proposed, they should be analyzed according to the factors described on page 137. The sponsor should also learn whether soft dollars (directed commissions) are allocated for research, office expenses, or marketing.

Legal Issues

Investors may want to inquire about any regulatory violations by the manager, any relevant lawsuits, and any side letters between the manager and other investors.

Conflicts of Interest

Potential conflicts include investments by the manager and any commissions or fees which could be earned by the manager other than the advisory fee.

SIZE OF THE MANAGEMENT ORGANIZATION

There is little to indicate that the size of the organization, with respect to either number of employees or assets under management, should be an important consideration in choosing an investment manager. Large organizations clearly have more resources, yet it is questionable whether they can necessarily bring these resources to bear to the benefit of individual clients. Smaller organizations have few resources, yet may be better able to coordinate these resources. They also may have a wider range of investment opportunities since they can purchase securities of smaller companies, and can move in and out of the market more easily. One argument, having little merit, raised against smaller organizations is that the portfolio will be in jeopardy if the key manager dies. Just as "a stock doesn't know who owns it," "a portfolio doesn't know who runs it." In the event of the passing of the key manager the sponsor can hire a replacement. This may be awkward at the time but it is a small risk to the fund and one worth taking to have the right manager.

CHOOSING THE INDIVIDUAL MANAGER WITHIN THE INVESTMENT MANAGEMENT FIRM

Thus far this chapter has dealt with the organizational and structural aspects of choosing investment managers. It is, perhaps, equally necessary to recognize the importance of the personal side of the equation. The sponsor should be almost as careful in choosing the individual within the investment management organization as it is in choosing the organization itself. This decision should be based on three factors: the individual's experience, his other work load, and intangible personal qualities.

Hopefully, the individual who actually manages the sponsor's fund will have had experience in managing portfolios during several market cycles. It is only after seeing several periods of dramatic over- and undervaluation of securities, and the passing in and out of favor of a number of investment fads, that most people are capable of exercising good investment judgment. Such judgment is a combination of a healthy skepticism, objectivity, humility sufficient to permit changing one's mind when the facts so dictate, the ability to keep one's eye on long-term goals despite the daily contradictions and confusions of the marketplace, and the ability to act independently and decisively when this is warranted by the conditions.

As to work load, it is important that the sponsor and its portfolio achieve adequate attention. This requires that the portfolio manager not have overly burdensome responsibilities in administration, marketing, or managing other portfolios. In the organizations which manage portfolios most intensively (and charge the highest fees), portfolio managers may have only 5 to 10 clients. In large organizations which have many clients of moderate size, portfolio managers may be responsible for many times this number of accounts. The sponsor should know in detail the work responsibilities of its portfolio manager before entering into an investment management agreement.

The third factor to be considered in choosing an individual investment manager is not easily measurable. This intangible includes the ability of the individual manager to communicate with the sponsor, his personal motivation in learning about the sponsor and attempting to do a good job, and his general willingness to respond to the sponsor's and the fund's needs. This does not mean that the individual should be an errand boy for the sponsor, spending his time seeking information unrelated to the fund. But a certain willingness to put in extra effort on behalf of the client is a most desirable attribute in the individual manager.

ADMINISTRATIVE SUPPORT FOR THE INVESTMENT MANAGER

Although the investment manager's primary responsibility is to make investment decisions, it is extremely important that he or she have adequate accounting and reporting facilities. The required services are discussed in Chapters 2 and 17. In addition, it is helpful if the manager has the ability to create special reports which the sponsor may require from time to time. Finally, inquiry should be made as to the investment manager's ability to control short-term cash investments, particularly if the manager is not also the custodian of the assets, and as to the extent to which the manager's statements are reconciled with those of the custodian to provide a cross-check on accounting errors.

USING CONSULTANTS TO CHOOSE INVESTMENT MANAGERS

Since the choice of investment managers is so critical, and since the investment management field is both fragmented and specialized, many sponsors consider it desirable to use outside consulting services to assist in the management selection process. A wide variety of such services is available, ranging from those which provide assessments of purely intangible factors to those which have detailed information on the performance of accounts and the qualifications of personnel. In selecting consultants, care must be exercised to ensure that the particular needs of the sponsor are within consultants' capabilities. It should also be recognized that choosing the manager who will have the best performance is not much easier than choosing the stocks which will rise the most. Thus, the sponsor should be realistic about what it expects to accomplish through the use of the consultant.

PERFORMANCE-BASED FEES

There are four logical methods upon which to calculate fees: hourly fees based on services rendered, fixed dollar fees for a given time period, fees based on assets managed, and incentive fees based on results achieved.

Hourly fees for services rendered are not used in investment management. Perhaps this is because the services rendered to all clients are similar and therefore it is not feasible to distinguish value supplied to one client versus that provided to another, or possibly because sponsors wish to be able to measure their costs in advance. Fixed dollar fees for a given time period are possible, but have not found use in investment management. The most common form of payment is a fee based on assets, which typically declines as the size of the client's account increases. However, performance-based incentive fees are becoming increasingly common.

Rationale

The two rationales for performance-based fees are to provide an incentive to managers and to align payment with results. Some investors feel that the best people and best effort can be attracted with performance fees. The implication is that by providing the opportunity for the manager to make a higher fee, one will attract the best managers and will extract the best effort from those managers, leading to performance worth the higher fees.

The second rationale, aligning payment with results, has much more modest expectations. It does not assume anything about the relationship between fees and performance, but rather focuses on fairness, so that in years with good results the payment is larger than it is in years with poor results.

Types of Fees

There are two types of performance fees. The fulcrum fee is based on a performance standard related to the market for the asset being measured. The "normal" fee is paid for achieving the benchmark, and an increment of fee is added or subtracted for each unit of performance above or below the index. The "percent of profits fee," sometimes called the venture capital type performance fee, is literally a percentage of the profits earned. Here effectively, the benchmark is zero and the manager receives a percentage of any gains above that amount.

Types and Structure

Since fulcrum and percent of profits performance-based fees have different structures, the two structures will be discussed separately.

Fulcrum Fee
In structuring a fulcrum fee, it is important to consider the benchmark, time frame, base fee, incremental fee, decremental fee, and caps and floors.

The time period should be long enough to eliminate random fluctuations in portfolio value but not so long as to exceed the normal investment time horizon. A minimum of one year and a maximum of five years seems appropriate, with three years being adequate and perhaps optimal.

The choice of the *benchmark* is crucial. If the performance fee is to provide an incentive, or if it is to fairly align payment with results, the results must be measured against a standard which represents the goal of the fund. A diversified portfolio is the ideal benchmark. The more specific the manager's assignment, the more specific must be the benchmark. For instance, a small cap growth manager can be expected to outperform the Standard & Poor's 500 over a period of time, but during any shorter period the results can be extremely different. Thus, an index of small cap growth stocks is much more appropriate than the Standard & Poor's 500 for this purpose.

The *time frame* can be fixed or rolling. It can start over at the end of the time period or continue onward, by dropping off old periods as new ones are added. To the extent it is rolling, the time frame can be shorter.

Once the benchmark and time frames are chosen, it is necessary to address the fees themselves. The *base fee* is the one which is paid if unexceptional results are achieved. It can be arbitrarily chosen, it can be an amount representing the alternative, such as the cost of an index fund, or it can be related to the manager's overhead or cost of being in business. The index fund choice suggests that the manager's unexceptional results could have been achieved with an index fund, and thus the fee of the index fund is appropriate. Choice of a cost-based method suggests that the investor wants the manager to be able to remain in business and pay its overhead, and to receive special reward when it does an above average job.

In addition to the base fee, the investor and manager must also agree on a *performance fee*. This can be symmetrical, that is, the same amount incremented for good performance as is reduced or decremented for bad performance, though it need not be. The increase or decrease over the base can also be proportional (linear) or it can rise and decline in an increasing or decreasing percentage. The increase or decrease over the base can also be calculated on percentages or dollar gains in the investment portfolio.

Finally, it might be appropriate to have a floor and a cap, such that the maximum fee cannot exceed a certain level nor can the minimum fee fall below a certain level.

Percentage of Profits Performance Fees

While fulcrum fees are based on performance relative to an index, percentage of profits fees are based on absolute results. The absolute result can be a zero gain, in which case the fee is a pure percentage of profits. It can also be subject to a hurdle rate of return or a preferred rate of return. If there is a hurdle rate, the manager receives none of the profits below the hurdle rate. For instance, the manager might receive 50 percent of the profits above the hurdle rate of 10 percent per year. At a 10 percent gross return the manager receives 0 percent, but at 12 percent gets 1 percent, at 15 percent gets 2½ percent, and so on. Alternatively, the manager might be entitled to one third of profits subject to the investor receiving a preferred 10 percent return. In this case, the first 10 percent goes to the investor and the next 5 percentage points go to the manager, at which time the manager will have received one third of the profits. Any profits above 15 percent are allocated one third to the manager and two thirds to the investor.

The hurdle rate or preferred rate can be a fixed amount, such as in the examples above, or variable. Common variable standards are the returns of Treasury bills, money market returns, or the Standard & Poor's 500, or those returns plus 100, 200, or 300 basis points.

The performance fee can also be a fixed percentage or it can vary depending upon performance. For instance, the fee might be 10 percent of the first 10 percent of profit, 20 percent of the next 20 percent, and 30 percent of amounts over 20 percent.

In addition to the performance fee, there is usually a base fee in a percentage of profits arrangement, which is paid irrespective of performance. Rather, the percentage of profits is on top of the base fee. Rarely is there a decremental fee, so the base fee is fixed. The floor fee is thus the base fee, and there are no caps on how high the fees can rise. However, usually there is a loss carry-forward or "high water" mark. This provides that the manager does not receive a percentage of profits in year two until any loss in year one is made up. For instance, if the fund starts with $100 and declines to $90 after one year, there is no incentive payable in year two until the fund rises back to the $100 or previous "high water" mark. Any excess value over $100 is subject to the performance fee.

Percentage of profits fees are most common in limited partnerships. Here, the fee is structured as a disproportional allocation of profits to the general partner, which is also the manager of the fund.

Concerns

While appealing in many ways, performance-based fees generate concerns of which investors should be aware. The structure should reward excellent performance by the manager but not random market movements. This makes choice of the benchmark important and suggests an extended time frame, preferably with a rolling measurement period, an increment over the benchmark before the performance fee starts to accrue, and a cap on the maximum performance fee payable. The structure should not induce the manager to take more risk in order to have a higher return. This suggests a longer time period for measuring results, a symmetrical fee which takes away as much for bad performance as is given for good performance, and measurement of risk of the manager relative to the benchmark. Further, the risk level of the portfolio should be measured before and after the incentive fee is introduced. Since the fees paid are based on performance, the importance of measurement and measurer are increased. Definitions of the performance period and methodology should be determined prior to the measurement period. Finally, the sponsor (and the investment manager) should be sure that the fee arrangement is legally permissible.

Incentive Fees May Affect a Sponsor's Costs

If the sponsor structures the fee to achieve a fair sharing of fees based on performance in good and bad times, it may be able to lower fees. Since a standard must be established for determining when a performance fee is payable, the opportunity is provided for setting a benchmark which is above the normal market portfolio. For instance, a U.S. equity manager might be expected to achieve the return of the Standard & Poor's 500 plus the amount of its fees plus 100 basis points. By establishing the bogey in this manner, the sponsor effectively can reduce the average fee, since on average managers cannot be expected to outperform the overall market.

If the sponsor is skillful in choosing managers, the overall level of fees paid may rise with the introduction of performance fees. If the managers would have done a good job anyway, there is no benefit to the fund from the higher fee. Further, some managers may want to receive a higher fee level for taking the risk associated with a performance-based fee. A careful analysis should be made of the break-even between normal and performance-based fees, and the cost and benefit of good and bad performance.

Finally, it may be appropriate to consider that if incentive fees really do encourage managers to work harder, if your manager offers incentive fees to its clients but you have chosen not to take them, your managers may be working harder for other clients of the firm than they are for you.

Should Performance-Based Fees Be Established
for Sponsor Representatives?

If the concept of performance-based fees is appealing, perhaps such a compensation arrangement should be created for internal managers, as well. This requires that pension officers and others with responsibility for "managing the managers" have a substantial degree of discretion as to how investments are made. If the responsible parties have this discretion, an arrangement can be created, subject to the structure described above as to benchmark, time frame, and fees. The caveats about minimizing the impact of random events and accounting for risk also apply.

APPENDIX

MANAGER SELECTION QUESTIONNAIRE

A. *Company background and general description*

1. Number and location of offices
2. Year founded
3. Employees

	Number	Average Number of Years of Professional Experience
Portfolio managers		
Equity only	——	——
Bond only	——	——
Balanced	——	——
Research analysts	——	——
Economists	——	——
Marketing	——	——
Trading	——	——
Administration	——	——
Other	——	——
Total	══	══

Number added —— lost —— in past two years

4. Company is
   Bank ____
   Insurance company ____
   Registered investment adviser ____
   Other ____

5. Ownership of company
   Employee percentage ____
   Is company affiliated with a bank, insurance
   company, broker or dealer, mutual fund?
   (Circle appropriate reply)
   Name the parent company.
   Name any mutual funds managed.

6. Clients

	Total Number	Largest Assets	Smallest Account	Smallest Account	In Last Two Years, Number of Accounts Added	Lost
Employee benefit						
Corporate	____	____	____	____	____	____
Jointly trusteed	____	____	____	____	____	____
Foundation	____	____	____	____	____	____
Personal trust	____	____	____	____	____	____
Individual	____	____	____	____	____	____
Mutual funds	____	____	____	____	____	____
Other	____	____	____	____	____	____
Total	====	====	====	====	====	====

7. Number of accounts per portfolio manager ____
   $ ____ assets per manager

8. Company objective for annual growth of assets
   under management?
   0–5% ____   5–15% ____   15–25% ____
   Over 25% ____

9. What, if any, maximum asset limit is planned? ____

10. Minimum account size:
    With no cash flow expected? ____
    With 10 percent annual cash flow? ____

11. Has company been profitable in each of last three years? Yes ____ No ____
    Please enclose a recent financial statement.

12. Does company have formal plans and budgets?
    Yes ____ No ____

B. *Investment philosophy*

1. Asset types managed

	Total Assets	Approximate Percentage of	
		Total Discretionary Assets	Total Employee Benefit Assets
U.S. securities (active management)	____	____	____
Fixed income	____	____	____
Equities	____	____	____
Privately placed	____	____	____
Bonds	____	____	____
Equities	____	____	____
Options	____	____	____
Real Estate	____	____	____
Mortgages	____	____	____
Equities	____	____	____
Other	____	____	____
Market (index) funds	____	____	____
Equities	____	____	____
Bonds	____	____	____
Venture capital	____	____	____
International	____	____	____
Equities	____	____	____
Bonds	____	____	____
Total	$ ____	$ ____	$ ____

2. Management style

	Balanced Fund	Equity-Oriented Fund	Bond-Oriented Fund
a. How important is market timing (changing asset allocation or mix) to your management philosophy?			
Very important	———	———	———
Somewhat important	———	———	———
Not important	———	———	———
b. Does your choice of stocks emphasize:*			
Income	———		
Growth	———		
Assets	———		
Quality	———		
Large companies	———		
Small companies	———		
Natural resources	———		
Low P/E	———		
Other (describe)	———		
c. If you expect to outperform the market over a market cycle, would you likely outperform it:			
In the upcycle?	———		
Downcycle?	———		
Equally likely	———		

*If more than one is checked use 1 for most important, 2 for second most important, etc.

d. Does you choice
of bonds
emphasize:*
  Issuer type
    Corporates
      Industrial   _____
      Utility   _____
      Finance   _____
    U.S. Treasuries   _____
    U.S. govern-
      ment
      agencies   _____
    Foreign gov-
      ernments   _____
    Foreign corpo-
      rates   _____
  Maturity
    Over 20 years   _____
    10–20 years   _____
    Under 10 years   _____
  Quality
    AAA   _____
    AA   _____
    A   _____
    BAA   _____
    Under BAA   _____
  Coupon
    Above current   _____
    Current   _____
    Discount   _____
  Turnover
    High   _____
    Low   _____

*If more than one is checked use 1 for most important, 2 for second most important, etc.

3. Relative importance of investment input

	Balanced Fund with Full Discretion on Percentage in Equities	Equity-Oriented Fund	Bond-Oriented Fund
Asset allocation			
Monetary economic	⎯⎯	⎯⎯	⎯⎯
Interest rate forecasts	⎯⎯	⎯⎯	⎯⎯
Other economic	⎯⎯	⎯⎯	⎯⎯
Valuation	⎯⎯	⎯⎯	⎯⎯
Technical	⎯⎯	⎯⎯	⎯⎯
Security selection			
Industry factors	⎯⎯	⎯⎯	⎯⎯
Fundamentals of security	⎯⎯	⎯⎯	⎯⎯
Valuation	⎯⎯	⎯⎯	⎯⎯
Technical	⎯⎯	⎯⎯	⎯⎯
Trading/swapping			
Among sectors	⎯⎯	⎯⎯	⎯⎯
Within sectors	⎯⎯	⎯⎯	⎯⎯
Total input	100%	100%	100%

4. Organization for decision making

	Equities	Bonds
Committee		
Sets policies as to asset allocation	⎯⎯	⎯⎯
Establishes approved list of securities	⎯⎯	⎯⎯
For equities, sets industry or sector	⎯⎯	⎯⎯
For bonds, sets maturity or issuer types	⎯⎯	⎯⎯
Team	⎯⎯	⎯⎯
Individual manager	⎯⎯	⎯⎯
	100%	100%

5. Portfolio control
   Would portfolios with identical objectives tend to have
       identical security positions?
   Are risk and diversification controlled quantitatively
       or intuitively?
   How many securities would typically be held in a:
       $10 million stock portfolio? _____
       $10 million bond portfolio? _____

C. *Available investment resources* (sources of information
   for investing)

   1. Economics
      Monetary economics
          Percentage supplied internally _____
          Percentage supplied by external sources _____
          Names of individuals and/or organizations most
          heavily utilized:
              (1)
              (2)
              (3)
      Other economics
          Percentage supplied internally _____
          Percentage supplied by external sources _____
          Names of individuals and/or organizations most
          heavily utilized:
              (1)
              (2)
              (3)

   2. Stock market level
      Percentage supplied internally _____
      Percentage supplied by external sources _____
      Names of individuals and/or organizations most
      heavily utilized:
          (1)

(2)

(3)

3. Bond market level

Percentage supplied internally _____

Percentage supplied by external sources _____

Names of individuals and/or organizations most heavily utilized:

(1)

(2)

(3)

4. Industry trends

Percentage supplied internally _____

Percentage supplied by external sources _____

Names of individuals and/or organizations most heavily utilized:

(1)

(2)

(3)

5. Common stock selection

Percentage supplied internally _____

Percentage supplied by external sources _____

Names of individuals and/or organizations most heavily utilized:

(1)

(2)

(3)

6. Bond selection or swaps

Percentage supplied internally _____

Percentage supplied by external sources _____

Names of individuals and/or organizations most heavily utilized:

(1)

(2)

(3)

7. Economic, stock market, or portfolio models
   Percentage supplied internally _____
   Percentage supplied by external sources _____
   Names of individuals and/or organizations most
   heavily utilized:
   (1)
   (2)
   (3)
8. Other resources (name and describe)
   (1)
   (2)
   (3)

D. *Administration and fees*

1. Accounting reports provided
   a. Data
      Valuations
         Monthly _____   Quarterly _____
         Trade date or settlement date?
      Cash or transaction statements?
      Performance
         Total portfolio _____   Equity _____
         Bonds _____
         Time weighted _____
         Dollar weighted _____
         Comparison? versus? _____
      Commentary on reasons for each purchase and
      sale?   Yes _____   No _____
      Commentary on investment outlook?
         Yes _____   No _____
   b. Whose system? _____
   c. Reconciled with bank statement?
      Yes _____   No _____

2. Fees on account of size
   1mm $ ____
   5mm   ____
   10mm   ____
   20mm   ____
   50mm   ____
   100mm   ____
3. Can brokerage be directed?

E. *Performance*

   1. Time-weighted returns

	1988	*1989*	*1990*	*1991*	*1992*
Balanced funds					
Number included	____	____	____	____	____
Equity funds					
Number included	____	____	____	____	____
Bond funds					
Number included	____	____	____	____	____

   2. Are funds weighted equally or by value? ____
   3. Are the results typical, above the average, or below the average of those experienced by your clients? ____

This questionnaire prepared by: Name _____
                                Telephone _____

Information as of (date) _____ .

CHAPTER 9

CHOOSING INVESTMENT MANAGER STYLES

There are very few old geniuses.
Old Wall Street Saying

ACTIVE EQUITY STYLES

Significance of Style

If two managers are attempting to achieve the same goal (for instance, beating the return on the S&P 500) but do so using different approaches, they are said to have different *styles.* It is important for sponsors to understand manager styles so that the sponsor can structure a portfolio that has the desired risk/return and other characteristics, to avoid hiring the wrong manager, and to avoid terminating managers who should be retained.

Risk/Return Characteristics
Depending on the manager's style, it might have more or less risk, and might correlate more or less well with other managers or sectors of the sponsor's overall fund. If the sponsor is to be able to structure the portfolio as desired, it must understand the characteristics of the components. Broadly speaking, this means understanding the manager's style.

Avoiding Hiring Wrong Manager
A wrong manager is one which does not have a rational investment methodology (since its method is not likely to work), has an approach which

the sponsor does not understand (since the sponsor will not be able to fit the manager into a portfolio profile, and the manager may be terminated at the wrong time), has a style too close to that of others of the sponsor's managers, or invests in a way with which the sponsor is not comfortable.

Avoid Terminating Manager which Should Be Retained
A manager which should not be terminated is one which fits the sponsor's profile, and has a rational, understandable approach, but which the sponsor does not in fact understand. The sponsor might terminate the manager if it thinks the manager's performance is bad, when the performance is actually acceptable or even excellent. For instance, if the manager has been hired to invest in small capitalization stocks, it would not likely fare well compared to the average manager during a period when small cap stocks badly underperform the market. For the sponsor to have the courage to retain the manager, it must have a full understanding of the manager's style.

ANALYZING STYLE

Two ways of looking at style will be explored here, a traditional approach and a factor approach.

Traditional Style Analysis

Active management styles can be defined in terms of economic approaches, value, and growth styles.

Economic Approaches
Investment managers, broadly speaking, use one of two economic approaches: top down or bottom up. The top-down approach involves analyzing the economy and attempting to identify the areas which have either the most favorable or the least favorable prospects, and weighting portfolios accordingly. The bottom-up approach involves purchasing those securities which have the highest potential return and constructing a portfolio from these stocks. Bottom-up and ''bottoms up'' are terms that are sometimes confused. ''Bottoms up'' is a toast, associated with alcoholic beverages, and hopefully is not related to stock selection.

Bottom-Up Styles

Four different bottom-up styles have been identified, relating to income, growth, value, and size of the stocks preferred.

The *income* style involves purchasing stocks in order to maximize current income or income growth. Investors utilizing this style will focus on yield (annual dividend divided by price), stability of dividends, and growth of dividends. Stability of dividends is primarily a function of stability of sales and earnings and of the company's cash position. Growth in dividends is a function of growth in sales and earnings and of the relative need to plow back earnings into the business as opposed to distributing them to shareholders.

The *growth* style involves buying companies with rapidly growing sales and earnings or cash flow which are enhancing their value by reinvesting profits in the company. The growth philosophy can be contrasted to the income orientation by observing that the income investor wants to receive its return currently, whereas the growth stock investor is willing to achieve its return, with compound interest, in the future. A growth company is one which has been plowing back earnings and is presumably witnessing a high rate of growth in sales, earnings, and either dividends or the ability to pay dividends.

The *value* style, articulated by the analysts Graham and Dodd, is one in which the investor tries to buy assets at a discount to market price. Typical measures of asset value are book value or owner's equity (assets minus liabilities), net working capital (current assets minus current liabilities), quick assets (cash on hand plus accounts receivable minus current liabilities), and "net" assets (current assets minus all liabilities).

Some investors have a preference for larger companies, others for smaller companies. Investors preferring larger companies typically point to the greater diversification and stability frequently found in the larger, older companies, and they also point to the usual higher liquidity of larger companies in the marketplace. It is easier to buy and sell shares in larger companies because more of their shares are outstanding and because more investors are interested in them. Investors who prefer smaller companies typically point to the fact that many institutions prefer companies with large capitalizations and more opportunities for high return are therefore likely to be available among smaller, less popular companies. Historical results tend to confirm the benefit of investing in companies with small capitalizations. For instance, for the period 1926 to 1991, small capitalization stocks returned 11.6 percent per year as compared to 10.1 percent per year for all common stocks (R. G. Ibbotson Associates, Inc.). Investors should make the distinction, however, between small companies and companies with a small market value. Included in the latter are large companies whose stock prices have declined severely. If these companies witness a turnaround, their stock prices can rebound sharply. The returns in this case are more closely related to a value style than to a small company style.

The styles can be fragmented further or combined. For instance, growth investing can be split into large and small cap growth, income can be tilted toward high yield or fast-growing yield, and growth can be combined with quality to distinguish high-quality growth from speculative growth. Any description or combination is possible, as long as it makes sense in the context of the investor's portfolio.

Factor Approach

Manager styles can be looked at in a slightly different way. A manager's style can be characterized as a reflection of the manager's view of the *rules the stock market uses to price stocks.* The manager looks for factors, or the key variables in determining prices, as well as a model, which tells how to measure and combine the factors to predict future stock prices, or at least future performance relative to the market, and how to combine the chosen stocks into a portfolio. For example, a value manager might determine that the ratio of price to earnings is an important factor in determining future performance. The manager's model defines earnings as the latest 12-months' earnings adjusted for special charges, and the model screens a database for stocks which have low P/E ratios. These stocks are then combined into a portfolio using constraints to avoid excess concentration in any industry.

Among the factors which are frequently used are those from the income statement (sales, earnings, cash flow, and dividends). Those from the balance sheet include book value and net working capital, and the factor ''return on equity'' relies on both income statement and balance sheet measures.

Some factors relate to industries or economic sectors, some to broad economic variables like interest rates and oil prices, and some to the stock market (large and small capitalization).

Managers can also be distinguished by the number of factors used. Managers who use a few factors frequently try to find stocks which have those factors, whereas managers who rely on many factors typically emphasize the way the market is currently pricing the factors. For instance, managers who favor low cap stocks look for a universe of low cap stocks, whereas multifactor managers look at the current pricing of low cap stocks relative to high cap stocks or relative to growth stocks to see if low cap stocks are cheap now or not. If they are cheap, low cap stocks are emphasized; if not, they are deemphasized. These managers also have a scheme for weighting the factors as to importance.

Managers must have a view of the market's decision rules, and this view is reflected in the manager's formula or model. The depth of the model, and the extent to which it is based on human judgment or mechanical rules, is insightful, as is the degree to which the model is altered over time or whether it can be overridden by the manager.

Many of these rules are based on the concept of mean reversion, which says that things may vary from average but they tend to return to average. Low P/E or low price/book stocks are seen as being out of favor, for whatever reason. As time passes, they come into greater favor, and their prices rise, so the P/Es and P/Bs return to average. Growth stocks do not operate on mean reversion, but rather on the idea that earnings will grow, and stock prices will rise, even if P/Es don't change. Investors who shun growth stocks frequently do so because the investors feel high growth rates cannot be maintained for long periods, but rather growth itself will revert to the mean.

Managers can also be distinguished by whether they use historical or forecast measures of factors, and whether they use internal or external sources of information in their forecasts.

ACTIVE BOND STYLES

The approaches to bond management are partly but not completely analogous to the styles in managing equities. Almost all bond investing is for income, and no growth is possible with bonds because their final maturity value is fixed at the time of purchase. However, undervalued bonds may be sought; quality is, of course, important in bond purchases, and some investors prefer the issues of larger or smaller organizations for reasons similar to those employed by equity managers. Four management activities can be performed by bond managers, and it is helpful to understand these methods in order to understand bond management styles.

EXHIBIT 9–1

When yields decline, longer term bonds rise more sharply than do shorter term bonds.

	Coupon	Maturity	Level of Interest Rates		Percentage Change in Price
			8 Percent: Price	7 Percent: Price	
Bond A	8%	One year	100	101	1%
Bond B	8	Two years	100	102	2

If interest rates decline from 8 percent to 7 percent, each bond is worth roughly 1 percent per year more than the prevailing rate. To equalize this change, the one-year bond rises about 1 percent and the two-year bond rises about 2 percent (ignoring call provisions and compounding).

The four activities are swaps based on interest rate anticipation or market timing, swaps between sectors of the market, swaps based on the valuation analysis of individual bonds, and market inefficiency swaps.

Rate Anticipation Swaps
If rates are expected to decline, bonds with longer term maturities will have higher rates of return than will bonds with shorter term maturities, and vice versa (see Exhibit 9–1).

Sector Swaps
Investment managers may identify changes in the historical spread relationship between sectors of the bond market. For instance, an investor may recognize that historically U.S. government bonds have traded at x basis points below those of triple A issuers. If the current relationship is such that the spread is below x basis points, the investor may wish to buy the government bond. This is because, regardless of the level of interest rates, if the spread widens, the investor would have been better off in the government (lower yielding) bonds. If the spread widens because the government yield declines, the investor will have a capital gain on the government bond. If the spread widens because the triple A bond rises in yield, the triple A bond will suffer a capital loss, which will give it a lower return than that of the government bond. Similar swaps can be made between short-term and long-term bonds; among industrial, utility,

---

EXHIBIT 9–2

Swapping between bond sectors occurs when sector yield spreads are "excessively" narrow. Assume that the yield spread between governments and corporates has historically ranged between −0.05 and −1.00 percentage points (5 and 100 "basis points").

Current Market

Government Yield	Corporate Yield	Spread
8.00%	8.10%	−0.10%

Investor decides to swap from corporates to governments because he feels that the spread will widen, in which case he will be better off in governments.

If the spread widens by the government yield declining, the government bond will rise in price.

If the spread widens by the corporate yield rising, the corporate bond will decline in price.

---

and financial bonds; and between bonds with high and low coupons (see Exhibit 9–2).

Swaps Based on Bond Valuation Analysis

The third method of active bond management is to view the companies which issue bonds as to their creditworthiness, with the thought of selling bonds which are declining in creditworthiness and of purchasing bonds which are rising (see Exhibit 9–3). Viewed another way, this method emphasizes the default risk of the issuer. Factors to be considered in looking at default risk relate primarily to funds available, both cash on hand and cash being generated by the business, relative to the bond charges, including interest and the payment of principal.

Market Inefficiency Swaps

A fourth activity for increasing the return on a bond portfolio is to look for situations in which bonds of similar characteristics sell at dissimilar yields due to imbalances in the marketplace. Such situations can occur when bond dealers develop excessive long or short positions and wish to lighten their holdings in order to reduce their risk, or when sinking fund

EXHIBIT 9–3

Bonds with improving credit will outperform other bonds.

Current Market Yields of AA-Rated Bonds

Strong	Average	Weak
8.40	8.50	8.60

Bond X, trading at an 8.60 yield to maturity, has a new product which is selling well and improving the company's cash position, with the result that investors view the bond as an "average" AA rather than a "weak" AA. The yield declines to 8.50, and the bond rises in price.

---

purchases are made in order to meet agreements to reduce the amount of bonds outstanding over a prescribed time, or when issuers of new bonds offer higher rates to attract buyers. In these circumstances, market inefficiency swaps may be made for a small gain in yield, perhaps even three to five basis points.

Managing High-Yield Bonds

High-yield ("junk") bonds can be fashioned into portfolios which meet a variety of objectives. Junk bonds of small, young, growing companies have characteristics of growth stocks. Bonds of companies with hidden assets or earning power take on the character of value stocks. Bonds of companies which have suffered reversals but which are showing improvement are similar to turnaround equity investments.

Junk bond portfolios can also be constructed with a bias toward income or with an orientation toward appreciation. This is a function of the financial condition of the issuer, the price of the bond relative to redemption (usually par), and whether interest is paid in cash or is deferred.

Finally, managers can specialize within the quality spectrum, anywhere from near-bankruptcies to high-quality subordinated debt.

In addition to the types of bonds owned, managers can emphasize their own strengths. These include credit research, covenant analysis, and trading, even though all managers should have capabilities in all three.

Market Timing

An active style which appears to be used by most managers at some point, but by few managers with great emphasis, is market timing. By market timing is meant changing the allocation of assets from stocks to bonds to cash equivalents in order to avoid losses in the worst performing category and to emphasize investment in the category which will produce the highest returns. Market timing can be viewed as either defensive, to preserve capital, or offensive, to maximize return. Because of compound interest, a manager who is successful in maintaining portfolio value need only achieve average returns in favorable periods in order to have extraordinary overall results (see Exhibit 9–4). Thus the potential for high returns is available, though actually achieving them is another matter.

Four methods of market timing have been identified: traditional economic, monetary economic, technical, and valuation. The traditional economic approach involves looking at employment, production, government spending, and so on, and deciding when the economy will be expanding and contracting its physical production. The intent is to be invested when the economy is expanding and to reduce investments when the economy is contracting.

EXHIBIT 9–4
Results obtained from investing $100 each in stocks, bonds, and Treasury bills and from perfect and perverse (always wrong) timing, 1/87–12/91 (5 years)

Successful timing the market can produce enormous benefits for a fund.

Index	Ending Value	Compound Annual Rate
S&P 500	203.90	15.3
Salomon Broad Bond Index	158.08	9.6
90-day U.S. Treasury bills	139.32	6.9
Perfect timing*	364.08	29.5
Perverse timing*	74.53	(5.7)

*For perfect timing, at the beginning of each quarter the portfolio is 100 percent invested in the index which will have the highest return for the quarter. For perverse timing, investment is in the index which will have the lowest return.

Source: Evaluation Associates Inc.

The monetary economic approach is similar, except that instead of viewing the physical growth of the economy the investor analyzes the economy's monetary growth. In simplest terms, this school of thought suggests that consumers (including business and government) use money to purchase needed goods and services and that the excess available after such purchases goes into securities. When the available supply of money is growing faster than the demand for goods and services, the excess (initially) moves into securities. The purchase of securities leads to higher prices, lower yields, and the enhancement of asset values. If monetary growth is below the physical growth of the economy, interest rates rise and lower security prices result. There are two ways in which this process can be frustrated. The first way is a decline in the velocity of money. That is, excess money, instead of being spent or invested in securities, lies fallow in consumers' pockets or bank accounts. The second and far more significant way occurs when the excess money is absorbed not by rises in security prices but by rises in the prices of goods and services inflation.

The technical method of market timing involves viewing historical patterns of prices and estimating when market sectors are undervalued or overvalued based on those patterns. Viewed another way, the technical approach looks at the supply and demand factors for stocks and bonds over and above the fundamental causes of changes in supply and demand.

The valuation method of market timing may use either an absolute or a relative approach. An absolute valuation approach suggests that when common stock yields rise or price/earnings ratios decline to certain points, stocks are attractive. A relative valuation approach suggests that when the differential between the yield on stocks and the yield on bonds reaches a certain level, stocks are attractive relative to bonds.

Modern Portfolio Theory

Modern portfolio theory (MPT) is a process for quantifying risk and return in investment portfolios. Traditional investment practice utilizes quantitative or intuitive judgments to set investment policies, choose individual securities, and structure portfolios. For traditional investors, the best portfolio is the one which contains the best securities and the emphasis is on return. MPT portfolio management, on the other hand, is quantitative rather than intuitive, and it emphasizes the portfolio rather than the securities held.

MPT began when Harry Markowitz discerned that portfolios can behave quite differently from the securities of which they are composed and that rational investors should be primarily concerned with their portfolios rather than with the securities owned. Markowitz noted that the impact of a security on a portfolio is dependent on three things:

1. The security's return.
2. The security's risk or uncertainty of return.
3. The movement (covariance) of the security in relation to the movement of every other security in the portfolio.

A strange-sounding but correct implication of this theory is that adding a risky security to a portfolio will frequently make the portfolio less risky. An even stranger implication is that adding a risky security to a portfolio may reduce the portfolio's risk even more than would adding a conservative security. The determining factor is how each of the proposed additions to the portfolio correlates with each other stock. If the stock being added is highly correlated with the other stocks in the portfolio, it does little to reduce the portfolio's risk. On the other hand, if the stock being added is highly uncorrelated with the other stocks in the portfolio, it reduces the risk of the portfolio. That is, if the new stock tends to move down when the portfolio moves up and tends to move up when the portfolio moves down, it will reduce the portfolio's risk. This phenomenon, the diversification effect, was described in Exhibit 3–1 in the example of the arms suppliers and in Exhibit 4–1 in regard to the benefits of foreign diversification.

Four types of equity models are described: the Markowitz or covariance model, the Sharpe or single-index model, the multi-index capital asset pricing model (an expansion of the single-index model), and the arbitrage pricing theory model. Under the Markowitz model the investor attempts to estimate the rate of return of each security being considered, its risk, and its covariance or comovement with each other security. With this information an investor can assemble a group of portfolios, each of which has the highest level of return for its level of risk or the lowest level of risk for a given level of return.

The investor can then choose from its so-called efficient portfolios the one which best balances its desire for return with its tolerance for risk. This method is the theoretically most correct way to invest, but it is not easy to implement due to the large number of estimates required and the tendency of optimizers to overweight data which are not close to average. If these data are the result of an error, or if the future is significantly different from the past, the resulting portfolios can be far from "optimal."

The Sharpe or single-index beta model greatly simplifies the measurement problem, though with some loss of accuracy. This approach suggests that each security can be viewed in relation to the market rather than to each other security, thus greatly reducing the number of correlation estimates which must be made. An investor then chooses a level of risk (beta) in relation to the market and attempts to find the portfolio which best meets the client's needs. Presumably this means some combination of highest return and least probability of deviating from the return anticipated, based on the portfolio's risk level. In other words, the investor might say that it would like to beat the market on a risk-adjusted basis by 1 percent per year, assuming that it is not likely to do worse than the market by one half of 1 percent per year. Any number of combinations of these parameters can be viewed by the investor, and a choice can be made, based on its perception of its requirements.

The multi-index model is similar to the single-index model in viewing each security in relation to the market rather than to each other security. The difference between the single-index model and the multi-index model is that the former has only one market index whereas the latter has more than one. This might mean that in addition to a securities market index the investor would have a second index which measures interest rates, industry effect, or some other economic variable.

The arbitrage pricing theory model describes the way prices of assets are set and suggests that there are general factors which impact most assets. The factors which are important and their weights thus determine how individual securities move. In mathematical form, the APT is similar to a multi-index capital asset pricing model except it does not rely on critical assumptions regarding the market portfolio, borrowing and lending at the risk-free rate, the need to ignore taxes, and the assumption that all investors have an identical, single-period time horizon.

Portfolio Insurance

Most investors recognize that risk and return are related such that the greater the risk of a portfolio the greater the expected long-run return. Investors who have long time horizons usually can bear substantial risk, but some have needs such that their portfolios must not fall below a certain value or must achieve a minimum rate of return. To meet these minimum requirements, this type of investor may feel compelled to maintain an extremely conservative risk policy. It may even invest totally in short-term U.S. government securities. While this strategy may be very effective in meeting the minimum requirements, it eliminates upside potential, and ultimately can be very expensive for the investor. Portfolio insurance is a technique which was designed to help investors seek a minimum return while attempting to achieve a higher return.

Portfolio insurance is a dynamic hedging strategy based on options pricing theory. Typically the investor divides its funds between a risky and a safe asset. If the risky asset does well, there is less chance than before that the investor's portfolio will decline to what it views as a critical level. In this case, the investor can afford to increase the portion of its funds allocated to the risky asset in order to achieve more upside capture if the risky asset continues to rise. If the risky asset performs poorly, there is more chance than before that its portfolio will decline to the critical level. In this case, the investor cannot afford to have so much of its funds invested in the risky asset, and the allocation to the safe asset must be increased. This protects it if the risky asset continues to decline. By properly increasing its allocation to risky assets after they rise and increasing its allocation to safe assets after risky assets fall, the investor can reduce the possibility that its portfolio will decline below the critical level when risky assets fall and attempt to secure substantial upside capture when they rise.

Portfolio insurance is greatly dependent on the ability to execute transactions at the expected prices. Any discontinuities in pricing can lead to a serious failure in the procedure. In the stock market crash of 1987, some investors found portfolio insurance to be unworkable, and others complained that it created extra downward pressure on the market. For these reasons, it has become distinctly less popular, although dynamic hedging strategies continue in use, and this use may grow.

PASSIVE APPROACHES TO INVESTING

Passive approaches to investing are frequently referred to as index funds or market funds, although strictly speaking the market fund is only one type of passive portfolio. Index approaches assume that the market is essentially efficient and consequently investors are not rewarded for attempts to find undervalued securities, or that the risk of trying to outperform the market is now worth the risk of underperforming it.

In both active and passive approaches to investing, performance is defined on a risk-adjusted basis, and transaction costs and management fees are recognized as having a negative impact on return. All such costs must be considered by investors who pursue active strategies which attempt to find undervalued securities.

Investors who establish index funds must consider a trade-off between the ability of such funds to track the index and the transaction and administrative costs involved in doing so. If these costs were nonexistent, the investors would hold portfolios which precisely mirrored the index. For example, an investor attempting to track the S&P 500 index would own each of the 500 stocks in exactly the same proportions as their proportions in the marketplace. As soon as the investor received additional cash, either through contributions or divided income, it would invest the cash balance by buying each of the 500 stocks in the same proportions. However, in the real world there are costs, so investors frequently decide to own fewer than the entire list of securities (except for the S&P 500 index), and when they make purchases with small cash inflows they usually buy fewer stocks than even the number on their reduced list. A constant trade-off must be made between the cost and the benefit of making a transaction (the benefit being reduced tracking error).

Characteristics of the Passive Portfolio
Passive portfolios can be broad representations of the universe being tracked, specific replications of a particular index, or subsamples of the index. The latter can be created by holding the securities with the largest weightings; holding assets based on major subsectors, such as industries or economic sectors; or attempting to balance factors such as size, sensitivity to interest rates, or price/earnings ratio.

Tilted Portfolios
An additional way of using index fund technology is to invest passively in or "tilt" toward a subset of the market. For instance, an investor can decide to own rapidly growing companies, low-beta conservative stocks, high-yielding stocks, and so on.

Enhanced Indexing
Not surprisingly, as indexing has become more popular, investors have tried to construct portfolios which are very similar to an index but which

are hoped to have incremental return. Among these are index arbitrage (exchanging stocks for futures of the same asset, such as the S&P 500); holding fixed-income securities and index futures, hoping to profit from a high return on the fixed-income component; and over- or underweighting certain stocks or factors about which the investor feels it has special knowledge.

In addition to simply purchasing an index fund as a style of investing, sponsors can utilize index funds as part of an active/passive strategy. The active/passive strategy involves placing a portion of the fund's assets in an index fund, where diversification is obviously very high, and placing the balance with one or more managers who will invest at a low level of diversification in a short list of securities which are expected to have high risk-adjusted returns. Theoretically, the fund could place 80 percent of its assets in an index fund and the remainder with 10 active managers, each of which invested all of the assets under its discretion (2 percent of the total fund) in one stock. This might make sense from the fund's point of view, but it is doubtful whether any investment manager would be willing to succeed or fail based on one judgment.

Alternatively, the sponsor could decide the amount in equities and then find as many active managers as it thought could add value. It would then fund the active managers and index the balance of the assets.

The case for a passive strategy or passive/active strategy is quite strong if one considers that large portfolios with active managers, when viewed as a whole, tend to look very much like index funds, except that they have higher management and transaction costs.

Fixed-Income Management Techniques

Three techniques will be discussed: dedication, immunization, and contingent immunization.

Dedication
Dedicating a bond portfolio means matching cash inflows and outflows. The technique involves purchasing a portfolio of bonds whose combined coupon payments and maturities will exactly equal the year-by-year cash requirements of the fund. This technique can be used to meet any cash need, but fund sponsors have found it particularly useful in respect to so-called retired lives of pension plans. Once a group of people reaches retirement, it is possible to estimate fairly accurately the amount

of cash required each year to meet their benefits. Since it is known that the retirees will not have terminated employment, died, or become disabled before retirement, and since their pension benefit is known, the only variable is how long they will live. This life expectancy can be estimated accurately if the group is large enough.

During periods of high interest rates, dedicated bond portfolios have been used to reduce contributions to a pension fund. Since the current bond rate was above the assured rate of return, assets were sufficient to pay all currently recognized future liabilities. However, this idea was based on two fallacies. First, since stocks have a higher long-run return than bonds, emphasizing bonds will increase future costs. Second, the cost of a pension plan is a function of benefits payable, administrative costs, and rate of return achieved. Even if bonds rather than stocks are held in the plan, the return achieved is the same whether the bonds are immunized or not. Thus, it is only the timing of contributions which can be impacted by setting up the dedicated bond portfolio, not the ultimate size of the contribution.

Immunization

Bond portfolios have a peculiar attribute. If interest rates rise, a holder of a bond finds that two things happen. First, it suffers a capital loss as investors increase the discount rate and thus decrease the present value of the cash flows provided by his or her bond. On the other hand, as coupon interest is received, the investor will achieve a higher rate of return on this reinvested coupon than was expected before the rise in interest rates. It so happens that there is a mathematical relationship between the two such that in controlled circumstances an investor can establish a bond portfolio in which capital gains and losses will be offset by decreases or increases in income on reinvested coupon. The "controlled circumstance" is when the duration of the cash inflows equals the duration of the cash outflows, at which point the portfolio is "immunized" against changes in interest rates.

Duration as a Measure of Maturity.   Whereas the normal measure of maturity considers only the time from the present to the time of repayment of the bond's principal, the duration measure recognizes that payments from coupon also impact a bond's behavior. Thus, two bonds will have different characteristics even if they have the same maturity if one has a higher coupon, and thus returns more money to the investor earlier than the other. The duration measure combines both the notion of

the size of the cash flow and its timing by looking for the point at which the investor has received half the present value of the cash flows from the bond. The present value of each payment, including the last one, to the investor is weighted by the time until the payment is received; an average is then taken of the weighted values. This average is the measure duration.

Contingent Immunization

While investors are anxious to take advantage of high interest rates, they also find it desirable to try to outperform the return provided by a "buy and hold" portfolio. This has led to the idea of contingent immunization. An investor can establish a rate of return below which it would find it uncomfortable to fall. If this rate is below the current interest rate, the portfolio can be contingently immunized. The portfolio can be actively managed until its value falls below the amount needed to immunize. For example, suppose rates are 10 percent and the investor wants to earn at least 8 percent. Its manager can trade the portfolio actively in hopes of achieving profits. If the portfolio's return falls below 8 percent for a long enough period that the 8 percent return is in jeopardy, the manager then immunizes by choosing a portfolio of securities which has a duration equal to the investor's remaining time horizon.

A comment should be made about quality of securities. All these tactics assume the bonds owned are "money good." This has led many investors to consider only Treasury or U.S. government agency securities. However, as always, it is tempting to try to achieve an even higher rate of return by moving down on the quality scale. The wisdom of doing this depends upon how long it will be until the funds are required (the longer it is, the more quality deterioration can occur) and the penalty for failing to meet the target relative to the benefit of exceeding it.

PUT AND CALL OPTIONS

With the standardized procedures developed by the Chicago Board of Trade in 1972, options became readily marketable, making them much more widely used in the investment community.

A *call option* is the right to buy 100 shares of stock at a specified price for a specified amount of time. For instance, if a stock is selling at 60, an investor might purchase for $400 the right to buy

100 shares at 60 for the next six months. This means that (ignoring commissions) if the stock rises above $64 per share, the owner of the option will have a gain. Since his investment is only $400, the gain can be a very large percentage of his equity. Similarly, any loss will probably be a large percentage of his capital. However, the investor might say that by buying the option he can have most of the benefits of the upside potential without risking nearly as much money as if it had bought 100 shares at $60 for $6,000.

The short-term nature of the option and the option's high volatility relative to the equity invested make purchasing calls rather speculative and hence generally inappropriate for tax-exempt portfolios. However, in certain circumstances, it may be perfectly appropriate for tax-exempt investors to sell options to other investors and speculators. If a fund owns the 100 shares of the stock, it can sell the option to the speculator without acting imprudently. In this case the fund receives $400 income and is entitled to the dividends paid on the stocks even during the period when the call is outstanding. If the stock rises dramatically, the fund loses the benefit of the dramatic increase. If the stock falls sharply, the fund will still own the stock, but it will have the $400 as a cushion against the loss. In either case the fund has the opportunity of selling the stock and buying back the option contract if it wishes to remove itself from the transaction. Experience indicates that stocks go up and down but that they do not go either to the moon or to zero, and consequently a steady option-writing program can provide income and reduced volatility to the portfolio. However, it is doubtful that any investment medium can provide above-average risk-adjusted returns over the long run. Rather, it is likely that covered call writing changes the shape of the distribution of returns, cutting off the upside, protecting the middle range of returns, and retaining the downside. Exhibit 9–5 demonstrates the impact of a covered option on a portfolio.

The above example assumed 100 shares of stock long versus 100 options sold. It is also possible to sell more or less than 100 options for each 100 shares of stock owned.

Two interesting uses of options have been developed. The first involves owning a combination of calls and low-risk Treasury bills or commercial paper. A fund might invest 10 percent of its assets in calls and 90 percent in Treasury bills. This approach permits reasonable participation in a strong market rise through the calls, while protecting capital in the event of a large decline through the short-term securities. The interest

EXHIBIT 9–5
Impact of change in stock price on value of "covered call" portfolio (assume ownership of 100 shares of stock and short sale of option to purchase 100 shares)

Value of Stock, Option, and Portfolio with Several Months Remaining Before Option Expires | | | | | | Value of Portfolio Just before Option Expires | |

A	B	C	D	E	F	G	H
	Price of Option to Buy 100 Shares at 50*	Portfolio Value	Percentage Change from Base			Portfolio	Percentage Change from $45 cost
Stock Price			Stock	Option	Portfolio	Value	
50	5	45	—	—	—	50	11.1
48	3.5	44.5	-4	-30	-1.1	48	6.7
46	2	44	-8	-60	-2.2	46	2.2
40	nil	40	-20	-100	-11.1	40	-11.1
30	nil	30	-40	-100	-33.3	30	-33.3
52	6	46	4	20	2.2	50	11.1
54	7	47	8	40	4.4	50	11.1
60	12	48	20	140	6.7	50	11.1
70	21	49	40	320	8.9	50	11.1

*i.e., "strike price" is 50

1. If the stock price remains unchanged, declines, or rises slightly, the investor is better off having written the option. This can be seen by comparing columns D and H.

2. If the stock is at or above the strike price at the time option expires, the investor's gain is the value of the option in excess of its conversion value. In this case the option's conversion value was "0" when its price was 5 and the stock price was 50, so the investor's gain was 5. His total investment was 50 for the stock less 5 for the option proceeds, for a net total of 45.

3. The covered portfolio is less volatile than the stock alone (compare columns D and F).

4. As the stock price declines, the portfolio volatility rises, since the option value gets smaller and smaller (i.e., the portfolio value is completely dominated by the movement of the stock price) (compare columns D and F).

5. As the stock price rises, the portfolio volatility declines, since the option value rises faster than the stock value (i.e., the impact of the stock price rise is increased by the rise in the option price) (compare columns D and F).

6. The relationship between the stock and option prices depends on the strike price, the stock volatility, and the level of interest rates. If these factors are constant, the option price decreases (as the square root of the time remaining) as the expiration date nears.

income on the short-term investment may even be enough to pay for the calls, in which case there is no risk to principal.

The second use involves selling puts. Whereas a call is an option to buy stock at a certain price during a certain period of time, a *put* gives the holder the right to sell his shares at a certain price for a certain time interval. Viewed from the point of view of the option seller, the writer or seller of a call has the liability to deliver shares to the holder of the call during the time interval. Thus, if the stock rises greatly in price, the investor who has written the call has a substantial liability. (If the investor owned the shares, this liability would be offset by the increase in the value of the shares that he owned.) The put seller, on the other hand, has guaranteed to purchase shares from the put holder, and consequently he has the liability of purchasing the shares at the agreed-upon price even though they may be far below that price in the marketplace.

This may be a less serious problem than it seems to be if the put seller sells puts only on securities which he is anxious to own. In other words, if a stock is at $50 and the investor feels that this is an attractive purchase price, he should be willing to receive a fee of $3 or $5 per share to guarantee to purchase the stock at $50. If the stock goes to $40 and the put is exercised, the investor still ends up paying $50, as he would have without entering into a put transaction, but at least he received the three- or four-point premium for having agreed to give the put holder the right to sell the shares to the investor at $50. The put seller is disadvantaged if unfavorable news is released regarding the stock. In that case, the stock will decline and the put will rise in price. The seller can cut its loss by buying back the put, just as a stockholder can cut its loss by selling the stock.

GUARANTEED INVESTMENT CONTRACTS

Guaranteed investment contracts can be purchased in competitive biddings by the sponsor, with or without aid from a consultant, or can be managed by an independent investment manager. The investment manager has the advantage of being in the market frequently and thus is able to take advantage of aberrations in the market and is better able to understand new products and their variants. The manager may also have a superior ability to monitor the creditworthiness of the GIC issuers. The investment manager's fee must be compared against the potential value added. Since GIC contracts are issued on a competitive basis and are subject to accurate analysis, the value which many sponsors find in GIC managers may relate to convenience and comfort provided by having an outside fiduciary rather than having higher return.

Since there are not widely accepted indexes of GIC performance, it is necessarily difficult for sponsors to evaluate the benefits of independent managers. This is unlike the problem of stocks or bonds. With those securities, it is reasonable to assume that the sponsor would own securities with the average return, rather than the best or worse return. However, since GICs are subject to a purchase through bids, it is more logical to assume that the sponsor would have picked the highest bid at any point in time. However, it is not logical to assume that all sponsors could have purchased GICs at the highest rate, since the capacity of the insurance company offering the highest rate is necessarily limited. Until this conundrum is solved, it will be difficult for sponsors to measure the performance benefits associated with professional GIC managers.

REAL ESTATE INVESTMENTS

Investments in real estate can be made either in mortgages or in direct ownership. Mortgages are reasonably straightforward, though care must be exercised in reviewing the collateral, the ability of the borrower to repay, the marketability of the collateral in case of default, and any special terms. Equity ownership can involve 100 percent participation by the sponsor, partnership with other investors or with the developer, or, increasingly, commingled funds. Because of illiquidity and lack of fungibility of real estate (each piece of real estate is unique, rather than fungible or identical), investing in real estate is different from purchasing securities. On the other hand, real estate returns are not highly correlated with those of securities; hence, real estate can be a very attractive investment. Chapter 5 deals more extensively with real estate investing.

CHAPTER 10

MEASURING INVESTMENT PERFORMANCE

If it can't be measured it doesn't exist.
Paraphrase from Lord Kelvin

The science of measuring the performance of investment portfolios began with a study by the Bank Administration Institute in 1968. This study, called *Measuring the Investment Performance of Pension Funds,* was made by a group of investment professionals and academics at the instruction of the Bank Administration Institute, a trade association of banks. Part of the impetus for the study was, in the view of some observers, the fact that bank trust departments, which had traditionally managed almost all investment funds for wealthy individuals and pension funds, were losing business to investment counseling organizations. Some of the banks which were losing their assets to these competitors felt that the investment counseling organizations were achieving superior investment performance by increasing the risk of the securities owned. Since risk-adjusted performance measurement was virtually nonexistent at that time, the sponsors of portfolios had been unaware of the increased risk that they were taking in order to achieve higher rates of return. Thus, it was felt desirable to have a prestigious and qualified group prepare an authoritative report on the appropriate method for analyzing investment performance. The BAI study made considerable progress in this regard. It drew four main conclusions:

1. Measurements of performance should be based on asset values measured at market, not at cost.

2. The returns should be "total" returns; that is, they should include both income and changes in market value (realized and unrealized capital appreciation).
3. The returns should be time-weighted.
4. The measurements should include risk as well as return.

Market values were required in performance measurement so that at any point in time the fund sponsor could accurately see the value of its portfolio and measure the changes in its value. It was acknowledged that fixed-income securities had a maturity date and that holders of such securities could expect to achieve the rate of return indicated at the time of purchase if they held them until maturity. However, it was felt that, if the returns of one portfolio were to be comparable with those of another, both portfolios must be measured at their fair market value. In retrospect, it seems obvious that total rates of return should have been used, but at the time many organizations were viewing the income from their portfolios in one light and capital appreciation in another. For taxable investors, this makes some sense, though even such investors must consider both capital changes and income. For tax-exempt investors, the distinction is of very little consequence. Therefore, the appropriateness of using total returns is unassailable.

The reasons for using time-weighted rates of return are not as obvious. The time-weighted rate of return is designed to eliminate the effects on the portfolio of the timing and magnitude of external cash flows, whereas the alternative, the internal or dollar-weighted return, includes the impact of any such external contributions or withdrawals. The rationale for the distinction and for the use of the time-weighted return is that what is being subjected to a performance analysis is not the fund's results but the activities of the manager. Since the manager presumably does not have control over the timing of contributions to and withdrawals from the portfolio, it is not appropriate to attribute to it the impact of these cash flows.

The decision to measure risk and return was simple in theory but difficult in practice. This was because a theoretical framework for measuring risk was lacking and because at that time few investors had the capability for manipulating sufficient data easily enough to develop risk measures even if such a framework existed.

CALCULATING THE RATE OF RETURN

A *rate of return*, or, for succinctness, a *return*, is the percentage profit or gain achieved for holding an investment or a portfolio for a particular time. *Price* or *capital returns* are the changes in the value of assets, excluding income. *Income returns* are the gain or profit from dividends or interest. *Total returns* are the sum of price or capital returns and income returns. In its simplest form, a return is calculated by subtracting the difference between the beginning and ending value and dividing this amount by the beginning value. The result will be the decimalized return, which can be converted to a percentage return by multiplying by 100. Alternatively, the return can be calculated by dividing the ending value by the beginning value, subtracting 1, and multiplying by 100 to show the percentage return. Both of these methods are demonstrated below for a security which rose in value from $100 to $105.

$$\text{Return} = \frac{\text{Ending value} - \text{Beginning value}}{\text{Beginning value}} = \frac{105 - 100}{100} = \frac{5}{100}$$
$$= 0.05 \times 100 = 5\%$$

$$\text{Return} = \left(\left(\frac{\text{Ending value}}{\text{Beginning value}} \right) - 1 \right) \times 100$$
$$= \left(\frac{105}{100} - 1 \right) \times 100 = 1.05 - 1.00 = 0.05 \times 100 = 5\%$$

Complications enter the process from two sources: the need for accurate valuations and the need to handle cash flows properly. The need for accurate valuations is obvious, since if we improperly measure either the beginning or ending value, we will obviously not have a true rate of return (unless by chance we have made a proportional error in both). The only other difficulty which can arise with valuations stems from the number of valuations required. The more frequent the intervals over which return information is required, the more frequently the portfolio must be valued even if there are no cash flows. If there are cash flows, the accuracy of the return calculation will be increased by having more frequent valuations.

This leads to the second complexity, namely the need to handle cash inflows and outflows to and from the portfolio. At this stage, let us consider only a total portfolio rather than dealing separately with such sectors as equities or fixed income. Clearly, if a contribution has been made to the portfolio, our simple calculation of rate of return breaks down: A portfolio which started with $100 and ended with $120 did not have a 20 percent gain if the sponsor contributed an additional $20 during the period. The fund in this case had a zero percent rate of return, as can be seen from the example below:

$$\text{Gain} = \text{Ending value} - \text{Contributions} - \text{Beginning value}$$
$$= \$120 - \$20 - \$100 = 0$$

Now let us see what would have happened if the fund started with $100, the sponsor added $20, and the fund ended with $130. We know that there is a gain of $10, but the return could have been anywhere between 8.3 percent and 10 percent. If the gain came before the arrival of the $20 contributioñ, then 10 percent is the correct return; if the gain came after the contribution, then 8.3 percent is correct (see Exhibit 10–1). If the gain came partly in each period, then we must have further information or make some assumption before we can state the return earned. The information that we require depends on whether we are calculating time-weighted or dollar-weighted returns. If a time-weighed return is needed, the required piece of information is the value of the portfolio at the time of the cash flow. If a dollar-weighted return is desired, the necessary

---

EXHIBIT 10–1
Timing of Cash Flow Affects Rate of Return

Beginning value = 100
Ending value = 130
Cash flow = 20

Case 1: Cash flow came before gain

$$\text{Return} = \frac{\text{Ending value} - \text{Beginning value} - \text{Cash flow}}{\text{Beginning value} + \text{Cash flow}}$$
$$= \frac{130 - 100 - 20}{100 + 20} = \frac{10}{120} = 8.3\%$$

Case 2: Cash flow came after gain

$$\text{Return} = \frac{\text{Ending value} - \text{Beginning value}}{\text{Beginning value}}$$
$$= \frac{110 - 100}{100} = 10\%$$

---

information is the exact time at which the cash flow occurred. This will be discussed further below.

TIME-WEIGHTED VERSUS DOLLAR-WEIGHTED RATES OF RETURN

The time-weighted return (TWR) shows the value of one dollar invested in a portfolio or a portfolio sector for the entire period. The dollar-weighted return (DWR) shows an average return of all the dollars in the portfolio or the portfolio sector for the period. The DWR reconciles the beginning dollar amount of the fund plus the cash contributions with the ending value of the fund. The TWR intentionally ignores the fact that money is contributed to or removed from the fund and looks only at the money in the fund during each period.

Consider an investment cycle in which a fund has high returns for one period and negative returns for the next period. If the portfolio has more dollars working when the return is low, the return on the average dollar will be low; in this case the TWR will be higher than the DWR. On the other hand, if more dollars are in the fund when the returns are high, the return on the average dollar will be high; consequently, the DWR will exceed the TWR. In both cases the TWR will be the same. If the fund manager had no control over the number of dollars in the fund, he should be measured on the basis of his time-weighted returns, not the fund's dollar-weighted returns.

Understanding of the distinction between the two types of returns can be enhanced by noting when the two will be identical, and by seeing an example. The TWR and the DWR will be identical when there are no cash inflows or outflows or when the return earned during the period is constant. Since the distinction arises only when there are contributions to or withdrawals from the fund, if there are no such cash flows, the two types of return will be the same. Also, if the return is constant during the entire period, there can be no difference between the two types of return.

Calculating the Time-Weighted Return

The time-weighted return is calculated by measuring the rate of return during a number of subperiods (presumably quarterly or monthly) and "linking" or "chaining" the interim returns (see Appendix, "Mathematics Refresher''). For example, if the fund earned 6 percent in period 1 and 8 percent in period 2, the time-weighted return is

$$[(1.06 \times 1.08) - 1] \times 100 =$$
$$1.1448 - 1 = 0.1448 \times 100 = 14.48\%$$

To calculate a time-weighted return, it is necessary to measure or estimate the value of the portfolio at the end of the first year when the cash flow took place. A simple example may serve to demonstrate differences in the two types of returns. Suppose a portfolio begins with $1,000 at the beginning of year 1, receives $100 at the end of the year, and has $1,200 at the end of year 2. If we know that the value of the portfolio was $1,050 just before the cash flow was received, we can easily calculate an accurate time-weighted rate of return, as follows. The return for the first year is $1,050 divided by $1,000, which equals 1.05, or 5 percent. The second year's return is calculated by taking $1,200, the ending value, and dividing it by $1,150 (the sum of $1,050 plus $100 equals $1,150). This return is 1.043, or 4.3 percent. The return for the two years is thus 1.043 times 1.05, which equals 1.095, or 9.5 percent.

The dollar-weighted return is calculated on an ''iterative'' or trial-and-error basis. In effect, the dollar-weighted calculation raises the question, ''What is the rate of return which can be multiplied by the beginning value and the interim cash flows in order to equal the ending value?'' Or more precisely, ''What rate of return per period equates the initial value of the cash flow received to the ending value?''

In the example above, the iterative procedure, figuratively speaking, asks what rate on $1,000 for two years plus the same rate on $100 for one year equals $1,200. Let's try 10 percent and see what happens. Ten percent of $1,000 for one year is $100, so at the end of year 1 and before the contribution we have $1,100. After the $100 contribution we have $1,200, which earns 10 percent, or $120, for year 2, providing an estimated total ending value at a 10 percent rate equal to $1,320. Since $1,320 is greater than the actual ending value of $1,200, the rate we used must have been too high. If 10 percent is too high, let's try 5 percent. Five percent of $1,000 is $50; 5 percent of $1,050 is $52.50; 5 percent of the $100 contribution is $5; and adding the $100 contribution we get a total of $1,207.50. Again the results exceed the actual ending value, so a lower return must be tried. The procedure keeps doing this until a return is calculated which leads to an ending value close enough to $1,200 to be acceptable. Thus, the dollar-weighted return takes into account both performance and the impact of the timing of cash flows on performance.

The following example demonstrates convincingly the difference between the two types of return. Both funds start with $100 and have the same investment manager, and the manager keeps both funds 100 percent invested in General Motors stock at all times. General Motors' price and the contribution to the two funds are as follows:

1. Beginning price: 50; each fund buys two shares.
   Value Fund A: 2 shares @ 50 = 100
   Value Fund B: 2 shares @ 50 = 100

2. One year later price rises to 100; Fund A receives $100 contribution and buys one share @ 100.
   Value Fund A: 3 shares @ 100 = 300
   Value Fund B: 2 shares @ 100 = 200

3. One year later price declines to 50.
   Value Fund A: 3 shares @ 50 = 150;
   cost = (2 × 50) + (1 × 100) = 200; loss = 50
   Value Fund B: 2 shares @ 50 = 100; cost = 2 × 50 = 100;
   gain = 0

Time-weighted return = 0 in each fund.
Dollar-weighted returns:
  Fund A = −18.1%
  Fund B = 0%

Fund A showed a loss and had a negative dollar-weighted return. Fund B broke even and had a 0 percent dollar-weighted return. Both funds had a 0 percent time-weighted return. Fund B had no contributions, and thus its dollar-weighted and time-weighted returns were identical. The manager clearly made the same contribution to each fund, since it made exactly the same investments in both funds. The TWR reflects its contribution. The DWR in Fund A reflects both the contribution of the manager (0 percent) and the timing of the contribution, which happened to come when the stock was at a high price.

CALCULATING THE RETURNS ON PORTFOLIO COMPONENTS

Equities

The technique for calculating returns can be applied to all asset categories, with only procedural rather than theoretical questions to be answered. The first such procedural question in measuring returns on equities is what to include in this category. A typical definition of equities would include common stocks, convertible preferred stocks, convertible bonds, warrants to purchase stocks, and options. Other definitions are perfectly acceptable as long as all parties are aware of the classification being used. The need for valuations is the same for all asset categories, and cash flows must also be dealt with. In the case of an individual asset category, such as equities or fixed-income securities, the cash flows are the purchases and sales. In other words, a cash flow into equities is an equities purchase and a cash outflow is a sale. Just as the increased value in the total portfolio resulting from contributions is not attributable to return, so a purchase of equities is not attributable to equities return. Assume, for example, a beginning value of 100, an ending value of 120, and a purchase of 20.

$$\text{Gain} = \text{Ending value} - \text{Purchases} - \text{Beginning value}$$
$$= 120 - 20 - 100 = 0$$

Equities purchases and sales are treated in the same fashion as are total portfolio contributions and withdrawals. An additional factor, dividends, must also be considered, since part of the return of an asset category is its income. This subject can cause confusion, since one could properly argue that income should be counted in the total portfolio return if we are measuring "total return." The distinction to be drawn is that cash, the normal form of income payment, is part of the total portfolio but that cash is not part of the equities portfolio. The total portfolio is defined to include all assets, including cash, but the equities portfolio can consist only of equities. Calculation of the return, including income, is demonstrated in this example:

$$\text{Gain} = \text{Price gain} + \text{Income gain}$$

$$\text{Equity return} = \frac{\text{Ending equity value} - \text{Equity purchases} + \text{Dividends} + \text{Equity sales}}{\text{Beginning equity value}}$$

Thus, it can be seen that the $5 dividend received on the $100 worth of stock has led to a 5 percent gain, just as would have been the case had the $5 come from capital appreciation. However, the return has been calculated as though we were viewing a total portfolio, since the ending value, $105, consists of $100 in equities plus $5 in cash. Thus, the true position of the portfolio at the end of the period is as follows: $100 stock plus $5 cash equals $105 total.

Presentation of the true portfolio position leads to an intuitive difficulty, namely that we all tend to think of the $5 dividend as a positive cash flow to the equities portfolio, whereas in fact the $5 is a positive cash flow to the total portfolio but a negative cash flow to the equities portfolio. This can be substantiated in several ways. First, the $5 increase in cash had to come from somewhere, and since it did not result from an external contribution it must have come from the only other source within the portfolio—equities. Since there were no external cash flows, the internal cash balance must net out to zero, which can occur only if the +$5 in cash is offset by a −$5 in equities. Second, we know that the portfolio gained 5 percent during the period and that equities were the source of this 5 percent gain. The only way in which an asset can start out with $100, end up with $100, and have a 5 percent return is if 5 percent of the value of the assets are withdrawn during the period. Finally, since we are drawing no distinction between income and appreciation in our calculation of return we can view the situations in which no dividend was paid but the shares rose 5 percent in value and 5 percent of the holdings were sold. In this case we would obviously treat the sale as a negative cash flow, and logically, therefore, we must treat the dividend in the same way.

Dividends should be assumed to be received on the date when a new purchaser is not entitled to them.

The next issue, the handling of stock splits and stock dividends, should be simple now that the principles have been established. Clearly, return is not enhanced by a stock split or a stock dividend, so no special consideration need to be given to these events except to be certain that the asset price used in the valuation is consistent with the number of shares owned. In other words, if 100 shares of a $50 stock are owned and a two-for-one split takes place, the new position is 200 shares at $25. In both cases the investment is worth $5,000, so there has been no impact on return. This may sound elementary, but it must be remembered that the receipt of the extra 100 shares by the investor invariably occurs well after the stock begins trading at the new price. This is because the company must know who owns its shares at the time of the split in order to distribute the shares properly. Consequently, a time lag exists which can cause errors in a custodial statement if the statement shows the old number of shares and the new price.

Bonds

The return on fixed-income (bond) investments is calculated very similarly to the return on equities. That is, it is calculated after adjusting for purchases, sales, and income. The principal distinction lies in accounting for accrued interest. Whereas the value of a common stock investment is merely the market price times the number of shares owned, there are two components to the value of a bond. These are the capital value (or number of bonds owned times price per bond) plus the accrued interest. Since misunderstandings regarding accrued interest can occur, it is well to discuss this area further.

The holder of a bond is contractually entitled to receive interest, usually semiannually. Since the bondholder is entitled to this interest, the value of the bond increases every day by that day's accrued interest. When a bondholder sells a bond two thirds of the way through the interest period (four months) it receives two thirds of the semiannual coupon from the buyer, with the buyer receiving the one third to which it is entitled plus the two thirds which it paid the seller at the end of the six-month coupon period. Thus, the value of the bond increases every day by the amount of accrued interest until the payment period, when the process starts all over again. Although some distortion in return is possible if there are large purchases or sales in a period within a fixed income portfolio (see discussion of anomaly in the appendix to this chapter), accrued interest should not be a problem in calculating return as long as it is treated consistently. That is to say, if the beginning value of the portfolio includes accrued interest, the ending value must also include accrued interest. It is preferable to include accrued interest in asset valuations wherever possible.

Cash Equivalents

Calculating returns on cash equivalents is no different, in principle, from calculating returns on stocks and bonds. If the cash equivalent is a discount instrument, the market value of the asset includes both accrued interest and capital changes such that a proper rate of return can be calculated from this value. If the instrument carries a coupon, the coupon must be treated just like any other income to a portfolio subsector, namely as a negative cash flow to that subsector and a positive cash flow to the cash holdings of the portfolio. Practical considerations in measuring returns on cash equivalents are shown on p. 63.

Commingled Funds

Commingled funds represent a special case in that they are single securities from the point of view of the fund owner. That is, although a commingled fund may own stocks, bonds, cash, or cash equivalents in any proportion, all of the assets within the commingled fund are treated as part of the portfolio's value. Hence the effect of the commingled fund on the return of the overall pension or endowment fund will be considered by merely accounting for changes in the value of the investment in the commingled fund and in the number of shares or units owned.

Caution must be taken regarding the treatment of income distributions from commingled funds. A commingled fund can treat income in one of three ways. One alternative is to retain the income within the portfolio, in which case the commingled fund's net asset value is enhanced by the amount of income per share. This causes no problem to the sponsor, since it includes the market value (equals number of shares times net asset value per share) in the value of its fund. A second alternative is for the fund to distribute its income to shareholders in cash. In this case the net asset value of the share declines due to the distribution, and thus the sponsor must treat the cash received as a negative cash flow from the commingled fund and an increase in cash within the sponsor's fund. The third alternative is for the sponsor to choose to have income distributions automatically reinvested in new shares. In this case the net asset value of the fund declines but the number of shares owned by each holder increases proportionately, so that the value of the investment is maintained at the same level before and after the income distribution. Fortunately, since many tax-exempt funds have no need for income, it has become customary for most commingled funds to retain and reinvest income within the commingled fund. A sponsor which wishes to receive a distribution merely sells enough shares to achieve the amount of cash required.

APPLYING PERFORMANCE MEASUREMENT TECHNIQUES TO REAL PORTFOLIOS

We have established that the dollar-weighted return is the average return on all dollars invested, whereas the time-weighted return is the result obtained from calculating the internal rate of return for subperiods between cash flows and "linking" or "chaining" the subperiod returns to find the return for the cumulative period. When we turn to real portfolios we find two practical restraints to accurate calculation of time- and dollar-weighted returns:

1. The valuation statements may not be produced as frequently as desired. The accuracy of the return calculation will be reduced if there are large cash flows and, for instance, only quarterly rather than monthly valuations are available.

2. Cash flows may take place at any time, not just at mid-month. There is obviously a different impact on a portfolio from a $100 contribution in the middle of the month than from a $100 contribution at the end of the month. On a practical basis, however, most performance measurement systems do not permit the treatment of cash flows on each of the 250-odd days possible.

It is not feasible to have reporting periods other than by calendar month, as the whole system of analysis in this and other countries is based on annual periods. Furthermore, since we are dealing with a time-related concept, namely rate of return per period, it makes sense to have the reporting done on a calendar month or quarter basis. This creates a problem, since we will not normally have appropriate valuations on the date of cash flows.

In addition to the "exact" method, which requires valuations at each cash flow, there are three methods for calculating time-weighted returns. These are:

1. The linked internal method.

2. The regression method.
3. Apportioned contribution methods.

The *linked internal method* involves measuring the internal rate of return for each period between valuations (in this case quarterly) and linking or chaining the results, as demonstrated in the Appendix Mathematics Refresher, page 325. This method assumes that the return within each quarter is uniform. Even though we know that dollar-weighted returns are not usually good estimates of time-weighted returns, if we break up the subperiods sufficiently and if there are no large cash flows during a period when the market had a large return, this method will yield adequate results.

The *regression method* is the most accurate way of calculating rates of return when valuations are available only quarterly. This method involves estimating the value of the portfolio at interim periods within the quarter, such as monthly, on the assumption that an estimate of the monthly valuation is more useful than the linked internal method's assumption that the rate of return during the quarter was equal each month. An estimate of the interim market value can be made if two things are known: the rate of return on the market during the monthly subinterval and the relationship (beta) of the portfolio's return to the market's return. If we know that the portfolio is, for instance, 10 percent more volatile than the market and that the market rose 10 percent during a month, we can assume that the portfolio's value was more likely to have risen by 11 percent than by either the 10 percent which the market earned or the average of the quarter, as would be assumed by the linked internal method.

An astute reader may recognize both the logic of this approach and the dilemma it poses. We are trying to calculate the portfolio's rate of return, and in order to do this we need to know the relationship between the portfolio's return and the market's return, which requires our knowing what the portfolio's rate of return was! This dilemma can be solved by using the trial-and-error method of trying to find a portfolio beta which will result in an ending value of the portfolio, arrived at by estimation, as close as possible to the actual ending value. The regression method is limited in that it is ordinarily not possible to develop a useful measure of beta without having had at least six to eight quarters of valuations. When 12 to 20 quarters of valuations are available, the regression method gives quite satisfactory results. According to the BAI study, for funds having quarterly valuation statements and monthly cash statements, the expected annual errors in return using the linked internal method and the regression method are 0.48 percent and 0.17 percent, respectively.[1]

The apportioned methods are hybrid approaches to performance calculations. They have a simplicity about them, both conceptually and in carrying out the calculations, which gives them considerable appeal. These methods say, in effect, that the ending value is composed of the beginning value, gains from income and appreciation, and contributions. The contributions cannot be treated as gains, so an adjustment must be made for them. Further, the amount of time that the contributions were in the portfolio must be recognized. Therefore, the beginning or ending values will be adjusted by a portion of the contributions. The adjustment can be the exact portion of the period for which the funds were available, thus leading to a return which is "weighted by the time" that funds are available.

APPENDIX

STRANGE BUT TRUE INVESTMENT RESULTS

Experience with the results of hundreds of performance measurement studies indicates that almost any combination of anomalous results is possible. These strange results can cause great frustration to those unfamiliar with how they come about and can cast doubts on valid and useful measurement techniques. These correct but nonintuitive returns can derive from such causes as:

1. Changes in the allocation among equities, fixed income, and cash equivalents.
2. Dollar-weighted versus time-weighted factors.
3. Compound interest.
4. Accrued interest.

---

[1]*Measuring the Investment Performance of Pension Funds for the Purpose of Inter-Fund Comparison* (Park Ridge, Ill.: Bank Administration Institute, 1968), p 25.

5. The use of total returns rather than just income.
6. Conceptual misunderstandings (e.g., all assets not accounted for—thus Equities plus Fixed Income equal Total Portfolio because of cash).

Changes in Allocation

One of the strangest things that can occur within a portfolio is for the return of the total portfolio to fall outside the return of the equity and fixed-income portions. An extreme form of this event occurs when the equity and fixed-income returns are up and the total portfolio return is down. The extreme form is apparent from the following example, which is taken from the results of a jointly trusteed retirement fund.

	Percent Return		
Year Ended	Equities	Bonds	Total Portfolio
12/75	19.8	8.1	−2.0

The portfolio had a loss on a time-weighted basis in 1975 even though equities and fixed-income securities showed gains. This seemingly impossible occurrence can take place if three things happen:

1. The rates of return on the asset sectors (equities and fixed income securities) fluctuate greatly (see Exhibit 10–2).
2. The allocation between equities and fixed-income securities changes greatly (i.e., the fund policy changes or the investment manager tries to time the market) (see Exhibit 10–3).
3. Time-weighted rather than dollar-weighted returns are being measured (see Exhibit 10–4).

Dollar-Weighted versus Time-Weighted Factors

A second major area of confusion occurs when the portfolio shows a negative time-weighted return but the portfolio has shown a positive gain (or vice versa). In other words, the sum of the initial value plus the net contributions is below the ending market value, thus indicating that a pos-

EXHIBIT 10–2
Quarterly Portfolio Returns: Sector Returns Vary Greatly

Quarter Ended	Equities	Bonds	Total Portfolio
3/75	15.5	3.5	4.7
6/75	12.4	2.3	3.4
9/75	−16.5	−1.0	−13.5
12/75	10.5	3.1	4.6
Year	19.8	8.1	−2.0

Note that for each quarter the total portfolio returns were in the range between the equity and bond results.

EXHIBIT 10–3
Valuations and Cash Flows: Significant Changes in Allocation (as Percentage of Total Portfolio)

Quarter Ended	Valuations		Purchases (Sales) at End of Quarter	
	Equities	Bonds	Equities	Bonds
12/74	10	90		
3/75	11	89		
6/75 (before transactions)	12	88		
6/75 (after transactions)	82	18	70	(70)
9/75 (before transactions)	79	21	(59)	59
9/75 (after transactions)	20	80		
12/75	21	79		

itive investment gain has been achieved. This case demonstrates the fundamental distinction between time- and dollar-weighted rates of return. The case may occur if the portfolio's return was lower when a smaller amount of money was invested in the portfolio and higher when more money was invested in it. If the cumulative effect of the portfolio returns is such that the down cycle does more harm than the up cycle does good, the overall portfolio return will be negative. This apparent anomaly occurred in many portfolios during the period 1973–76. The cumulative effect on $1 invested throughout the poor years 1973 and 1974 was not overcome by the market improvements in 1975 and 1976, yet the portfolio had a great deal more money invested in the latter years due to

EXHIBIT 10–4
Source of Total Portfolio Return

Quarter Ended	(Equity Allocation	×	Equity Return)	+ (Bond Allocation	×	Bond Return)	= Total Portfolio Return
3/75	0.10		15.5%	0.90		3.5%	4.7%
6/75	0.11		12.4	0.89		2.3	3.4
9/75	0.82		−16.5	0.18		−1.0	−13.5
12/75	0.20		10.5	0.80		3.1	4.6
			19.8			8.1	−2.0

The movement of large amounts of money between sectors at the wrong time led to small allocations to equities in the first, second, and fourth quarters, when equity performance was good, and to a high allocation to equities in the third quarter, when equity results were poor. Consequently, the poor results in the third quarter overshadowed the good results in the other three quarters.

increased contributions. The result was negative time-weighted returns and positive dollar-weighted returns.

Compound Interest

When an investor views his portfolio he sometimes wonders why the results in up and down quarters appear to be equal or perhaps favoring the upside but the portfolio's cumulative return is negative. This results because of the impact of negative returns on an investment portfolio. If a portfolio rises 10 percent one year and declines 10 percent the next, it would appear that the investment has maintained its original value. However, a quick run through the numbers indicates that this is not the case. A $100 investment which achieves a 10 percent return will have $110 at the end of the period, for a gain of $10. A decline of 10 percent leads to a loss of $11 and an ensuing value of $99, or an overall loss for the two periods of $1. The greater the volatility of the portfolio, the more apparent this phenomenon will be. We can see this in Exhibit 10–5, wherein returns are shown for various percentage gains and commensurate percentage losses.

It sometimes appears that the last year's results dominate portfolio returns over the cumulative period. That is, a portfolio which did very well in the last period seems to have done well cumulatively, and similarly a portfolio which did badly in the latest year appears to have a poor

EXHIBIT 10–5

Result of Equal Percentage Gains and Losses			Gain Required to Recoup Losses	
Gain	Loss	Cumulative Loss	Loss	Gain Required
5%	−5%	−0.25%	−5%	+5.26%
10	−10	−1.00	−10	+11.1
15	−15	−2.25	−15	+17.6
20	−20	−4.00	−20	+25
25	−25	−6.25	−25	+33.3
30	−30	−9.00	−30	+42.9
33⅓	−33⅓	−11.11	−33⅓	+50
40	−40	−16.00	−40	+66.6
50	−50	−25.00	−50	+100
75	−75	−56.3	−75	+300
100	−100	−100.00	−100	+Infinity

cumulative result. It can easily be seen that the apparent phenomenon does not really exist. Each year's returns count equally with each other year, so it makes no difference whether the portfolio did well in the first period or the last. This is indicated by the following example:

	Year 1	Year 2	Cumulative
Fund A	−5	+15	$0.95 \times 1.15 = 1.0925$, or 9.3%
Fund B	+15	−5	$1.15 \times 0.95 = 1.0925$, or 9.3%

Accrued Interest

An anomaly can occur in which returns on bond portfolios which have heavy contributions are lower than those of portfolios invested in the same bonds but with static or negative cash flows. This results not from any complexity of mathematics but rather from limitations in the evaluation process. The source of the problem is the way in which accrued interest is treated in the performance measurement process. When an investor sells a stock it has no right to subsequent dividends that the company pays, regardless of the fact that it may have held the stock for almost the full 90-day period between quarterly dividends. (For this analysis we exclude consideration of the five-day period prior to the payable date for the dividend, during which the purchaser is entitled to the dividend payment.) That is, a buyer who has held the stock for only a few days may still be entitled to the full quarterly dividend. This is because the company does not have a contractual obligation to pay the dividend, and consequently the buyer cannot hold the seller accountable for it. (Of course, the market price action reflects the presence or absence of the dividend to each party.)

The bond issuer, on the other hand, has a contractual obligation to pay interest, usually semiannually, and thus the holder of a bond should receive interest for each day that it holds it. Let us assume that a bond pays interest on January 1 and July 1 and that a purchaser buys the bond four months into this period. The seller is thus entitled to four months of interest and the buyer to two months. If we assume that the bond has a 6 percent coupon, the seller is entitled to 2 percent interest and the buyer to 1 percent, representing their respective portions of the semiannual 3 percent payment. When July 1 arrives, however, the holder of the bond will be the purchaser and he will at that time receive 3 percent interest from the issuer. In order to properly compensate the seller, the buyer must at the time of purchase pay the seller the accrued interest of 2 percent. Thus, if the bond were traded at par, or 100 percent of value, the buyer would pay $102 to the seller, of which $2 would be interest and $100 principal.

To measure performance, it is necessary to treat the 2 percent interest that the buyer paid as interest paid, or negative interest income. This is not a long-run problem, in that each party is properly compensated for his investment, but for the quarter ended June 30 the purchaser's portfolio, assuming a $100 value at March 31 before the bond purchase was made, will show a negative return of 2 percent. For the six-month period through September, the return will be correct, since as soon as July 1 arrives the $3 semiannual interest payment will be received, representing repayment of the $2 paid out and the $1 interest due. However, a distortion occurs for the one period, causing an understatement of return for the period. If there are no additional purchases, the problem corrects itself, but for rapidly growing (or declining) bond portfolios the problem persists, with growing portfolios having an understated return and shrinking portfolios an overstated return. The distortion remains with the portfolio if the fixed-income portion of the fund continues to grow. If the fund in the above example were to double on June 30, the portfolio would be penalized by 2 percent ($2 ÷ $100), whereas the correction would be only 1 percent ($2 ÷ $200). Thus, the fixed-income portion of the fund would be affected in its time-weighted rate of return until such time as there was a substantial liquidation of bonds. Total portfolio return would also be affected, with the extent dependent on the size of the bond portfolio as a percentage of the total portfolio.

Total Returns

An apparent anomaly can occur for investors who are unaccustomed to viewing total rates of return, especially in fixed-income portfolios. For example, assume that the portfolio has a yield of 7 to 8 percent and that the total return for the period is dramatically different, perhaps minus 2 percent to plus 15 percent. Dramatically varying total rates of return result, of course, from changes in the capital value of the portfolio rather than changes in interest income. Changes in the level of interest rates can cause large changes in capital value even in portfolios with no default risk. The impact of interest rate changes on a portfolio is largely a function of the portfolio's maturity structure. This can be demonstrated by looking at the rate of return on individual bonds of different maturities as interest rates change (see Exhibit 10–6).

EXHIBIT 10–6
Percentage Changes in Bond Prices, Assuming a Current Coupon 8 Percent Bond (i.e., all bonds start out at par) and Rate Changes to Those Shown

	New Level of Interest Rates			
Maturity	6 Percent	7 Percent	9 Percent	10 Percent
1	1.8	1.0	−1.0	−1.8
3	5.4	2.6	−2.6	−5.0
5	8.4	4.1	−3.9	−7.6
10	14.7	7.0	−6.5	−12.2
15	19.4	9.1	−8.0	−15.3
20	23.0	10.6	−9.2	−17.0
25	25.6	11.6	−9.8	−18.2
30	27.5	12.4	−10.3	−18.9

These are the percentage price changes due to an instantaneous shift from 8 percent to each of these interest rates. If the shift is not instantaneous, the total return of the investment should be considered. This total return will include the price change and the income received during the period measured, as well as income on that income.

Exhibit 10–6 shows that bonds with longer maturities are more volatile than bonds with shorter maturities. A simplified example (which does not precisely take compounding into account) may assist in understanding this process. Let us assume that the general level of interest rates rises from 8 percent to 9 percent. Let us further assume that we own three bonds in our portfolio, all of which have 8 percent coupons at the beginning point, with one bond having a one-year maturity, the second bond having a two-year maturity, and the third bond having a three-year maturity. We will also assume that the change in interest rates comes right after we purchase the portfolio.

Looking at the one-year bond, an investor would see that the general level of interest rates provides for a 9 percent return for one year and that the one-year bond provides only an 8 percent return. For this bond to have a competitive return in the marketplace it must also yield 9 percent. In order for it to yield 9 percent the investor would have to make 1 percent in appreciation in addition to the 8 percent in interest. For the investor to make 1 percent in appreciation over a one-year period, the $100 value of the bond would necessarily have to drop to $99. Thus, this bond would show an instantaneous negative return of 1 percent.

The investor would apply the same analysis to the two-year bond, but in this case he would not be satisfied with a purchase price of $99, since this would yield him 8 percent per year in interest but only one half of 1 percent per year in appreciation. To achieve the 9 percent return he must have a 1 percent per year return from capital appreciation, or a 2 percent return for the two years. He would thus be willing to buy the 8 percent two-year bond at $98, with the bond showing an instantaneous return of minus 2 percent in comparison to the minus 1 percent return of the one-year bond.

Carrying the analysis to the three-year bond, we immediately recognize that the investor would be willing to pay only $97 for this bond, which would then have an instantaneous return of minus 3 percent. Recognizing that, if interest rates declined, the longer term bond would have a positive rate of return greater than that of the one-year bond, we can see the impact of changes in interest rates on bonds of different maturities and the fallacy of expecting the income return to closely correlate with the total return when a portfolio is being measured.

We have thus determined that results of almost any kind can be achieved, and that there is usually a good reason for them!

CHAPTER 11

COMPARING INVESTMENT PERFORMANCE

Success is largely a function of the standard for comparison.

Although virtually all sponsors are interested in comparing the results of their funds with appropriate benchmarks, it is not easy to determine the appropriate benchmarks. In general terms there are four useful standards against which portfolios can be measured:

1. Comparison with an absolute goal.
2. Comparison with market indexes.
3. Comparison with other portfolios.
4. Comparison with a custom or "normal" portfolio.

COMPARISON WITH AN ABSOLUTE GOAL

When a choice is presented as to which of the four standards is appropriate, almost all fund sponsors will choose the first. That is, almost all will agree that the most important measure of the fund's success is whether it meets its objectives. In the case of a pension fund the objective is to return at least as much as the assumed rate. For an endowment fund the objective is to provide sufficient capital or income to meet the needs of the sponsoring organization. Although achieving these goals is certainly important, in practice this method of comparing results is rather unsatisfying. A brief example will demonstrate why.

In both of the periods shown in Exhibit 11–1, the fund has a target rate of return of 6.0 percent. In an absolute sense the fund met its

EXHIBIT 11–1

Period	Market Return	Fund Return
1	+50%	6.1%
2	−50	5.9

objective in the first period and failed to meet it in the second period. However, virtually all fund sponsors and investment managers would feel that the fund performed well in the second period and poorly in the first. This is because the returns of investment portfolios are dominated by the returns of the market, particularly in the short run. Consequently, practically all funds will fail to meet their stated objectives in a poor year and will exceed them in a good year. Similarly, even the best managers frequently show negative returns in bear markets and even the poorest managers generally show positive returns in strong bull markets. Thus, although meeting the absolute goal of the fund is certainly important, there is a need for additional benchmarks in order to understand the activities of the fund and to assess whether the manager is doing a good or a bad job in light of the market environment in which it is operating.

COMPARISON WITH MARKET INDEXES

In order to look beyond the problems associated with the absolute goal, it is desirable to measure the market environment so as to assess its impact on portfolios. Since most funds invest in more than one asset type, it is appropriate to measure the impact of the market on the various sectors of the portfolio.

Equity Portfolios

The performance of the equity portion of portfolios (common stocks, convertible securities, and warrants or options) can be appropriately measured against any one of a number of stock market indexes. Among these indexes are the Standard & Poor's 500, Standard & Poor's 400, New York Stock Exchange Index, American Stock Exchange Index, Value Line Index, Indicator Digest Average, Dow Jones Composite Index, and Wilshire 5000 Index. A summary of their composition and construction is presented in the appendix to this chapter.

Bond Portfolios

Fixed-income or bond portfolios can be appropriately compared to bond indexes, including the Salomon Brothers Index, the Lehman Brothers Kuhn Loeb Indexes, the Merrill Lynch Indexes, and the Moody's Index. Two points should be made about the ways in which bond portfolios and indexes differ from those for equities. First of all, the bond market is not a unified market in quite the same way as the stock market is. This is because the fixed maturity of bonds creates a spectrum of risk and return quite apart from the characteristics of the bond issuer. Whereas AT&T common stock is AT&T common stock, an AT&T bond with two years until maturity is a quite different investment from an AT&T bond with 30 years until maturity. For this reason it is not easy to find a bond index which is truly representative of the market. Second, because of this maturity characteristic and because an investor may have a fixed time horizon, it is possible for an investor to choose bonds which are appropriate for its portfolio but unrepresentative of the bond market as a whole. Consequently, this investor may find that even a bond index which is truly representative of the bond market may not be an appropriate benchmark for comparing performance. Fortunately, indexes describing the returns of the various sectors of the bond market are becoming increasingly available.

Cash Equivalents

The return on cash equivalents (short-term investments or money market instruments) can be compared to the returns on U.S. Treasury bills, certificates of deposit, commercial paper, and banker's acceptances. The rate on U.S. Treasury bills is readily available and is easy to measure with high precision. For funds which take credit risk in their cash equivalent portfolios, the Donoghue money market index is also appropriate.

Not Readily Marketable Assets

Private placement returns can be measured against bond market indexes, and real estate equities can be measured against the Frank Russell index. More exotic investments typically do not have indexes which permit class comparison of results.

Total Portfolios

The total fund typically consists of investments in various market sectors, and consequently there is no total portfolio index which is appropriate for all investors. However, it is possible to construct a "custom" index which is useful in measuring a given investor's results. This index is constructed by looking at the composition of the fund and weighting market indexes accordingly. For example, if a portfolio consists of 60 percent stocks and 40 percent bonds at the beginning of a certain quarter, we can use an index for that quarter which consists of 60 percent of the return on an equity index plus 40 percent of the return on a bond index. If the investor switches to 70 percent equities and 30 percent bonds at the end of the quarter, we might consider the "market" return for the total portfolio for the second quarter to be equal to 70 percent of the equity index's return and 30 percent of the bond index's return. The "market" return for the two-quarter period could then be calculated by linking or chaining the market return of the individual periods. Alternatively, the market index could be calculated by using the average percentage in equities and the average percentage in bonds, in this case 65 percent and 35 percent, respectively. The stock and bond index returns for each quarter would then be weighted 65 percent and 35 percent, respectively, and chained.

Both methods are useful and sensible. The method using quarter-by-quarter returns measures selection but not timing. The average method measures both selection and timing, because in each quarter the measurement considers not only the difference between the equity and fixed-income returns in the portfolio and those of the indexes but also the difference in the proportions of the two. This is shown in Exhibit 11–2.

The custom index has two limitations. First, the index of each fund will be different, reflecting the fund's composition. Consequently, there is no total portfolio index which is appropriate for all portfolios. Second, since there are no widely published indexes covering private placements

EXHIBIT 11–2

Custom index at actual allocation measures selection only:*

	Period 1	Period 2	Average	Cumulative (not compounded)
(1) Percentage in equities	60	70	65	
(2) Percentage in bonds	40	30	35	
(3) Equity index return	10	20		
(4) Bond index return	5	10		
(5) Custom index return	$[0.6(10) + 0.4(5)]$ $6 + 2 = 8$	$+ [0.7(20) + 0.3(10)]$ $+ 14 + 3 = 17$		+25
(6) Fund return	10	19		+29
(7) Fund return − Custom index return at actual allocation = Return from security selection and choice of risk level of securities	+2	+2	+2	+4

Custom index at average allocation measures selection and timing:*

	Period 1	Period 2	Average	Cumulative
(1)–(4) Same as above				
(5) Custom index return	$[0.65(10) + 0.35(5)]$ $6.5 + 1.75 = 8.25$	$+ [0.65(20) + 0.35(10)]$ $+ 13 + 3.5 = 16.5$		+24.75
(6) Fund return	10	19		29
(7) Fund return − Custom index return at actual allocation = Return from selection, choice of security risk level, *and* timing	1.75	2.5	2.125	4.25
(8) Impact of timing = Custom index at actual allocation − Custom index at average allocation = 25.0 − 24.75 = +.25				

*Selection is used here to include not only security selection but also choice of the risk level of the stocks and bonds owned.

199

and other less marketable assets, it is difficult to reflect the portfolio's full composition if the fund contains such assets.

Dollar-Weighted Indexes

The preceding discussion of market indexes assumed a time-weighted approach, namely that we were looking at one dollar invested throughout the period and not considering any impact from external cash flows. An alternative approach to the use of indexes is to assume that return equaled the return on the index but that the portfolio had cash flows equal to those which actually occurred. In this case the question being asked is, "How much money does the fund have relative to the amount that it would have had had it invested in a certain index?" This approach can be used in a variety of ways for the total portfolio and for the sectors of the portfolio. Logical ways in which the concept can be applied are as follows.

Total Portfolio
The assumed ending value of the portfolio can be calculated under the assumption that the fund is 100 percent invested in an equity index, 100 percent in a bond index, 100 percent in a cash equivalent index, or any combination of weightings. The same calculation can be made by assuming that the portfolio is invested in the average commingled equity fund, the average commingled fixed-income fund, the average separately managed balanced fund, the best fund, the worst fund, and so on. Another application of this approach is to see whether the fund kept up with its assumed or actuarial rate of return or with the consumer price index. A special case of this analysis can be carried out to see whether the fund achieved a profit or a loss from investments. In this case the fund's ending value is compared with its beginning value plus net contributions and the question implicitly asked is, "Did the fund achieve a return above or below 0 percent?"

Equity or Fixed-Income Portfolios
The same multitude of possibilities exists for comparing the actual ending value of equity and bond portfolios with assumed ending values under various assumptions, as exists for the total portfolio. Logically, one might compare the actual ending value for an equity portfolio with the

results which would have been attained had the fund been invested in equity indexes, equity commingled funds, or the equity portions of separately managed funds. The same approach can be applied to fixed-income funds, only using fixed-income indexes and funds to provide the alternative rate of return which might have been achieved.

In summary, comparing portfolio returns to those of market indexes is a useful function that can be carried out by comparing a sector of the portfolio to the appropriate market index and by comparing the total portfolio return to an index weighted in the same proportions as the portfolio.

COMPARISON WITH OTHER PORTFOLIOS

Although comparing portfolio results to those of market indexes has considerable use, there is still something lacking, both conceptually and emotionally, when only market indexes are used as comparisons. The conceptual problem is that even though the market indexes are supposedly representative of the "market," each index is, in fact, a specific portfolio with characteristics which may or may not be representative of what real funds are like. Further, the market indexes have no transaction costs associated with them, and real portfolios obviously incur a certain amount of transaction costs. This creates a negative bias for fund results as compared to those of market indexes. As an example of the limitation of using market indexes as a sole benchmark for comparison, we can see how the Standard & Poor's 500, viewed as a portfolio, would have compared to a sample of large corporation equity portfolios for the years 1982 to 1991 (Exhibit 11–3). As can be seen, the Standard & Poor's 500 was not a good representation of the "average" managed equity portfolio, which many people believe that a market index should be.

In addition to the conceptual objections to using only market indexes for comparisons, there is also an emotional objection. Human beings tend to be greatly concerned with how they fare in comparison with other persons in similar circumstances. For both reasons, fund sponsors have come to count on comparisons between their fund results and those of other funds. Consequently, a knowledge of this area is important to all fund sponsors.

EXHIBIT 11–3
S&P 500 Ranked versus Performance of Equity Portion of Large Corporation Retirement Plans

	1982	1983	1984	1985	1986	1987	1988	1989	1990	1991
S&P 500 Rank	49	35	11	61	38	41	52	16	31	74
	1982–91	1983–91	1984–91	1985–91	1986–91	1987–91	1988–91	1989–91	1990–91	1991
S&P 500 Rank	26	24	23	30	30	32	40	43	48	74

Source: SEI Corporation

Equity Portfolios

Portfolios containing only equities should be compared to other similarly constructed portfolios. That is, an equities versus equities comparison is by far the most appropriate basis for comparing the results of an equity portfolio with those of other portfolios. Both the fund and the sample should be either tax-exempt or taxable. In almost all cases in which performance measurement services are provided, the portfolios measured are tax-exempt retirement or endowment funds.

Equity-Oriented Portfolios

A portfolio can be called an equity-oriented portfolio if it is invested in either equities or cash reserves that will be invested in equities at an appropriate time. It is important to distinguish between an equity-oriented portfolio, which conceivably could be 100 percent in cash equivalents, and an equity portfolio, which by definition is always 100 percent in equities. The appropriate comparison for equity-oriented portfolios is other equity-oriented portfolios. That is, portfolios which can be invested in either equities or cash equivalents should be compared to similar funds.

However, it is not easy to find such a sample for separately managed portfolios. This is because most funds own stocks, bonds, or cash equivalents, and in the reporting process often do not distinguish their cash equivalent reserves for equity investing from their cash equivalent reserves for fixed-income investing. Thus, adding the portfolio's cash to the equity sector to calculate an "equity-oriented" return would be misleading, in that some or all of the cash equivalents in the account may, in fact, be in reserve for the purchase of fixed-income investments.

Fortunately, an alternative solution is at hand in the form of bank-commingled equity-oriented funds. Although these funds are typically called equity funds, they are more appropriately called equity-oriented funds since they contain both equities and cash equivalents. Mutual funds are also a source of information on the performance of equity-oriented funds, and precise information on mutual funds is widely available because these funds are required to calculate and publish their values daily. However, since mutual funds typically invest for individuals rather than tax-exempt portfolios, they are a less appropriate basis for comparison than are bank-commingled equity-oriented funds.

Bond Portfolios

Bond portfolios, consisting of intermediate-term and long-term bonds (but not cash equivalents) are appropriately measured against similar portfolios. The tax implications of the fund sponsor must be considered, since a portfolio with tax-exempt (municipal) bonds obviously cannot be compared to one with taxable bonds. This is usually not a problem because most funds desiring performance information are tax-exempt. Since the funds are tax-exempt, they own higher yielding taxable bonds.

Bond-Oriented Funds

Bond-oriented funds, unlike bond funds, can own both cash equivalents and bonds, whereas pure bond funds can own only bonds. Thus, as with equity-oriented funds, bond-oriented funds should be compared to similar funds. For the same reason, namely the availability of appropriate data, the results of bond-oriented funds can be compared to those of bank-commingled bond-oriented funds or mutual funds.

Cash Equivalents, Private Placements, and Other Assets

The returns on cash equivalents can be compared to the returns of "money market" funds which invest in taxable securities. The returns on private placements could be compared to the returns of the few insurance company private placement commingled funds, though these funds may also contain cash equivalents. As to "other assets," it is difficult to make use of comparisons due to differences in portfolios.

Total Portfolios

Total portfolios consist of assets from the various sectors of the overall marketplace. Thus, it is appropriate to compare the total returns of a fund with the total returns of many other funds. However, several cautions are in order.

First, returns (and hence comparisons) tend to be dominated by the risk posture of the portfolio and by the particular market results which occurred during the period being measured. A fund whose policy is to be

80 percent in equities will look very good in a period when the stock market rises and will look quite poor in a period when it declines. This may be fully attributable to the policy chosen by the sponsor rather than a reflection of the investment manager's skill.

Second, a problem arises regarding how to treat investments which are in less readily marketable securities. One alternative is to include these assets in the total portfolio, recognizing that some investors have large investments in these "other assets" and that other investors have none at all. Recognition must also be given to the fact that some of these assets are valued at historical or amortized cost, and others at some estimate of market value. The quality of these estimates affects the quality of the total portfolio return and hence the usefulness of the comparison. An alternative treatment is to exclude less readily marketable assets from the "total portfolio" for comparing results to other portfolios. Although this solves the question of the accurate measurement of returns, it can be misleading in that not all of the portfolio's assets are accounted for. Perhaps the only solution in this case is to choose a method and to be sure that the portfolio is being measured on the same basis as the funds in the comparative universe.

Third, commingled funds are generally not appropriate comparisons for total portfolios. This is because the total portfolio, which is assumed in this case to be a balanced fund, is not structured in the same way as the commingled funds, which are usually oriented to either equities or bonds. (Obviously, if the total portfolio contains either no equities or no bonds, then the commingled funds are appropriate comparisons. For this discussion, however, such a portfolio would not be regarded as a total portfolio but as an equity- or bond-oriented fund.) The fallacy of using commingled funds to compare total portfolio results is the same as the fallacy of comparing equity-oriented funds to equity-only funds, namely that the differences in allocation among stocks, bonds, and cash equivalents will have an important bearing on how the fund performed in a particular market environment. In a rising market, a balanced fund will tend to underperform bank-commingled equity funds and to outperform bank-commingled bond funds. Since stocks will return more than bonds, the funds with the highest percentage in equities will have the greatest returns. In a down market the reverse will be true. Again, the problem is measuring the investment policy rather than the investment performance of the fund.

In summary, the principal concern in comparing portfolio results with the results of others is to find a sensible comparative universe. The best way to do this is to compare the fund being measured with funds which are as close as possible to it in construction—equities to equities, bonds to bonds, and total portfolios to total portfolios. Funds containing equities plus cash equivalents should be compared to similar portfolios, as should funds containing bonds plus cash equivalents. In this way the most reasonable comparisons of returns can be made.

COMPARING RISK AND RISK-ADJUSTED RETURNS

Once an appropriate risk measure has been chosen (see Chapters 12 and 13), comparing the performance of portfolios becomes quite straightforward. The percentage in asset categories, such as equities, of one portfolio versus another can be readily compared. Similarly, the beta, or variability, however measured, of one portfolio can be directly compared with that of other portfolios. Of course, this assumes that the fund sponsor has available information on the risk measures of other funds.

Comparing risk-adjusted returns, like comparing risk, is straightforward. The only requirements are that the portfolio's measurement of risk-adjusted performance be similar to that of the sample and that the classification of assets also be similar. For instance, meaningful comparisons cannot be made if the portfolio's equity sector is defined to exclude convertible securities, but the comparative sample defines equity to include convertibles.

COMPARING FUNDS WITH SIMILAR OBJECTIVES
OR OF SIMILAR TYPES

The idea of comparing one's fund with other funds that have similar objectives is very appealing. This is especially true since many fund sponsors are hiring managers with specific styles which cannot easily be compared with more diversified portfolios or with specialized portfolios with different structures or objectives. Unfortunately, developing a workable definition for "similar objectives" and finding a large enough sample of funds which fit the objectives are two formidable problems. All funds have as their general objective making money without losing money. More eloquent statements suggest as objectives maximizing return without undue risk of loss of principal. These definitions of objectives are of little help since they include all funds rather than just "similar" funds.

In theory it is possible to compare funds based on their level of risk, such as the percentage in equities. In practice it is not possible to find a sample of funds with exactly the same asset allocation as the sponsor's fund, so typically a range of allocations is considered. In other words, a fund with 63 percent in equities would be compared with funds having between 60 percent and 70 percent in equities. However, in a volatile period there can be substantial differences between funds having 60 percent in equities and funds having 70 percent in equities. Also, if the fund being measured has a very high or a very low percentage in stocks, there will probably not be many similar funds in the same category.

An alternative might be to construct an artificial total portfolio sample by taking a sample of balanced funds and assuming that each hypothetical fund in the sample had the equity and fixed-income returns of the real fund but the asset allocation policies of the sponsor's fund. Although a bit awkward to calculate, this alternative has some merit. However, most of the benefit of this procedure could be gained merely by comparing the sponsor's equity to the sample of other equity funds, and making a similar analysis for other asset categories.

Criteria other than the percentage in equities could also be used for establishing similarity of objectives. Among such criteria are the age level of employees covered by pension funds or the riskiness of the company's capital structure and the size of cash inflows or outflows.

It makes sense to compare the results of commingled equity funds with those of other commingled equity funds, and similarly for bond funds and other fund types. However, the rationale for this type of comparison is related to the asset type and policy rather than any characteristic of the sponsor. It is also possible to compare profit-sharing funds with other profit-sharing (but not pension) funds, Taft-Hartley pension funds with other Taft-Hartley pension funds (but not corporate pension funds), and similarly for public pension funds and endowment funds. Although this makes intuitive sense, experience indicates that very few differences between funds are attributable to the sponsor's organization type other than that Taft-Hartley funds and public funds tend to have lower percentages in equities than do corporate pension funds. This is probably the only area in which a comparison by fund type provides useful information. Even so, it is still appropriate to compare equity funds with an equity funds sample, bond funds with a bond funds sample, and the timing scores of funds with the timing scores of other funds.

Normal Portfolios

A normal portfolio is one which is created as a special benchmark. It replaces more general standards, such as broad market indexes or averages of other funds. For example, a normal portfolio for a high quality growth stock manager might consist of the largest 25 growth companies in the Standard & Poor's 500 index. By measuring the performance of these 25 stocks, a sponsor would have a benchmark which is more relevant to the performance of the growth manager than would an index which contains small capitalization or cyclical companies.

COMPARING PORTFOLIO RESULTS TO THOSE OF OTHER PORTFOLIOS MANAGED BY THE SAME INVESTMENT MANAGER

If it is appealing to know how one is faring compared with his or her peers, as broadly defined, it is especially interesting to know how one's portfolio is performing compared to similar portfolios managed by the same organization. Or, more precisely, it is interesting to know whether or not the sponsor's portfolio is performing worse than those of other clients of the manager firm. Of course, there might be very good reasons for differences. First, the needs of the sponsoring organization may be different. One fund might have a very different liability structure in its pension plan than another. One fund might be a profit-sharing as opposed to a pension fund, in which case employees receive periodic statements as to the value of their investments, and payout to employees may be in a lump sum as opposed to over a period of years. Contributory funds might be treated differently by a manager from noncontributory funds. One organization may have restricted securities or company stock which biases results. Finally, the views and prejudices of the sponsoring organization may lead to different portfolios. All these factors tend to cloud the issue which the sponsor is trying to determine, namely whether or not its investment officer is providing as astute management as are others in the firm.

APPENDIX

COMPOSITION AND CHARACTERISTICS OF VARIOUS STOCK AND BOND INDEXES

Since portfolios are so frequently compared to market indexes, and since sponsors, investment managers, and consultants place considerable weight on such indexes, it is worthwhile to understand more about them. It should be noted that:

1. No one index is useful for all purposes.
2. Each index is composed of a certain list of securities that are weighted in a specific way, and if the list contained other securities or a different weighting scheme, the results would be different.
3. Each index has flaws or limitations.

Creating indexes involves deciding what is to be measured, choosing a list of representative securities, choosing methods for weighting the securities, changing the list of securities, treating income, and establishing the frequency and timing of index availability. Characteristics of the major stock indexes follow (see also Exhibit 11–4).

Standard & Poor's 500
Goal is to measure the pattern of common stock movements; 500 large companies are included; changes are made in the list of securities by a committee at Standard & Poor's; weighting is by capitalization; available daily as to capital changes and quarterly about one week after quarter end, including dividends.

Standard & Poor's 400 Mid Cap
S&P 400 Mid Cap Index measures return of 400 middle-sized companies (in market capitalization).

Dow Jones Averages

Industrials. Designed to measure movements of industrial companies—includes 30 large industrials; changes made rarely, generally to

EXHIBIT 11–4
Common Stock Indexes

Index	Number of Securities	Weighting	Calculation Technique	Base Year
U.S. Equity				
Standard & Poor's 500	500	Market value	Sum of market values	1941–43 = 10
Standard & Poor's 400 Mid Cap	400	Market value	Same as S&P 500	1990 = 100
Dow Jones Industrials	30	Price	Sum of prices divided by number of companies adjusted for historical splits	Started 1927 (an average, not an index)
Dow Jones Utilities	15	Price		
Dow Jones Transportation	20	Price		
Dow Jones Composite	65	Price		
New York Stock Exchange	All companies 2,426 issues as of 12/31/91	Market value	Market value of all listed shares, adjusted for capitalization changes	December 31, 1965 = 50 (approximate average share price)
American Stock Exchange	All companies 908 issues as of 12/31/91	Market value	Same as NYSE except that NYSE subtracts the value of dividends from the index on ex-date, whereas ASE does not	August 31, 1973 = 100

EXHIBIT 11-4 (continued)

Index	Number of Securities	Weighting	Calculation Technique	Base Year
Value Line	1,667 issues as of 12/31/91	Equal	Geometric mean of daily price relatives	June 30, 1961 = 100
Wilshire 5000	5,000	Market value	Same as S&P 500	December 31, 1970 = $798.439 billion
Russell 2000 Small Stock	2,000	Market value	Same as S&P 500	December 31, 1978 = 130
World Equity Morgan Stanley Capital International (M.S.C.I.)	1,504	Market value	Same as S&P 500	January 1, 1970 = 100
U.K. Equity Financial Times 100 (FT-SE 100)	100	Market value	Same as S&P 500	April 10, 1962 = 100
German Equity DAX	30	Market value	Same as S&P 500	December 31, 1987 = 1000
French Equity CAC	250	Market value	Same as S&P 500	December 31, 1981 = 100
Japanese Equity Nikkei-Dow	250	Equal	Same as Dow Jones	January 4, 1968 = 100
EAFE Morgan Stanley Capital International	1050	Market value	Same as S&P 500	January 1, 1970 = 100

211

reflect mergers or acquisitions; weighting according to price of shares; available daily for price changes.

Utilities. Covers utility companies; otherwise same as Dow Jones Industrials.

Transportation. Covers transportation companies; otherwise same as Dow Jones Industrials.

Composite. Amalgamation of Industrials, Utilities, and Transportation indexes.

New York Stock Exchange Index
Represents market value of all common stocks on New York Stock Exchange; issues included changed according to listings and delistings from the NYSE; capitalization weighting; available daily as to price.

American Stock Exchange Index
Reflects value of shares on American Stock Exchange; all issues on ASE included; issues changed when listing so requires; capitalization weighted; available daily as to price.

Value Line Index
Goal is to represent typical price movements of stocks in Value Line Universe; changes in securities made at discretion of Arnold Bernhard & Co.; weighting is equal, calculated as a geometric average (rather than adding up the values and dividing by the number of securities, the index multiplies daily price relatives and takes the nth root of the ensuing value); price relatives are then compounded to compute the index; available daily as to price. Note: A geometric index always underperforms the corresponding arithmetic index.

Wilshire 5000
Represents the market value of all common stocks on the New York Stock Exchange, American Stock Exchange, and over-the-counter markets; changes at discretion of Wilshire Associates; weighted by capitalization; price index and total performance index available; published weekly as to price.

Russell

The Frank Russell Company measures stock returns on the 3,000 largest U.S. stocks by market capitalization. This group is further segmented into the top 1,000, and the next 2,000 (Russell Small Stock Index).

Bond indexes

A myriad of bond indexes are produced by Merrill Lynch, Salomon Brothers, Shearson Lehman, and Ryan.

CHAPTER 12

MEASURING RISK IN EQUITY PORTFOLIOS

Measurement of performance of pension funds should be in two dimensions: rate of return and risk. [1]

In Chapter 3, risk was discussed in general terms and defined as uncertainty of the rate of return. In this chapter more precise measurements of risk will be explored, and both traditional approaches will be considered. It is helpful to view traditional and quantitative approaches as being at different ends of the same spectrum rather than as opposing philosophies. The traditional measurements, such as price/earnings ratio and financial leverage, are causes of uncertainty of the rate of return. Standard deviation and beta can then be viewed as measurements of the uncertainty resulting from fundamental risk.

TRADITIONAL RISK MEASURES

Traditional or fundamental risk measures can be divided into two categories: company related and stock price related. Company-related factors pertain to the company itself, whereas stock price factors indicate the risk arising from the price that the stock market places on the company's characteristics.

---

[1] *Measuring the Investment Performance of Pension Funds for the Purpose of Inter-Fund Comparison* (Park Ridge, Ill.: Bank Administration Institute, 1968).

Company-Related Factors

Debt/Equity Relationship
The more a company has borrowed to finance its capital expenditures or operations, the greater is the company's risk. To avoid bankruptcy, a company must pay interest and principal to lenders before it can pay dividends to shareholders. Thus, although a highly leveraged position may contribute to a company's growth rate, it also increases the company's risk.

Stability of Sales and Earnings
An important measure of a company's risk is the stability of its sales and earnings. The greater their stability, the more confidence investors can have that the company will continue to operate successfully. Quality measurements for stocks, as well as bonds, reflect to a large extent the stability of a company.

Profit Margins
The greater the difference between revenues and expenses, the less risky a company is, all other things being equal. If costs rise unexpectedly, a company with narrow profit margins may become unprofitable, whereas a company with wide profit margins will just become somewhat less profitable.

Return on Equity or Return on Assets
The extent to which a company can profitably employ capital is an important risk measure.

Price-Related Factors

Price/Earnings Ratio
Probably the most common measure used by equity investors to establish the relative value of stocks is the P/E ratio. The more an investor must pay for each dollar of earnings, the greater is the risk of the investment.

Yield
The current return provided by a stock is also an important measure of risk. The greater the income provided by a stock, the less incentive investors will find to sell it during an unfavorable economic period.

Price/Book Value Ratio

In the same way that an investor can view its stock holding in terms of its earnings or yield, the investor can also look at the underlying assets of the company whose stock it is purchasing and relate them to the price being paid. Subtracting liabilities from the asset figure leaves the net worth, owners' equity, or book value of the shares. In a sense, the investor is looking at the liquidation value of the company and comparing that to its purchase price. Since the assets of the company are calculated on a historical cost basis, rather than on the basis of current market values, there are limitations to this approach.

Most basic texts in finance expand considerably on the financial ratios described above.

QUANTITATIVE RISK MEASUREMENT TECHNIQUES

Since quantitative approaches define risk as uncertainty of return, quantitative measurements attempt to calculate the degree of risk or uncertainty. This can be done by looking at either absolute or relative measures. The absolute measures include standard deviation, variance, and mean absolute deviation. Beta is a relative measure. These are all described in the appendix. The standard deviation, as the most common measure and one of the simplest, is described below.

Standard Deviation as a Measure of Uncertainty

When looking at a series of numbers describing the characteristics of some phenomenon, analysts usually think first of reducing the measurement to an average. However, in many cases additional information is required in order to analyze the characteristics of the phenomenon being measured. For example, a person desiring to cross a river would not find it sufficient to know only the average depth of the river. He would want to know the maximum depth of the river as well. Assume that the person was told that the river, which is 10 miles long, averages 1 foot in depth, but that the range is between zero inches and 10 feet. This would be additional useful information, since the person would then know that at some point the river is 10 feet deep. Suppose further that the person did not know precisely where he was going to cross, and that not every point in the river had been measured, because this was too expensive.

An intermediate step could be carried out by calculating the depth of the river at a number of places and establishing a distribution or pattern of the measurements. That is, it might be that roughly 90 percent of the river is 1 inch deep and that about 10 percent is 10 feet deep. On the other hand, it might be that 99 percent of the river is 1 foot deep, nine tenths of 1 percent is 1 inch deep, and one tenth of 1 percent is 10 feet deep. This distribution of measurements could provide very significant information to the person attempting to understand the characteristics of the river to be crossed. The standard deviation describes this distribution.

Another example is more relevant to the investment world. Suppose that an investment manager owns a portfolio containing 100 stocks. The manager's style is to preserve capital, and consequently he wishes to investigate closely all securities which are in an unfavorable price trend. He wishes to find a simple way of establishing which stocks are trading in an unfavorable pattern. He could review the list of "new lows for the year" each day in order to see whether any of his companies have traded at a lower price than they had during the previous year. However, this would require waiting until a stock went all the way down to its low point before the investigation process was initiated, by which time the fund would have been injured excessively. The investor could also keep track of stocks which have declined by a given number of points or a given percentage from some previous level. However, some stocks are more volatile than others, and just because they swing widely it is not necessarily serious if these stocks decline below their prior levels. The manager thus wants to have a measurement which shows when an individual stock is trading below its normal range. This could be done by calculating the average price of the stocks over a period and the extent to which the stock fluctuates around that average. For instance, a utility stock may average 60 and fluctuate between 57 and 63. A growth stock may average 60 but trade between 50 and 70. Thus, the utility would come under scrutiny when it declined below 57, and the growth stock when it fell to 50.

This technique can be applied to portfolio rates of return in order to measure the volatility or risk of the portfolios. A common stock portfolio might average a 10 percent return and fluctuate between −12 percent and +32 percent. A bond portfolio might average 8 percent and fluctuate between a 0 percent and a 16 percent total rate of return. Treasury bills might average 6 percent and vary between 4 percent and 8 percent. This distinction can be seen in Exhibit 12–1.

EXHIBIT 12-1
Variability of Return of Assets with Different Risk Levels

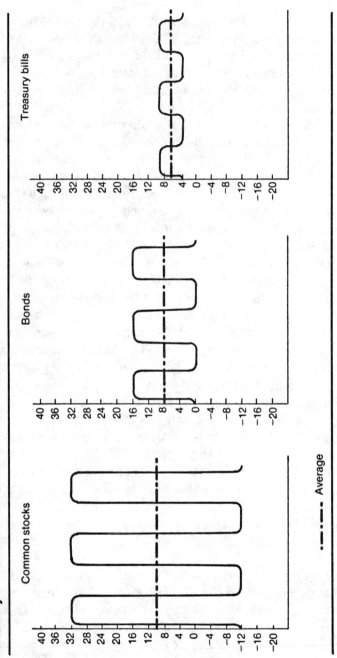

BETA

Using the standard deviation, the portfolio's variability or volatility is measured in relation to the average return. In the beta analysis the portfolio's volatility is measured in relation to the volatility of the market.

Beta is a calculation which results from making a "regression" analysis. Regression analysis is a statistical technique for relating two variables (see Mathematics Refresher in the appendix). In this case the two variables are the rate of return on a stock or portfolio and the rate of return of the market. As can be seen in Exhibits 12–2 through 12–6, the regression analysis, also called the characteristic line analysis, is made by plotting the rate of return of the security or portfolio against the rate of return of the market during the same period. Each of the graphs contains plots of the quarterly rates of return for hypothetical portfolios. The "line of best fit" is drawn in each case to fit as closely as possible the points plotted. For instance, in Exhibit 12–2, point A represents a three-month period in which the market rose 10 percent and the fund rose 5 percent.

A similar point is drawn to represent each quarter or month for which data are available. A line is then drawn which best fits these points. Much useful information can be acquired about a portfolio of equities by performing the characteristic line analysis. Of special interest

EXHIBIT 12–2

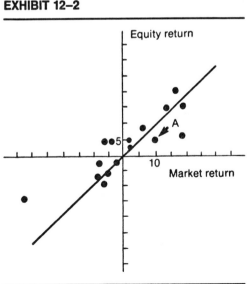

are the amount of market risk in the portfolio, the level of diversification, and the manager's contribution through stock selection (risk-
adjusted return). Alternatively, these factors are known as beta, R^2, and
alpha. Beta, or market sensitivity, is measured by the slope of the characteristic line.

Three portfolios will be considered for comparison purposes. The
first of these (Exhibit 12–3) is an index fund containing the market portfolio, that is, a portfolio containing all the stocks in the market balanced
in the proportions in which they appear in the marketplace. The second
portfolio (Exhibit 12–4) is an aggressive fund, containing many volatile
stocks, such as airlines and emerging growth companies. The third portfolio (Exhibit 12–5) is a conservative fund composed of stocks of utilities, and food service companies.

To understand how the characteristic line helps determine the market sensitivity or risk of the equity portfolio, it is helpful to recall how the
characteristic line is constructed. The return of the portfolio and the market is plotted for each quarter. In a quarter in which the market had a
return of 10 percent and the fund had a return of 15 percent, a point
would be drawn which is closer to the equity portfolio's (vertical) axis
than to the market's axis. Similarly, in a period in which the market went
down 10 percent and the fund went down 15 percent, a plot would be

EXHIBIT 12–3

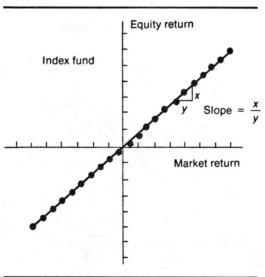

EXHIBIT 12–4

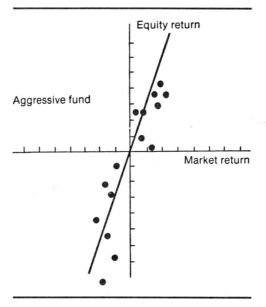

EXHIBIT 12–5

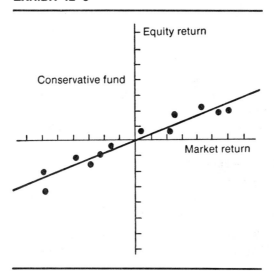

drawn closer to the axis of the fund. In this case the line would have a steep slope, characterizing a fund which is aggressive (moving up more than the market when the market rises and down more when the market declines). This can be seen in Exhibit 12–4.

Conversely, for a portfolio of conservative stocks, the plots would be drawn closer to the axis of the market, indicating that the fund rises less than the market in a rising period and declines less than the market in a declining period. Thus, the slope of the line determines the amount of market risk. This slope is measured by viewing the ratio between the vertical distance and the horizontal distance that the line moves, as is shown on the triangle in Exhibit 12–3. The slope may also be viewed as the percentage change in the portfolio that is expected for a 1 percent change in the market. In the case of the aggressive fund, a gain of 1 percent in the market would be accompanied by a gain of more than 1 percent in the fund, thus giving the fund a beta, or market sensitivity, greater than 1. The opposite is true for a conservative portfolio. The index fund, shown in Exhibit 12–3, has a slope of 1. When the market rises 5 percent, the fund rises 5 percent, which is not surprising, since the fund is identical to the market. The index fund thus has a beta of 1.0.

In the preceding discussion it was tacitly assumed that the portfolio was completely diversified, so that all of the risk in the portfolio was market risk. However, this is usually not the case. In most portfolios there are two types of risk: market risk and specific, or nonmarket, risk. *Market risk* derives from factors affecting the overall market and economy, such as interest rates, inflation, and unemployment. *Specific risk* relates to factors affecting the individual companies in the portfolio. Among such factors are the management of the company, the success of the company's new products, and the impact of foreign competition on the company's product line. It is important to distinguish between these two types of risk because market risk is inherent to investors in the stock market, but specific risk can be eliminated through diversification. This is because an investor can own many stocks with the thought that unusual specific factors affecting individual companies will offset each other. For example, one company may have especially bad results during a quarter, but another company may have surprisingly good results during the same period. These two factors offset each other, leaving the investor with a return which on average is what was expected.

Since there are two types of risk in a portfolio, it is important to measure both of them. We have discussed the significance of beta, or market sensitivity, as a measure of market risk. Beta measures the market risk and helps determine the expected rate of return of a portfolio, given a particular rate of return for the market. However, the beta measurement applies only to the market risk in the fund; it tells nothing about the amount of nonmarket, or specific, risk in the portfolio. The usefulness of the beta measurement thus depends on the percentage of the total portfolio risk which is represented by market risk. This can be seen by considering two portfolios, both of which have a beta of 1. The first of these portfolios is the index fund, which contains all the stocks in the market in the same proportions in which they exist in the marketplace. The second portfolio consists of a single stock which happens to have a beta of 1 but has had returns each quarter which are very different from those of the market. It might appear that the beta of 1 is something of a coincidence in this portfolio, since about half the time the fund's return was above what would have been expected and about half the time it was below what would have been expected for a portfolio with a beta of 1. It may be that the fund's return and that of the market were never very similar.

The plots for this portfolio are shown in Exhibit 12–6. It can be seen that the plots cover a broad range and do not fall into a neat linear order. This fund can be characterized as having a beta of 1 and a low

EXHIBIT 12–6

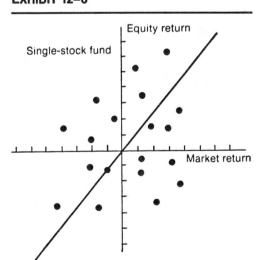

diversification level. Its condition can be described in two ways: First, we can say that the fund is not very diversified, and consequently its success or failure is highly dependent on the success of the stocks owned rather than on the general level of the stock market; second, we might say that we cannot have much confidence that the portfolio's return will be close to the return indicated by its beta level. Both statements say the same things but from different points of view. The points in Exhibit 12–3, the index fund, all fall precisely on the characteristic line, whereas the points in Exhibit 12–6, the individual stock, scatter widely about the line. In effect, the diversification measure describes the extent to which the dots fall close to the line. The standard error of beta, also called the standard error of estimate or the standard error of regression, shows the extent to which the dots are dispersed in relation to the line.

More frequently, the diversification measure is expressed as the R^2, also known as the coefficient of determination. This measurement, which is linked precisely to the standard error, shows the extent to which the regression line explains the relationship between the equity portfolio and the market. A measurement of zero shows no relationship, and a measurement of 1.00 shows a 100 percent explanation, as would be the case in an index fund.

A third factor which can be determined from the characteristic line is whether a manager was successful on a risk-adjusted basis in adding to the portfolio's return. This can be determined by looking at the intercept of the regression line (also called the alpha). Returning to the index fund in Exhibit 12–3, we note that the characteristic line goes through the origin, or meeting point, of the two axes. This indicates that the fund had a risk-adjusted return of 0.0 or, phrased another way, the manager neither added nor subtracted return through stock selection. This is what is anticipated with an index fund.

A manager who had success in stock selection on a risk-adjusted basis would find the characteristic line intercepted above the zero mark, as shown in Exhibit 12–7. We can think of this example intuitively by considering a fund manager who invested by starting with an index fund and each quarter sold those securities which were overvalued and placed assets obtained from the sale in securities which were undervalued, but in each case moving the assets in such a way as to maintain the beta of 1. Assume that this activity added 1 percent per quarter to the portfolio's return. In a quarter in which the market rose 10 percent, the fund would rise 11 percent. When the market declined 10 percent, the fund would

EXHIBIT 12-7

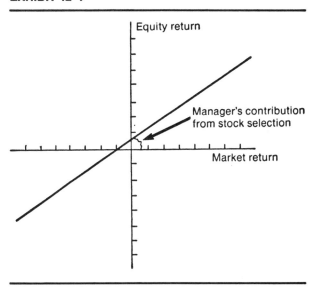

decline 9 percent, thus still achieving a return 1 percent better than the market. In this case the slope of the line is the same as that of the pure index fund, namely the 45 degree line with a slope of 1.0. However, the line would not go through the origin of the axes, but through the +1 percent mark on the vertical axis. This 1 percent per quarter represents the alpha, or the contribution through stock selection. The gain could have been achieved either by judicious choice of stocks or by increasing or decreasing the beta of the portfolio in anticipation of market movements (a form of timing).

An alternative way of viewing these ideas is shown in Exhibits 12–8, 12–9, and 12–10. Rather than looking at a regression characteristic line, we now look at a more familiar graph showing events over time. Exhibit 12–8 shows the stock market (or index fund) through one cycle. Exhibit 12–9 shows a portfolio with a beta of 1.5. The portfolio rises more rapidly than the market in rising periods and declines more rapidly than the market in declining periods. Exhibit 12–10 shows a portfolio with a beta of 0.8; the portfolio moves more conservatively than the market, dampening swings in the market in both directions. In both cases the portfolios have an R^2 of 100, that is, are highly diversified. The idea of diversification can be introduced by recognizing that the portfolio may not have

EXHIBIT 12–8

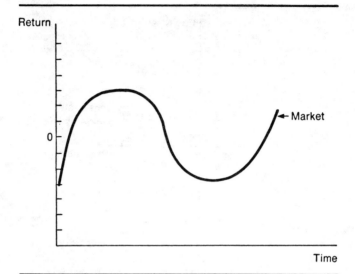

EXHIBIT 12–9

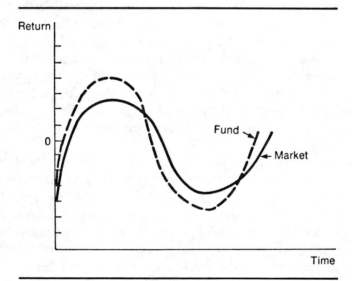

EXHIBIT 12–10

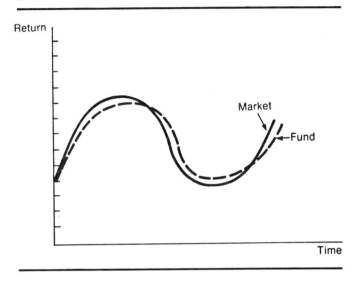

a return exactly equal to that indicated by its beta. Exhibit 12–11 shows a portfolio with a beta of 1.2 and an R^2 of 0.90. In this case the portfolio's expected rate of return is known, but its actual return will vary from the expected return. The width of the shaded area indicates a confidence span around the expected return. In this case, two thirds of the time (within one standard deviation) the portfolio's return is likely to be within plus or minus 4 percentage points of the expected return. For another portfolio (Exhibit 12–12) with a beta of 1.2, but containing only a few stocks and thus having a very low diversification, or R^2, level, this span is much wider. Finally, Exhibit 12–13 shows the portfolio whose manager had 1 percent per quarter risk-adjusted contribution through stock selection in a portfolio with a beta of 1.0. The actual average return is distinguished from the expected return for this beta level. We can also see the degree of diversification in the portfolio by viewing the shaded area.

The implications of the information provided by the characteristic line are extremely important to fund sponsors and investment managers. Two policy considerations are represented, and one evaluation of the manager's skill. The two policy considerations are the amount of market risk in a portfolio (beta, or market sensitivity) and the percentage of the total risk in the portfolio which is represented by market

EXHIBIT 12–11

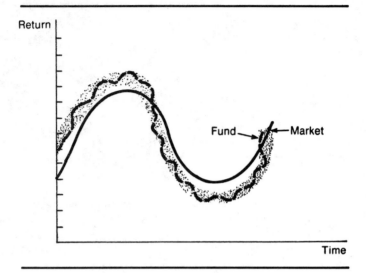

EXHIBIT 12–12

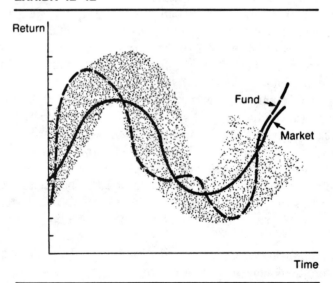

EXHIBIT 12–13

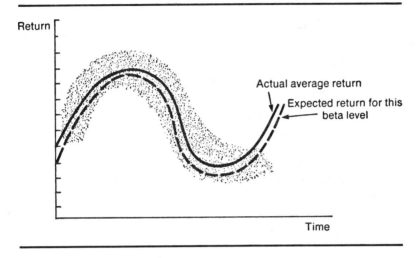

risk (diversification, or R^2). The beta, or market risk, question is one of whether or not the sponsor and the manager feel that it is appropriate for the fund to have an aggressive posture. This is largely a function of the characteristics of the sponsor, but it is also impacted by the percentage of the portfolio in equities. For example, a fund might choose to place 50 percent in aggressive equities rather than 60 percent in conservative equities.

The diversification issue is the extent to which the sponsor is willing to make the success of the fund a function of the success of the manager in finding undervalued securities, as opposed to allowing the movements of the marketplace to dominate the fund's return. This is not to say it is wrong to be undiversified and to depend on the investment manager's success in stock selection. The reason for hiring an investment manager, in most cases, is that the sponsor believes the investment manager will be able to find undervalued securities, or at least that the sponsor feels it is worth the risk of doing somewhat worse than the market on a risk-adjusted basis in order to try to do better than the market on a risk-adjusted basis. However, since it is possible to participate at low cost in equities through an index fund, the sponsor should have some reason for feeling that the manager will be successful in stock selection before they permit a manager to operate with a relatively low diversification posture.

Limitations of the Beta Measurement

Although the characteristic line beta analysis has considerable usefulness, there are some limitations which should be considered. First, the validity of the beta calculation is only as good as the "fit" between the two variables being measured, in this case the rate of return on the portfolio and the rate of return on the market. The closeness of the fit is measured by the R^2. Generally speaking, if the R^2 is below 50 percent, not much confidence can be placed in the measurement of the beta; if the R^2 is below 80 percent, not much confidence can be placed in the measurement of the alpha, or intercept (selection measurement).

The calculation technique is also limited if there is a significant change in the beta during the period being measured. If the manager owned highly aggressive stocks at one point in the market and conservative stocks at another point, it is not possible to distinguish between the movements attributable to the market (beta) and those attributable to selection (alpha).

Moreover, the beta measurement is of limited value in looking at an individual stock. This is because the R^2 is usually low, averaging about 0.3. Intuitively, we know that stocks are affected both by the market and by internal or industry factors affecting the company, and we see from the R^2 that about 70 percent of the risk or movement in the stock price is attributable to internal or industry factors and only about 30 percent to movements in the market. Consequently, although the beta measurement is useful for a stock, it is not appropriate to place much weight on the information supplied by the characteristic line analysis. As more and more stocks are added to the portfolio, the specific factors cancel, leaving the market factor to dominate. Thus, the beta measurement is quite useful for diversified portfolios.

MEASURING RISK-ADJUSTED RETURN

The characteristic line beta analysis makes possible the measurement not only of risk and diversification, but also of risk-adjusted return, through the alpha, or intercept, in the analysis. Two additional measurements of risk-adjusted return can be made, using either beta or standard deviation as measurements of risk. This will be explored in terms of the security market line.

The Security Market Line

The security market line relates return and risk. A chart is developed, showing return on one axis and risk on the other (see Exhibit 12–14). The market line connects points representing risk-free securities (such as U.S. Treasury bills) and the overall market. The point representing risk-free assets is on the vertical axis, indicating zero risk. The point representing the market is shown as having a greater degree of risk and also, at least in expectation, a higher rate of return. The measurement for risk can be either standard deviation (or a related measure) or beta. The risk

EXHIBIT 12–14
Market Security Line Analysis for Period Jan. 1987 to Dec. 1991

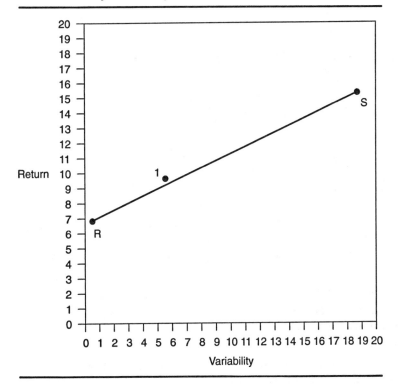

Source: Evaluation Associates Inc.
R–Risk Free 91 Day U.S. T-Bill.
S–Standard & Poor's 500 Index
1–SL Gov't Corp Bond Index

and return of an individual portfolio or security can be measured and placed in the market line framework. It is then possible to relate the amount of return achieved to the amount of risk taken. This is normally done by dividing the "excess return" (the return over and above the risk-free rate) by either standard deviation or beta. The former is called a Sharpe measurement, the latter a Treynor ratio.

ARBITRAGE PRICING THEORY

The capital asset pricing model (CAPM) is a theoretical model which explains returns on assets based upon a relationship between the asset and the market. Fundamental to the CAPM are certain underlying assumptions, including that investors have an identical, single-period time horizon, that investors can borrow at the risk-free rate, that there are no taxes, and that investors choose their portfolios on the basis of mean and variance of return. It is also possible to decompose, at least conceptually, the return of the market into the returns of the subsectors of the market, and thus present the CAPM in a multi-index rather than a single-index form. Mathematically, these two approaches are shown below:

1. Single-index model $R = rf + bM + e$
2. $R = rf + b1 * F1 + b2 * F2 \ldots + bn * Fn + e$

where R = return on a security, rf is the return of a risk-free security, b is sensitivity (beta), M is the return on the market, e is the error term, $F1$ is factor 1, and $b1$ is the beta or sensitivity of the security with respect to factor 1.

An alternative view of the process is contained within the arbitrage pricing theory (APT). Whereas CAPM describes how returns are generated, APT describes pricing relationships among securities. Its fundamental thesis is that assets with similar cash flows will sell at similar prices. Investors will adjust their portfolios until this relationship prevails by selling assets with relatively lower cash flows and buying assets with relatively higher cash flows, in effect arbitraging until no further profit opportunity is perceived because prices are "in line."

According to APT, prices of securities are determined based upon the factors which impact them and the degree of sensitivity the particular security has to the factor. No theoretical framework is required to justify the use of factors—they either contribute to the price of an asset or they do not. However, empirical research suggests that there are a number of factors significant to the pricing of most, if not all, assets, including changes in investors' perceptions as to rate of inflation, level of industrial output, attitude toward risk, and the structure of interest rates.

As with CAPM, there are also individual or specific factors which impact the prices of individual assets. Since the individual factors impacting one security do not impact other securities (i.e., the specific factors are "uncorrelated"), they tend to cancel each other out in portfolios with large numbers of securities. Hence, the price of a diversified portfolio is primarily influenced by the factors impacting the overall economy or market, as in the case with the CAPM.

CHAPTER 13

MEASURING RISK AND RETURN IN FIXED-INCOME PORTFOLIOS

Bonds are strange investments. When you own them you don't even know whether you want them to go up or down in value.[1]
Paraphrased from Professor Lawrence Fisher

The measurement of bond portfolios is extremely important to fund sponsors because of the enormous amount of money they invest in bonds and because of their increasing concern that assets be invested prudently and efficiently. Historically, bond "measurement" has meant measuring the rate of return, and possibly comparing results with a bond market index or with other portfolios. Although these analyses are important, they do not address one of the most significant factors that every fund sponsor and investment manager should be concerned with—risk. This chapter reviews why bond measurement is important, how risk and return are measured, why fund sponsors should be concerned with risk, and what the sources of risk are in bond portfolios. Finally, the chapter presents a number of methods for measuring risk and return in bond portfolios, using both traditional and new quantitative approaches.

---

[1] Bonds would rise in price only if interest rates declined. Although this produces a capital gain for the investor, it also means that bonds may be "called" and replaced with lower-yielding investments and that the return from the reinvestment of coupon will be lower.

RETURN

To begin the measurement process, the portfolio's rate of return must first be calculated. For this analysis, return is total rate of return on a time-weighted basis. Total rate of return includes income and realized and unrealized capital appreciation, with all assets measured at market value. Total rates of return are used because this makes it possible to perform analyses and make comparisons, and allows time to make changes in the portfolio if the results are not satisfactory. Using book values, whether or not they are amortized, investors cannot do much in the way of analysis, since they are not dealing with the true condition of the portfolio as of any point in time. For the same reason, it is not possible to compare the results of one fund to those of another fund or to a market index. Finally, if investors ignore the true value of the portfolio and consider only the book value, they are not likely to recognize problems with the portfolio in time to make changes.

Time-weighted rates of return are calculated in such a way as to distinguish the effects on the portfolio of the timing and magnitude of external cash flows. This places the focus on what the investment manager did with the portfolio rather than on what happened to the fund, and is appropriate for sponsors trying to "manage their investment managers."

RISK

There are many possible definitions of risk. It is possible to look at risk from loss due to default or change in quality rating, or potential loss if interest rates rise. *Risk* is defined here as the uncertainty of return or the uncertainty of the future value of the portfolio. The more uncertainty there is, the more risk the portfolio bears. For instance, we know that a 91-day Treasury bill has no risk for an investor with a three-month time horizon. On the other hand, bonds and stocks have uncertain returns to investors with a three-month horizon, since it is not known what the value of bonds and stocks will be three months hence. Thus, risk can be defined as the amount of uncertainty in the portfolio.

The sponsor of a fixed-income portfolio might reasonably ask why it should care about risk. There are three reasons:

1. If a fund has an inappropriate risk policy, its chances of meeting its objective are reduced. A good example is a small portfolio owned by a widow on behalf of herself and her children. Her goal is to receive income in order to pay her monthly bills. The widow's ability to bear risk is very low, and her need for income is high, so her portfolio should be structured to take these factors into consideration. The objectives of pension funds or other tax-exempt funds may not be as dramatically obvious as those of the widow, but nonetheless the investment objective is extremely important. Although it is no easy task to establish a correct policy, sponsors must be able to measure the risk of their investments in order to have any hope of establishing one.

2. A fund may be taking too much risk relative to the return it is achieving. Risk measures make it possible to calculate risk-adjusted returns in order to answer the question, "For the risk our investment manager took, did we achieve a high enough return?"

3. Bond prices can be volatile. As interest rates change, bond prices move significantly. This is because the present value of future cash flows changes as interest rates change.

The skeptic may ask why he should not ignore risk and instead merely compare his results to any or all of his assumed rate of return, a market index, or other portfolios. Although each of these comparisons is important, none is sufficient. Comparing a fund to its assumed rate of return is not adequate, since in periods when the market declines sharply, almost all portfolios will fail to meet their objectives. Similarly, in a sharply rising market, almost all funds will exceed their assumptions. Thus, the usefulness of this method is limited. It might be suggested that the limitations of comparison to the assumed rate of return can be compensated for by comparing a portfolio's results to a market index or to the results of other portfolios. The drawback of this approach is that the indexes or portfolios used as comparative benchmarks may be structured in a way which does not reflect the objectives, needs, or characteristics of the fund in question. Therefore, these comparisons, though certainly useful, are not sufficient.

SOURCES OF RISK IN BOND PORTFOLIOS

The first and foremost risk in bond portfolios is default. If the issuer does not pay interest and principal, the value of the bond is severely diminished. As a practical matter, the vast majority of bond issuers have been able to honor their commitments precisely. Furthermore, most investment managers concentrate on reasonably high-quality bonds, such that the risk of default is more noticeable in the differences in yield between high-quality and lower quality bonds than in the likelihood of real default. However, should the country witness a severe and prolonged depression, the number of bonds defaulting would increase considerably.

For bonds which are not likely to default, two types of risk or uncertainty are of interest: changes in the general level of interest rates and changes in the "spread," or yield differential, between sectors of the bond market. An additional risk is "call," or reinvestment risk, which occurs when interest rates drop sharply and remain down for a long period of time. In this case investors who own bonds with high coupons may find that issuers will sell new bonds at lower rates and use the proceeds to pay off the old bonds which require payment of a higher interest rate. Further, since the new level of interest rates is lower, cash received from coupon payments and from maturing bonds is reinvested at the new (lower) rates of interest, thus reducing the amount of money received and the return of the investor.

Other risks are introduced by special features of individual bonds. For instance, subordinated bonds place the investor in a position junior to other creditors in the case of default. Convertible bonds, which in many cases are more like equity securities than like fixed-income instruments, can be exchanged under certain circumstances for shares of common stock. For these securities the price of the common stock becomes an important determinant of the value of the bond, and consequently introduces a major uncertainty. Another source of risk occurs when bonds are subject to sinking funds. In many cases corporate bonds are offered with a requirement by the borrower to retire a portion of the issue prior to maturity, in order to reduce the amount of liabilities outstanding. Although this activity generally improves the creditworthiness of the bonds, the presence or absence of the issuer repurchasing bonds to meet sinking fund requirements introduces a modest but additional uncertainty in the marketplace.

Inflation risk is present for all assets denominated in money as opposed to goods or services. Since a bond has to be repaid in money it has inflation risk, whereas if a bond were to be repaid in soybeans it would not have general inflation risk.

CHANGES IN THE GENERAL LEVEL OF INTEREST RATES

In looking at the impact of changes in the general level of interest rates, four rules will be observed. First, when interest rates change, bond prices also change. Second, the change occurs in the opposite direction. That is, when interest rates decline, bond prices rise, and vice versa. Third, all other things being equal, bonds with longer maturities are more volatile than bonds with shorter maturities.[2] Fourth, bonds with lower coupons are more volatile than bonds with higher coupons. Exhibit 13-1 shows two bonds with similar coupons and different maturities. When the level of interest rates declines from 8 percent to 7 percent, both bonds rise in price, as indicated by the first and second rules. According to the third rule, the longer maturity bond rises more than the shorter one. The reason for this becomes apparent when we consider that a one-year, 8 percent bond pays 1 percent more than the going interest rate of 7 percent. Thus, investors in one-year bonds should be indifferent to whether they receive 7 percent interest and pay par or receive 8 percent interest and pay 101 (ignoring compounding, call features, and taxes). Similarly, an investor buying a two-year bond when rates are 7 percent expects to receive roughly 14 percent on his investment over a two-year period. When he purchases a bond with an 8 percent coupon, he receives 16 percent in interest and therefore is willing to lose 2 percent in principal in order to achieve the 7 percent per year prevailing rate of return.

The fourth rule is that lower coupon bonds are more volatile than higher coupon bonds for a given change in interest rates. This behavior can be traced to the fact that a bond returns both interest and a final maturity payment, and that for lower coupon bonds a smaller percentage of the return comes from coupon than is the case with a higher coupon bond. Thus, when rates change, the lower coupon bond must change more in price in order to offset the greater stability of return offered by the higher coupon payments of the high-coupon bond. Put another way, since the average time to repayment is farther in the future for lower coupon bonds, there is more impact from discounting their future cash flows.

---

[2]More precisely, it is the duration of a bond rather than its maturity which determines its volatility. Certain (hypothetical) discount bonds of extremely long maturities reach a point at which they become less volatile as maturity increases, since duration at this point is decreasing rather than increasing.

EXHIBIT 13-1

When yields decline, longer term bonds rise more sharply than do shorter term bonds.

	Coupon	Maturity	Level of Interest Rates		Percentage Change in Price
			8 Percent Price	7 Percent Price	
Bond A	8%	One year	100	101	1%
Bond B	8	Two years	100	102	2

If interest rates decline from 8 percent to 7 percent, each bond is worth roughly 1 percent per year more than the prevailing rate. To equalize this change, the one-year bond rises about 1 percent and the two-year bond rises about 2 percent (ignoring call provisions and compounding).

This principle can be seen from Exhibit 13-2, in which the impact on an 8 percent 20-year bond is compared to the impact on a 4 percent 20-year bond when the level of interest rates changes from 8 percent to 7 percent. Both bonds rise in price according to rules 1 and 2, with the lower coupon bond being more volatile, showing a 12.5 percent increase in price as compared to a 10.7 percent increase in price for the higher coupon bond.

Thus, for a given change in the general level of interest rates, the impact is greater for longer maturity bonds and for lower coupon bonds. These impacts can be combined (when quality is unchanged and when

EXHIBIT 13-2

When yields decline, lower coupon bonds rise a greater percentage than do higher coupon bonds.

	Coupon	Maturity	Level of Interest Rates		Percentage Change in Price
			8 Percent Price	7 Percent Price	
Bond A	8%	20	100	110.677	10.7%
Bond B	4	20	60.414	67.967	12.5

EXHIBIT 13–3

Changing spreads between different sectors are a source of bond volatility. When the spread between a higher yielding bond and a lower yielding bond widens, the lower yielding bond is the better performer.

Bond 1	Bond 2	Spread
8.00	8.10	−0.10

If the spread widens by Bond 2's yield rising, Bond 2 will sustain a capital loss, making Bond 1, the lower yielding bond, a better performer.

If the spread widens by Bond 1's yield declining, Bond 1 will sustain a capital gain, making it the better performer.

---

the shift in interest rates is uniform for all maturities) into a measure of duration. Duration measures the time it takes for the investor to receive back half of his or her money. It includes the timing of final maturity and the size and timing of coupon payments received in the meantime.

CHANGES IN SPREADS BETWEEN BOND SECTORS

In addition to changes in the general level of interest rates, a major source of volatility in bond portfolios is changes in the spreads between bond sectors. The five types of changes relate to maturity, quality, coupon, issuer type, and coupon area (premium or discount). Exhibit 13–3 shows two bonds with different yields. The difference in yields can be caused by a difference in maturity[3] (with longer term bonds typically having higher yields), quality (with lower quality bonds having higher yields), coupon (with higher coupon bonds typically having higher yields), issuer type (with financial and utility bonds generally having higher yields than industrials), and coupon area (with premium bonds typically having higher yields than discount bonds). The point is that

---

[3]Changes in yield spreads between maturities are typically referred to as changes in the shape of the yield curve.

bonds with different characteristics have different yields and that the difference in yield between these bonds can change. For instance, in Exhibit 13–3, bond 1 yields 8.00 percent and bond 2 yields 8.10 percent. We might assume that bond 1 is a AAA bond and bond 2 a AA bond of similar characteristics. There is no reason why this spread relationship must stay at 10 basis points; it could become wider or narrower, with either bond rising or declining in yield.[4] Such changes in the relationship between bond sectors can come at any time and be of almost any magnitude.

TRADITIONAL RISK MEASURES

Traditional measurements of risk in bonds can be divided into two general categories. The first looks at the underlying strength of the issuer, and the second looks at the characteristics of the bonds held. The measurements which describe the issuer can be further divided into those which relate the issuer's income or cash flow to the amount of debt service required each year and those which address the amount of debt relative to the amount of assets or equity.

Measurements of the ability to repay from operations include:

1. Earnings before interest and taxes divided by debt service. This measurement views the issuer's net income as an indication of ability to repay debt. Since interest payments are deductible they are included before taxes.
2. Cash flow divided by debt service. Similar to the previous measurement, this calculation also includes the cash available from noncash charges, such as depreciation.

Measurements relating debt to assets or equity include:

1. Debt as a percentage of total capital. This is perhaps the most traditional measurement of the amount of debt that an issuer can

---

[4]It is interesting to note that when spreads widen, the investor is better off owning a lower yielding bond, regardless of its other characteristics. If the spread widens because the higher yielding bond rises in yield, this bond will have a decrease in price. If the spread widens because the lower yielding bond drops in yield, this bond will have a capital gain. In either case the investor is better off owning the lower yielding bond. When spreads narrow, the opposite is true.

properly handle. These ratios differ considerably from industry to industry and should be considered in that context.

2. Debt as a percentage of equity. This similar measurement relates debt to equity rather than to debt plus equity. Both measurements could define equity as historical book value or market value less debt.

It is also desirable to consider profitability measures, such as profit margins and return on equity or return on total assets, as indications of the long-run ability of the issuer to pay.

In addition to these fundamental measurements, it is possible to use traditional risk measures in the form of maturity, coupon, quality, and issuer type. As discussed earlier, long-term bonds and low-coupon bonds are more volatile than otherwise similar short-term bonds or high-coupon bonds. High-quality bonds are less risky than lower quality bonds. As to issuer type, U.S. government securities are obviously of higher quality and hence less risky than corporate bonds. Among the three corporate sectors—industrial, financial, and utility—no category is inherently more secure than another.

AGGREGATING TRADITIONAL RISK MEASURES OF INDIVIDUAL BONDS INTO PORTFOLIO MEASURES

The measures discussed above are used primarily in analyzing individual bonds for their creditworthiness and their relative value. Fund sponsors are typically less concerned with individual securities and more interested in descriptions of the portfolio in its entirety. It is possible to use traditional measures for the total bond portfolio by measuring each bond and weighting the measurement for the percentage of the portfolio in that security. This can be done for each security, with the sum of the measurements of each security being representative of the portfolio. The aggregate number can then be compared with a similar number for the market as a whole, subsectors thereof, or other portfolios.

QUANTITATIVE TECHNIQUES FOR MEASURING RISK

Although the above measurements certainly provide useful information about a portfolio, they do not indicate its overall risk. At least three measures exist which might do this. First, the standard deviation of the portfolio's returns will be considered, as it was with equities. Second, the beta method for measuring risk in fixed-income portfolios will be discussed. Third, a model which measures the sensitivity of a portfolio to changes in the level of interest rates will be considered.

Using Standard Deviation in Market Line Analysis

The market line is a simple method of measuring risk as well as return in portfolios, as is shown in Exhibit 13–4. The vertical axis shows return and the horizontal axis shows variability as measured by the standard deviation of return. (Since standard deviation is an arithmetic, as opposed to geometric, concept, the returns shown are arithmetic rather than

EXHIBIT 13–4
Bond Portfolio Market Line Analysis for Period January 1987 to December 1991

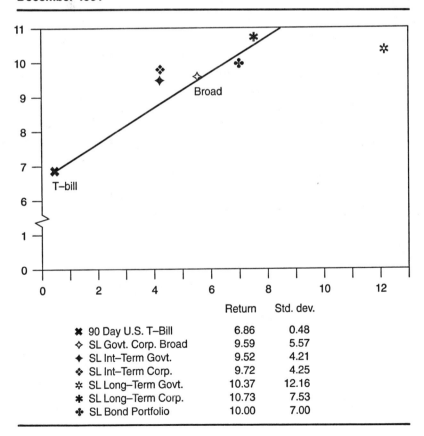

	Return	Std. dev.
✖ 90 Day U.S. T–Bill	6.86	0.48
✧ SL Govt. Corp. Broad	9.59	5.57
✦ SL Int–Term Govt.	9.52	4.21
❖ SL Int–Term Corp.	9.72	4.25
✳ SL Long–Term Govt.	10.37	12.16
✱ SL Long–Term Corp.	10.73	7.53
♣ SL Bond Portfolio	10.00	7.00

geometric. Although this changes the actual measurement of return somewhat, it does not in any way alter the concept of return.) It can be seen from this framework for measuring risk and return that the most desirable portfolio would be one which is represented by a point at the upper left part of the graph, signifying a low level of risk and a high level of return.

Utilization of the market line begins with measurement of the risk and return of Treasury bills and the overall bond market (the Broad index). Treasury bills had a return during the period 1987 to 1991of 6.86 percent and a variability of near zero for a one-quarter time horizon. The overall bond market, as measured by the Shearson Lehman Government and Corporate Broad Index had a return of 9.59 percent, with a variability of about 5½ percent. This risk measurement indicates that about two thirds of the time during this period we would have expected the bond market to have a return within 5½ percentage points of its average. Put another way, the bond market would have been expected to return between 4 percent and 15 percent about two thirds of the time. It should be noted that any return is theoretically possible but that a return above or below two standard deviations (plus or minus 11 percent, or outside the range of −1½ percent to +20½ percent) would occur only 5 percent of the time.

We have thus described two points on the fixed-income spectrum, the risk and return of Treasury bills and the risk and return of the overall bond market. We can now draw a market line showing the risk and return of "market" portfolios with a wide variety of risk levels. This is done by connecting the Treasury bill point with the bond market point and indicating that an investor could achieve a portfolio of any risk level and any return shown on that line merely by combining the appropriate proportions of Treasury bills and the bond market. In other words, a point halfway along the line would have a risk of about 2¾ percent and a return halfway between that of bills and that of the market. This portfolio can be constructed by allocating half of fund assets at the beginning of the period to bills and the other half to the bond market as represented by the index. Similarly, any other point on the line can be achieved by combining the appropriate amount of bills and bonds. It must be noted that in order to achieve a point to the right of the bond market, the percentage in Treasury bills must be negative; that is, the investor must borrow money, at the risk-free rate, and leverage its portfolio. Although this may not be a permissible alternative for most funds, it is at least a theoretical alternative and useful from an analytical point of view.

Having drawn a market line for the period January 1987 to December 1991, we note that during this period the line slants upward. This indicates that during the period there was a "premium" for bearing risk: the greater the risk that was taken, the better portfolios tended to do. This is the normal expectation, though in poor markets the line slopes downward, indicating that bearing risk detracts from return.

Beta Analysis

As shown in the equity analysis, the beta measurement presents the relationship between a portfolio's historic rate of return and the market's historic rate of return, with the slope of the line indicating how volatile the portfolio is relative to the market index. Exhibits 13–5 and 13–6 use the beta model to show the relationship between short-term government portfolios and long-term corporate portfolios, both in relation to a broad-based market index. It can easily be seen that the short-term government index has a much flatter slope than that of the long-term corporate index, demonstrating its lesser volatility or risk.

EXHIBIT 13–5

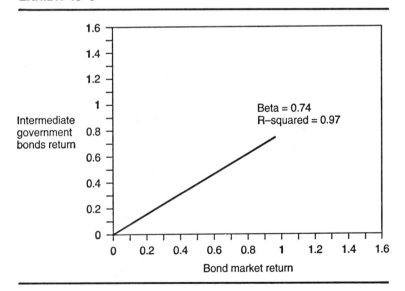

Bond market – Shearson Lehman broad index
Intermediate government – Shearson Lehman intermediate government
Timeperiod: 1/82–12/91

EXHIBIT 13–6

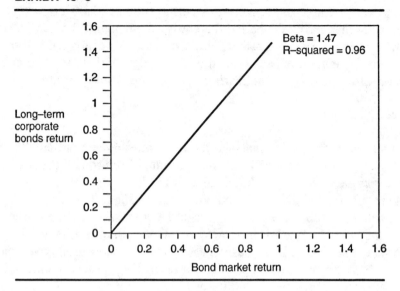

Bond market – Shearson Lehman broad index
Intermediate government – Shearson Lehman intermediate government
Timeperiod: 1/82–12/91

Certain difficulties arise in using the beta measurement for bond portfolios and hoping to make judgments from them. First, the choice of index makes a great deal of difference in the results achieved. Second, the portfolio's characteristics should be stable for the measurement to be highly useful. Since bond portfolios, if no action is taken, are constantly becoming shorter term and hence less risky, this creates difficulties with the measurement. Finally, as will be discussed later, because of these problems it is questionable whether the beta analysis can be expanded beyond risk to measure selection and diversification, as can be done with equity portfolios.

The Duration Model

Duration measures the average time required for the investor to receive its investment and the interest on it. It is similar to maturity, except that maturity considers only the timing and the amount of the final payment of a bond. Duration, on the other hand, also considers the

EXHIBIT 13–7
Duration of Selected Bonds at Market Yield of 6 Percent (in years)

Years to Maturity	Coupon Rates*			
	0.02	*0.04*	*0.06*	*0.08*
1	0.995	0.990	0.985	0.981
5	4.756	4.558	4.393	4.254
10	8.891	8.169	7.662	7.286
20	14.981	12.980	11.904	11.232
50	19.452	17.129	16.273	15.829
100	17.567	17.232	17.120	17.064
∞	17.167	17.167	17.167	17.167

*Coupon payments and compounding semiannual.

Source: Fisher and Weil, *Journal of Business*, October 1971, p. 418.

impact of the timing and magnitude of coupon payments. Consider the bonds shown in Exhibit 13–7. For long maturities, the high-coupon bonds have a considerably shorter duration than do the low-coupon bonds. The greater the duration, the more volatile a portfolio's return is with respect to changes in the general level of interest rates. In fact, for small changes in rates the relationship is proportional.

As was noted earlier in the chapter, longer maturity bonds are more volatile than shorter maturity bonds because the time period over which the discounting process takes place is much longer with longer maturity bonds. With low-coupon bonds the percentage of the total return represented by the final payment is much lower, and since the final payment is obviously the longest term payment received, the volatility of the portfolio or bond with respect to changes in interest rates is increased.

The duration measure has several limitations and these should be noted. First, there are risks to portfolios other than those associated with interest rate changes. Second, the precise measurement of the portfolio's volatility with respect to interest rate changes assumes a so-called parallel shift in the yield curve. In other words, if 20-year rates move 1 percent, then a similar change is assumed for 19-year bonds, 10-year bonds, 5-year bonds, and so on. Despite these limitations the duration measure is of considerable use in measuring the risk of fixed-income securities.

MEASURING RISK-ADJUSTED RETURN

The rate of return adjusted for the amount of risk taken, also known as the "manager's contribution," can be calculated by using each of the three measurements shown for calculating portfolio risk. Each of these measurements is discussed below.

Using Standard Deviation in Market Line Analysis

In the market line analysis a line was drawn representing the risk and return of portfolios consisting of various portions of Treasury bills and the market. This line can be viewed as an unmanaged or "naive" portfolio. In other words, it is possible to suggest that the line represents a market portfolio of a specific risk level, and that the market return for a portfolio of that risk level is the one shown on the vertical axis (see Exhibit 13–4). It is then possible to see whether the return of a specific portfolio is above or below that of the market portfolio of the same risk level. If the return is above the line, it can be stated that the portfolio achieved a risk-adjusted return above that of the market. If the return is below the line, the portfolio did less well than an unmanaged portfolio of the same risk level. As with all measurements comparing actual performance to a market index, it must be considered that the index has no transaction costs and that real portfolios do; consequently, all such measurements are somewhat biased against the investment manager operating in the real world.

Using Beta

Just as with equity portfolios, it is possible to use the alpha, or intercept, to measure risk-adjusted returns. However, this procedure is not recommended because of the segmented nature of the bond market; the impact on the portfolio of shifts in the bond yield curve; the varying results which can occur, depending on which index is used to represent the overall bond market; and the changing risk level of the portfolio which occurs as bonds become shorter in maturity and as coupon reinvestment and other funds added to the portfolio change its structure. All of these factors impact the measurement of risk in the portfolio and create the possibility that the alpha is showing a factor representing risk when it is supposedly demonstrating the impact of the manager over and above that indicated by the risk of the portfolio.

Using the Duration Model

With the duration measurement it is possible to calculate the sensitivity of a portfolio to changes in the general level of interest rates. With this information it becomes possible to attribute the sources of the portfolio's return to the market, the policy effect, the interest rate anticipation effect, the analysis effect, and the trading effect. In the duration model (Exhibit 13–8), the rate of return is shown on the vertical axis and duration on the horizontal axis. This is similar to the market line, except that duration rather than total variability is used as the risk measure. The market effect is the base point, and it represents the return which the market achieved during the period being measured. Moving up the line, the long-term average risk level of the portfolio is shown, the difference between the market return and the return of a market portfolio with the fund's risk policy being the policy effect. If the manager expects rates to change, it will probably shift the duration of the portfolio accordingly. In the example shown (Exhibit 13–8), higher risk was rewarded as the manager increased the duration of the portfolio above the long-run policy average and achieved a higher rate of return in the process. The difference between the return at the actual duration on the market line and the return at the policy duration, also on the line, is the interest rate anticipation effect. If the manager were successful in finding undervalued bonds, its favorable analysis effect would be shown as the difference between the rate of return of the initial portfolio, had it been held for the whole period, and a portfolio of the same duration on the market line. Finally, any difference between the actual rate of return earned and the return on the buy-and-hold portfolio is called the trading effect.

This analysis is extremely interesting, but unfortunately it has limitations. Because measurements are attributed so minutely, it is extremely important that the portfolios be valued precisely and that they be measured whenever any significant cash flow takes place. In other words, the rate of return must be precisely measured for it to be possible to attribute return to the various effects. Also, duration is not a complete measurement of the risk in a portfolio, since it leaves out quality factors. Thus, these factors will be attributed to other areas. In addition, the impact on the portfolio from sinking funds, calls, and redemptions will be

EXHIBIT 13–8
The Duration Model

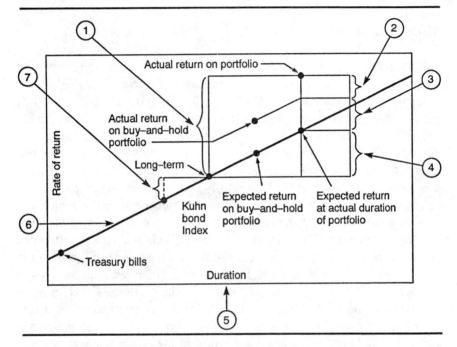

1. The management effect is the improvement in the investment performance of a passive strategy through active bond management. It is the difference between the total bond portfolio return and the expected return at the long-term average duration.
2. The trading effect is the result of the current quarter's trading, either through effective trade desk operation or short-term selection abilities. It is the difference between the total management effect and the effects attributable to analysis and interest rate anticipation.
3. The analysis effect, attributable to the selection of issues with better than average long-term prospects, is the difference between the actual return of the buy-and-hold portfolio at the beginning of the quarter and the expected return of that buy-and-hold portfolio.
4. The interest rate anticipation effect is attributable to changes in portfolio duration resulting from attempts to profit from and ability to predict bond market movements. It is the difference between the expected return at the actual portfolio duration and the expected return at the long-term average duration.
5. Duration, a measure of the average time to the receipt of cash flows from an investment, is a measure of the sensitivity of a bond's price to changes in interest rates. An increase in yields causes a percentage decrease in price equal to the duration time change in yield.
6. The bond market line is a straight line drawn through the return/duration of Treasury bills and the return/duration of the Bond Index.

EXHIBIT 13–8 (continued)

7. The policy effect is the difference between the long-term duration of a bond portfolio and the duration of a bond market index resulting from long-term investment policy, measured as the return at the long-term average less the return on the Bond Index.

Note: The buy-and-hold portfolio is the composition of the portfolio at the beginning of the quarter. It is used to differentiate between trading gains secured within a quarter and long-term analysis gains.

Source: Wilshire Associates; *Pension World*, June 1977.

attributed to trading, whereas they may be due to fortuitous causes. Naturally, since the market line is based on the return and the duration of the market index, precise measurements of the index must also be available. Finally, it should be noted that there is no generally accepted theory which suggests that a straight-line relationship should exist between return and duration. Although the analysis may be extremely ambitious, nonetheless the results being sought are entirely desirable.

MEASURING THE MANAGER'S CONTRIBUTION

One approach to bond measurement uses traditional measurements (see Exhibit 13–9). This method compares results to the market and to a buy-and-hold portfolio. The difference between the rate of return on the market and the rate of return on the beginning or buy-and-hold portfolio is considered to be the management differential. The difference between the rate of return on the beginning portfolio and the actual portfolio is called the activity factor. This analysis suggests that the return on a portfolio will equal its beginning yield to maturity if nothing else changes. However, interest rates may change, and this impact is measured by looking at the shift in the government bond yield curve from the beginning to the end of the period. The impact of this shift is called the interest rate effect. To the extent that the portfolio is weighted differently from the market, any changes in the relationship between quality and issuer type will also have an impact on the portfolio. The difference between the total rate of return of the beginning portfolio and the sum of the beginning yield to maturity, the interest rate effect, and the sector/quality effect is called the residual effect, or "other selection effect." Finally, the difference between the return on the beginning portfolio and the actual return is an activity or swapping factor.

EXHIBIT 13–9
Measuring Manager Contribution Using Traditional Analysis

Return analysis (beginning portfolio)

	Total Return		Adjusted Beginning Yield to Maturity		Interest Rate Effect		Sector/ Quality Return		Residual
1. Return of beginning portfolio	0.92%	=	2.14%	+	(3.84%)	+	0.80%	+	1.82%
2. Market return	(1.25)	=	2.06	+	(4.13)	+	0.87	+	(0.05)
3. Management differential	2.17%	=	0.08%	+	0.29%	+	(0.07)%	+	1.87%

Manager 1's static portfolio performed considerably better (+2.17 percent) than the market portfolio. This better performance was mainly attributable to 1.87 percent from "other selection effects," which occurred on several bonds. Also, about 0.29 percent additional return was experienced because of the shorter maturity of this portfolio (13.5 years) versus the market average maturity of 19.5 years.

Activity factor

Total reported return	versus	Return on beginning portfolio	=	Activity factor
0.30%		0.92%	=	(0.62%)

Account descriptors

	Market	Manager
Maturity	19.5 years	13.5 years
Coupon	7.9%	8.2%

Source: Russell Fogler and Peter O. Dietz, Frank Russell Company, Inc.

COMPARISON WITH A BASELINE PORTFOLIO

Some practitioners suggest that it is inappropriate to compare a portfolio's results to a market index or to the results of other funds. Rather, a fund's results should be compared to its objective. The objective is not a simple percentage or dollar amount but a portfolio which meets the needs of the fund sponsor. Assume that a certain fund with assets of $1 million is required to pay $80,000 per year to the sponsor for 10 years. In this case the baseline portfolio might be a U.S. government bond with an 8 percent coupon and a 10-year maturity. It is then possible to compare the results of the portfolio in any period to those which would have been achieved by investing in this bond.

This method has considerable appeal, though it is not easy to put into practice. First, it is not easy for most sponsors to articulate their needs as specifically as the method requires. Second, a portfolio must be found which meets these needs. Third, this portfolio must be measured along with the real portfolio. Nonetheless, at least conceptually, there is considerable merit to this approach. If nothing else, the method forces sponsors to investigate and articulate their needs.

CHAPTER 14

MEASURING MARKET TIMING

Timing is everything.
Old Wall Street saying

Most investors know in general terms what is meant by market timing—
the movement of funds from one asset category, such as equities, to another, such as bonds, in order to maximize returns and minimize losses.
However, measuring this phenomenon is extremely difficult since it is desirable to eliminate from the measurement the impact from securities selection, the risk level of the assets owned, and the sensitivities of those
assets to the period measured, the average allocation, and the beginning
allocation. Various methods for measuring market timing are discussed,
along with the pros and cons of each. For analysis, the methods for measuring market timing have been divided into three categories: changes in
portfolio value, the use of market indexes, and the measurement of cash
flow movements.

CHANGES IN PORTFOLIO VALUE

This method involves looking at the portfolio at the beginning of the period and calculating the return which would have been achieved had that
same portfolio been held throughout the period. That return can then be
compared with the actual return achieved to see whether or not the "unmanaged" buy-and-hold portfolio would have performed better than the
actual portfolio. Although this information can certainly be of interest, it
is really not a satisfactory measurement of market timing. First, this type
of measurement is very sensitive to the beginning point chosen. In other
words, if the period chosen were one year earlier or one year later, the

results might be dramatically different. Also, any aberration in the portfolio's structure at the beginning point impacts the result. More important, this measurement does not distinguish among market timing, the risk level of each asset category, and contributions through selection. Consequently, the measurement has serious deficiencies for sponsors which are trying to determine the contribution made by the manager in timing the market. The impacts of asset category risk level and selection are demonstrated below.

THE USE OF MARKET INDEXES

To overcome the biases caused by differences in asset category risk level and selection, it is possible to view the portfolio as being invested not in the actual securities held but in market indexes. In other words, if the portfolio were 60 percent in equities, 30 percent in bonds, and 10 percent in cash equivalents, we could assume that the portfolio was invested 60 percent in the S&P 500, 30 percent in a bond index, and 10 percent in Treasury bills. This appears to be a quite satisfactory solution to the biases introduced by measuring the actual portfolio owned. Someone might suggest that this is not appropriate, since a manager might go from cash into equities and choose a particular list of stocks which does extremely well, whereas the general market declines. According to general terminology, however, this manager would be deemed to have had especially high success in stock selection but not success in market timing.

Numerous methods can be derived for measuring market timing with the use of indexes.

The Beginning Allocation

It is possible to use the beginning percentage allocation among asset categories to see whether the portfolio would have performed better over time had the manager maintained the beginning allocation rather than causing or allowing the allocation to change as it did. Again, this method is very sensitive to the beginning point chosen. It would be possible to repeat this method for each year (or even each quarter or month) of the measurement period. That is to say, we could look at the results from a point starting five years ago, a second point starting four years ago, a third point starting three years ago, and so on. The difficulty with this approach is that the results might be positive for some years and negative for others, without there being an obvious way of averaging the results for the entire period.

Since this method is sensitive to the beginning point chosen, an improvement can be made by making the beginning point less arbitrary. For instance, if the beginning of a market cycle is used as the beginning point and the end of the market cycle as the end point, the period being measured is both rationally determined and the same for all portfolios. In this case the performance in a market cycle would be measured for the two hypothetical portfolios, one with the average allocation during the cycle and the other with the actual allocation. If the portfolio at the average allocation exceeded the portfolio at the beginning allocation, a positive timing score would result. A drawback of this method is that it cannot be utilized unless the portfolio was under the manager's control for at least the full market cycle being measured.

The Average Allocation

To avoid dependence on the beginning point, it is possible to use the average allocation during the period rather than the allocation of the beginning point. In other words, if the average percentage in equities, bonds, and cash equivalents is 60/30/10, a comparison can be made of the return which would have been achieved by investing in market indexes at the average allocations and comparing it to the return which would have been achieved by investing at the actual quarter-by-quarter allocation which occurred in the portfolio. This method has considerable merit, although, like all of the index methods discussed here, it suffers from two problems: the measurement is "period dependent" and it is sensitive to the level of average allocation. In other words, a manager who behaved exactly the same in one period as he did in another would show different timing results simply because the stock, bond, and cash equivalent markets behaved differently during the two periods. Furthermore, even if we look at only a single period, two funds with significantly different allocations will have different timing measures. This makes it difficult to compare managers over a given period. Such period dependence is the result of a phenomenon which might be called the "rebalancing effect," and serious students of performance measurement may wish to study this phenomenon, since it crops up in several different areas of performance measurement.

The measurement technique is looking at the difference between a portfolio which was rebalanced periodically to a certain allocation level and one which was not rebalanced. This means that, if the market rises, the percentage in equities increases and the rebalancing occurs by selling sufficient equities to rebalance to the desired level. If the market declines, the percentage in equities also declines, thus making it necessary to rebalance by purchasing additional equities. As long as the market heads in one direction, rebalancing hurts the portfolio. That is, as long as the market is rising, a policy of selling equities hurts the portfolio. Similarly, if the market is declining, a policy of purchasing equities hurts the portfolio. Thus, in periods in which the market goes straight up or straight down, the rebalancing strategy works poorly and the unbalanced portfolio will tend to outperform the rebalanced portfolio. On the other hand, if the market has wide fluctuations but ends up roughly where it started, the rebalancing strategy is effective in increasing returns. This is because the percentage in equities in a rising market is constantly reduced, and at such time as the market declines, the lower level of equities works to the portfolio's benefit. Conversely, in a declining market the policy of rebalancing by purchasing stocks increases the fund's return when the market rebounds to its original position. Thus, the rebalancing effect is different in each period measured due to the differences in what the market did during that period. Consequently, a bias is introduced into all measurements which involve rebalancing. Unfortunately, this includes almost all measurements of timing.

A variation of the measurement of looking at the average percentage in equities versus the actual percentage is to look at the average beta, or market sensitivity, of the total portfolio in comparison to the period-by-period beta. In other words, the expected returns could be calculated for a portfolio with a beta equal to the average beta over the period, and these returns could be compared to the expected returns from the quarter-by-quarter beta of the portfolio. Again, if the average returns exceed the returns quarter by quarter, a negative timing score results.

The Trend Line Allocation

One of the most difficult problems associated with the measurement of market timing is the need to distinguish between the discretionary activity of the manager and the policies dictated by the sponsor. If the sponsor dictates or suggests a change in the percentage in equities, the measurement of market timing must take this change in policy into account. Otherwise, an impact will be attributed to the manager which should be attributed to the sponsor. Similarly, if the manager changes the long-term policy as to percentage in equities, this change cannot easily be distinguished from attempts at timing.

Regrettably, there is no simple way to measure this phenomenon unless the sponsor precisely and before the fact states an investment policy. It is insufficient for it to give general guidelines, and there is no way to distinguish between the impact of such policy decisions on a manager and the results of subtle comments by the sponsor, such as, "I see you've been doing some buying lately; that surprises me, given the market's outlook." One means for eliminating the impact of these policy decisions involves looking not at the average allocation but at the trend line. If the average or trend over time is rising or declining, it is possible to measure the impact of the portfolio's being invested at a higher or lower allocation than that indicated by the trend line. Of course, there is still no way to distinguish between the sponsor's and the manager's impact.

The Perfect Allocation

It is possible to compare the results of a portfolio at actual allocation with the results of a portfolio which had perfect (or always wrong) allocation. That is, instead of the standard being the beginning point, the average, or the trend line, the standard would be the results obtained from having always been in the highest returning (or the worst returning) asset category. Unfortuntely, this measurement is not particularly useful, since it really measures the policy rather than the deviations from the policy which result from the manager's attempts at timing. In a period in which the stock market did well, portfolios with high percentages in equities would show up well under this score even if the manager's activities in deviating from this policy actually hurt the portfolio's results.

All of the measurements using the indexes are affected by the frequency with which the percentage in asset categories is measured and by the stability and magnitude of cash flows. If the portfolio's structure is measured only quarterly and there are large, infrequent cash flows, the measurement of the asset allocation is affected. For instance, if a portfolio is normally 50 percent each in stocks and bonds, and the annual contribution (equal to 10 percent of the portfolio) is received on March

28 and temporarily put in cash equivalents, the portfolio's allocation as of March 31 will be distorted, even though the distortion lasts only a few days.

MOVEMENT OF CASH

To eliminate the problems associated with viewing the percentage allocation, some people feel that it is better to look at the movements of cash. This can be done in two ways: looking at purchases and sales and looking at the disposition of new cash in the portfolio.

In applying the first method, if the fund's manager in a given quarter purchased $100 in stocks and sold $30, for a net purchase of $70, this would be regarded as an indication of greater commitment to equities, and hence the subsequent performance of equities would be tracked. Although this idea has merit in principle, there are drawbacks. The first is the difficulty of achieving sufficiently detailed information as to when the purchase took place. If the typical system of using mid-month cash flows is utilized, it is possible that the fund manager purchased securities early or late in the month, when the situation was more favorable than that suggested by use of the mid-month assumption. Even if the exact timing of equity purchases and sales could be shown, there would still be a need to average purchases on the 5th of the month with sales on the 16th in some intelligible fashion. And if this problem could be solved, there is the question of how long to track the purchases before deciding that the manager did well or poorly by making them. Should we view the change in the market over the next week, month, or year? Another important limitation of this method is that heavy contributions or withdrawals may dictate making purchases or sales at times when the manager would far prefer to be doing just the opposite.

The second method, tracking new cash added to the portfolio, has two limitations. First, if there is no cash flow activity at all, there is no measurement of market timing even though there may have been significant attempts at timing the market. Further, a contribution may be used to purchase stocks, whereas shortly before or after this purchase other, more significant sales of stocks may have been made. The disposition of contributions does not provide a satisfactory basis for measuring timing. An effort might be made to look at the allocation of contributions as well as the impact of purchases and sales in order to determine the impact of both. However, it is not clear how this would be done, nor would doing it solve the problems of measuring the timing of purchases and sales and the appropriate period for viewing their results.

DOLLAR-WEIGHTED VERSUS TIME-WEIGHTED RETURNS FOR ASSET CATEGORIES

For an asset category (but not for the total portfolio) it is possible to look at the difference between dollar-weighted and time-weighted rates of return. The latter assumes that equal amounts were invested in the asset category during the whole period, whereas the former weights returns by the amount of money invested. Thus, if money were moved in and out of the equity portfolio at propitious times, dollar-weighted returns for equities would exceed time-weighted returns. Conversely, if the timing were poor, dollar-weighted returns would be less than time-weighted returns. The measurement could be carried out for each asset sector, though there appears to be no way of combining the results of various sectors unless the portfolio had no external cash flows. If there were no such cash flows, it would be possible to translate the returns into dollars and then combine the dollars in various sectors into a total portfolio measurement. However, if there were external cash flows, there is no obvious way to calculate the average amount of money impacted by the differences between dollar-weighted and time-weighted returns.

DEVIATION FROM "OPTIMUM" AND PRESCRIBED POLICIES

It is possible to establish a "market line" which shows the risk/return relationship available in the marketplace over any period. A longer period could be broken up into shorter periods, over which risk/return ratios for stocks, bonds, and cash equivalents are each calculated. The investor's bogey would then become not the actual return of some hypothetical portfolio but rather the portfolio with the averge risk/return characteristics for the period.

Perhaps the only time market timing can be measured accurately is when the sponsor prescribes a policy and deviations from this policy are measured. If the sponsor says that the policy will be to invest 70 percent in equities at all times, it is possible to look at the return of a portfolio consisting of market indexes invested at the 70 percent level and to compare its return with that of a portfolio invested at the actual quarter-by-quarter allocations of the fund. Although this method is quite satisfactory in principle, in practice few sponsors prescribe policies sufficiently to permit such a measurement.

In summary, the measurement of market timing contributions is complex and no bias-free solution appears to exist. Perhaps the only solution, then, is to choose a measurement which is easy to understand and to openly recognize its limitations, so that no one will be misled. With this viewpoint in mind, comparing the return of hypothetical funds invested in market indexes at the average with the return of the actual allocations appears to be a satisfactory approach.

CHAPTER 15

CONTROLLING THE INVESTMENT PROCESS

This chapter deals with three subjects: establishing a management review process, conducting meetings with investment managers, and integrating multiple managers. In some respects this chapter is the most important one in the book. Observation indicates that the vast majority of sponsors have not established standards, either before or after the fact, as to what constitutes acceptable results. The consequences of this lack of standards are extremely significant for funds. First, investment managers operate in the dark since they do not know how they will be measured. Second, the sponsor's representatives are frequently uneasy because they do not know whether results are acceptable or what they should do about them. Third, in many cases inadequate managers are maintained and in other cases good managers are terminated. Finally, when a manager is replaced, the same difficulties arise in dealing with the new manager, and consequently the change may be of no benefit.

THE MANAGEMENT REVIEW PROCESS

There is no reason why the general techniques for decision making applicable to other management questions cannot be applied to fund measurement. These techniques prescribe that the manager of an organization:

1. Set objectives.
2. Set allowable tolerances around those objectives.
3. Measure results.

4. Establish responses to results below the allowable tolerances.
5. Carry out the responses.
6. Review objectives, tolerances, and responses.
7. Review the allowable tolerances.
8. Review the responses.

The difficulty of invoking this process in dealing with funds lies in the fact that the achievement of a specific objective, such as earning x percent each year, is frequently overwhelmed by the activities of the marketplace. Since a portfolio's return in any given year is dominated by the return of the markets for equities or fixed-income securities, very frequently a fund does not meet its objective. In other years the objective may be far exceeded, to the point where the specific objective is dwarfed.

A solution of this problem is the use of a relative objective. Results can be viewed not only absolutely but relative to some sort of benchmark, such as a market index or the performance of other funds. Of course, this only partly alleviates the problem, since a fund which outperforms the market may nonetheless be failing to meet its objective, with disastrous consequences for those relying on the fund.

Since both relative and absolute decisions are important to the control process, it is advisable to have both relative and absolute standards. We will thus analyze both relative and absolute measures and combine the two into a workable format.

Setting Objectives

Absolute measures are aimed primarily at ensuring that the portfolio provides sufficient assets to meet the fund's needs. Let us assume that the fund has a 6 percent assumed return, meaning that the fund's assets must grow by 6 percent per year in order to meet future fund needs. This assumed rate of return would be an appropriate absolute measurement. A slightly different tack can be taken by measuring the number of dollars that are required to meet benefits and then measuring whether the fund has increased by a sufficient number of dollars to meet the fund's needs.

Relative objectives might be established such that the fund's performance is equal to some market average, or the typical portfolio in a universe of funds, or some measure of risk-adjusted return.

Setting Allowable Tolerances

In determining allowable tolerances, two factors must be considered: the size of the tolerances and the time frame in which they develop. Unfortunately, these two factors are intertwined, since tolerances which might be acceptable over a three-year period might be unacceptable over a six-month or six-year period. The first thing to be done is to decide on the normal time horizon, the frequency of measurement, and the allowable tolerances for a normal period. Then tolerances should be established for periods shorter than the nominal period.

Normal Time Horizon
The decision on the time horizon over which to judge a manager can be stated as the following question: "How long must we observe a manager so that we do not allow it to injure the fund excessively during the short run while we attempt to be sure that we do not discharge it for poor short-term performance when it might be a top performer over the long run?" Sometimes the question raised is how long should a manager be retained before it is "fair" to terminate it, but this is really not the issue. The real issue is the interest of the fund, not whether the manager's feelings are being hurt or whether business is being taken away from the manager unjustly.

The most common answer to the question of time horizon is a market cycle. This period is chosen because it allows for differences in risk postures and investment styles. It is not sensible to fire an aggressive equity manager for having poor results over a six-month period if during that period the stock market declined sharply. Continuing with the manager over a complete cycle would allow its selection ability to show up in both good times and bad. As to different investment styles, some equity managers emphasize growth stocks, others income stocks; some large companies, others small; and so on. Similarly, bond managers have different styles with respect to coupon and maturity structures. The market cannot favor all of these groups at the same time. Instead, there is group rotation in each cycle during whch different types of stocks and bonds successively take their turns as good or bad performers. Thus, there is considerable merit to the idea of measuring a manager over at least a market cycle.

The second most frequent measurement period is three to five years. However, most of the sponsors which use this time horizon relate it to the length of market cycles. Virtually all sponsors agree that periods of one month, one quarter, or even one year are inadequate measurement periods unless calamitous results befall the portfolio, or unless the measurement standard is very similar to the portfolio.

The Frequency of Measurement

The most common frequency of measurement is quarterly, followed by monthly and annual frequencies. Given the logic of the market cycle as a time horizon, quarterly reviews seem appropriate, since this frequency is sufficient to spot disastrous results in time. Monthly reviews seem to be overkill for a sponsor which uses the market cycle measurement period, since the typical market cycle of 53 months implies reviewing results 53 times before making a decision on the manager.

An interesting anomaly results for sponsors and managers after the manager has been retained for the normal time horizon. At this point the horizon appears to shrink to the period of measurement. Assume that the normal time horizon is three years, the frequency of measurement is quarterly, and the manager has been employed by the sponsor for three years. In this case the measurement period presumably is moved ahead every quarter to encompass the most recent three years, after which the manager's three-year results are reviewed. Since the results of the quarter to be dropped from the earlier period are known in advance, the only unknown factor in the three-year measurement horizon is the current quarter. Consequently, to some extent the manager who has been employed for the sponsor's time horizon becomes subject to discharge after each quarter's results are measured.

Allowable Tolerances within the Normal Time Horizon

For absolute measures, the sponsor should determine how much damage the fund can tolerate before the sponsor's goals are placed in jeopardy. For instance, the sponsor might decide that if the fund lost 15 percent per year for three years, or if it lost x dollars, the sponsor would be seriously injured. This factor would then be considered in establishing the fund's investment policy, and the allowable tolerance might be set at a loss of 5 percent per year for two years, after which the asset allocation policies and the investment manager's activities would be closely scrutinized. Assuming that the investment manager was aware of this criterion two years earlier, it should have adopted portfolio policies which would have had a high probability of avoiding such losses.

Relative measures could be established such that the fund does as well as the market index or that it is the top two thirds of the funds in an appropriate comparative universe. A custom or tailored market index could be established reflecting the fund's policies. Thus, if a fund has a long-term goal of being 60 percent in equities and 40 percent in bonds, the appropriate market index would be 60 percent of the return of an equity index plus 40 percent of the return of a fixed-income index. The difficulty of using market indexes is that they sometimes act very differently from the average portfolio. It would be difficult to justify discharging a manager for failing to equal the market index in a period such as the five years ended 1991, when approximately 68 percent of equity fund managers failed to meet this objective (see Exhibit 11–3).

A combined relative and absolute measure is probably the most logical approach. It does not seem appropriate to fire a manager who is performing better than most other managers, even though market conditions are so bad that the fund falls far short of its objective. Conversely, if a fund greatly exceeds its objective in a favorable market environment, but the manager ranks near the bottom in performance as compared to other managers, its position should be reviewed. The approach favored here is to combine absolute and relative measures, as follows.

Absolute measures should be used in determining the fund's policy. That is, the maximum damage which the fund can tolerate should be calculated, and an investment or risk policy chosen which makes it highly unlikely that the damage will be incurred. Each year both the estimate of the maximum allowable damage and the investment policy for avoiding this result should be recalculated. If the fund's asset base has changed sufficiently, or if the sponsor's needs have changed enough, the risk policy should be adjusted.

Relative objectives are appropriate for measuring the manager as opposed to the policy. That is, it is probably desirable to view the market as being substantially unpredictable, and consequently the broad swings which impact fund results so dramatically should be viewed as beyond the manager's control. This makes it difficult to hold the manager responsible for absolute results. Hence the investment policy was established with absolute results in mind. However, it is entirely plausible to measure the results of the manager against those of other managers to judge whether the performance of the manager is adequate to justify continuing the use of his services. Chapter 11 provides appropriate measurements for comparing investment performance. Thus, we must decide here only how bad the manager's performance must be to justify discontinuing his services. Although everyone would like a manager to perform in the top percentiles, it must be recognized that the odds are against a manager's being above average for a long period. However, it is also unlikely that a qualified manager will remain in the bottom third of comparable managers for a full measurement horizon, so logically performance below the 60th or 70th percentile can be viewed as inadequate to justify continuing with a manager unless contrary reasons prevail.

The distinction between using absolute and relative objectives, respectively, for evaluating policies and managers appears to be quite appropriate, with one exception. That exception is the manager which views itself as being able to time the market. Such a manager will want broad latitude both in establishing policies and in selecting securities. Fortunately, this does not present a problem for the sponsor. If the manager is a successful market timer, it will do well relative to other funds and it will also have excellent absolute results, never coming anywhere near the poor results which would dictate a change in investment policy. On the other hand, if the manager were extremely unsuccessful at market timing, it would show up poorly in both relative and absolute terms. In utilizing such a manager, the sponsor must exercise care, since the fund will lack safeguards (i.e., an investment policy which limits asset allocation) to protect it when markets move adversely. Consequently, the sponsor should be especially careful in monitoring the manager's activities during bear markets.

Responses during Time Periods Shorter than the Normal Time Horizon

Measurements should be made more frequently than the normal measurement horizon when the sponsor has to be alert to a management organization which has been delivering extremely poor results. Absolute results which should push the sponsor toward a serious review of the manager's activities before the normal time horizon include absolute declines at the annualized allowable rate. If it were allowable to lose 10 percent per year for two years, certainly losing 10 percent in one year should be of concern. For relative results, performance below the 80th percentile for a one-year period should encourage the sponsor to investigate any changes in the manager's structure or style, as well as the reasons for having chosen the particular manager.

Responding to Results below Allowable Tolerances

When absolute results fall below the standard established in advance, it is necessary to decide whether the unsatisfactory results are due to market conditions or to the activity of the investment manager, since the action to be taken differs in each case. This distinction can be made by seeing what returns the fund would have achieved if it had invested in the market or if it had invested with the average manager at the fund's policy allocations and then comparing those results with the results actually received. Assume that the risk policy is to be 60 percent in equities and 40 percent in bonds. Further assume that during this period the average equity fund returned −30 percent and the average bond fund returned −2.5 percent. As can be seen in exhibit 15–1, a fund achieving average results in equities and bonds and having our policy mix of 60 percent equities would have returned −19 percent. It is now possible to analyze the three cases where actual results could be below minimum acceptable returns and attribute the arising shortfall to either the policy or the manager.

If actual results fall below the "average" fund with our policy, the manager has subtracted from performance. This is because the manager must have underperformed the "average" fund in equities or bonds, or in market timing, in order for the fund to have underperformed the "average." If the results of the "average" fund with our policy fall below minimum acceptable returns, then the policy is a reason for the shortfall. This is because we assume that, if we have chosen the policy properly, average managers using our policy will not fall below minimum acceptable returns.

In case A, actual results were below the minimum acceptable return of −15 percent, leading to a total shortfall of 5 percentage points. Since "average" results were below the minimum acceptable return, a shortfall exists due to policy, in this instance four percentage points. Since actual results were below "average" results, the manager provided an additional shortfall, one percentage point.

A similar analysis can be made for case B and case C, where actual results also fell below minimum acceptable results.

If the problem is with the policy, the choice of policy and of any changes in the structure of the marketplace must be reassessed. If it is assumed that no change occurred in the structure of the investment marketplace, then a decision must be reached as to whether the impairment of the fund's assets has been so great that it is no longer prudent to em-

EXHIBIT 15–1

Deciding whether unacceptably low returns are due to the manager or the risk policy.

Equity/bond risk policy: 60/40
Return of average equity fund: −30 percent
Return of average bond fund: −2.5 percent
Return of the total portfolio which had average returns in both equities and bonds and had our risk policy:

$$0.6 \times -30\% = -18\%$$
$$0.4 \times -2.5\% = -\ 1\%$$
$$\overline{\qquad\qquad -19\%\qquad\qquad}$$

The three cases where actual results are below acceptable are:

A.

5% total shortfall
- Minimum acceptable return −15% } 4% shortfall due to policy
- "Average" fund with our policy −19% } 1% shortfall due to manager
- Actual results −20%

B.

4% shortfall due to policy
- Minimum acceptable return −15% } 3% total shortfall
- Actual results −18%
- "Average" fund with our policy −19% } 1% gain due to manager

C.

3% shortfall due to manager
- "Average" fund with our policy −19% } 1% gain due to policy
- Minimum acceptable return −20% } 2% total shortfall
- Actual results −22%

ploy a policy whose risks are as high as those which led to the unsuccessful results. This procedure is not without its risks, however, for two reasons. First, when the market is low, it is easy to become discouraged and to view the future with pessimism. This might cause a conservative policy to be chosen at the worst time in the market cycle. It is not easy to determine whether a structural change has occurred within the market, such that the return or risk expectations which were used to create the original policy must now be rejected in favor of less optimistic ones.

During bear markets there is always a tendency to assume that what is being witnessed is something new, whereas bear markets have occurred every 3 or 4 years for the last 70. Nonetheless, the procedure described above is the relevant procedure for making a decision.

Although not totally satisfying, that procedure is at least a rational way of reviewing investment results, and since it has a defensible methodology it is likely to achieve better results than those currently employed by many fund sponsors. Nonetheless, the sponsor is not relieved of the difficult assignment of determining whether it is appropriate to become more conservative on a long-term basis after having witnessed a severe decline in assets, despite being fully aware that the decline may be reversed dramatically in the ensuing six months to two years.

If the manager fails to meet relative standards of performance, or if the preceding analysis indicates that the manager rather than the policy is the source of the fund's unsatisfactory results, then the manager should be reviewed in detail. Through the performance measurement techniques described in Chapters 10 through 14, it will be possible to determine whether the shortfall is within the equities or fixed-income area and whether it arose from poor security selection or timing or from asset volatility. Although difficulties with the results of a manager can presumably be addressed by replacing the manager, this can be an expensive and fruitless process. Thus, it is helpful to consider ways in which such difficulties can be corrected while still retaining the manager. If securities selection is at fault, it is possible to achieve enhanced results by minimizing selection through increasing diversification. That is, the more securities the fund owns, the less chance there is of making serious errors in choosing them, although if the manager is not successful in securities selection, it may not have a justification for its fees.

If market timing is leading to poor results, this can be corrected by attempting to keep the portfolio near the guideline asset allocations. Thus, if the policy is to be 60 percent in equities, the portfolio can be "rebalanced" each quarter or month to keep within close tolerance of this goal. If the volatility of each asset category is causing unacceptable results (presumably because of an aggressive policy during a declining market), this can be the result of either the sponsor's or the investment manager's choice. It is possible that a choice for the asset category of assets with a volatility significantly different from that of the market may be frustrating the overall asset allocation policy. That is, if the fund intends to be 60 percent in equities, it is important to know whether the equities owned are to be extremely aggressive or extremely conservative. This factor should be incorporated into the overall policy decision, and it should be treated in the same way as the policy determining the allocation between stocks and bonds.

Carrying Out Responses

In all phases of the review process, a practice of openness with the investment manager is urgently required. Because of its familiarity with investment markets it may be able to make important contributions to any adjustments of the risk policy. Also, if performance results are inadequate, the manager should be apprised periodically of the sponsor's awareness of the shortcoming (if the guidelines have been sufficiently well communicated to the manager, it will already be fully aware that there has been a shortfall).

Reviewing Objectives, Tolerances, and Responses

As with any management process, it is necessary to review investment procedures and criteria periodically to ensure that they are still relevant. This process should be carried out at least annually, should receive endorsement from the highest level in the organization, and should be communicated to all parties having an impact on the success of the fund.

CONDUCTING THE REVIEW MEETING

Since most of the contact between the sponsor and the manager will occur during periodic review meetings, it is vital to the control process that these meetings be as informative as possible. Typically, this is not the case.

Most meetings between sponsors and investment managers consist of a review of economic and market forecasts and comments on the purchases and sales made in the portfolio since the last meeting. These meetings are almost always controlled by the investment manager, with the sponsor's representatives listening attentively and occasionally asking questions. Too frequently the meetings, though pleasant and perhaps interesting, are unsatisfying and insubstantive. With relatively little effort on the part of the sponsor, significant increases in the usefulness of the meetings can be achieved.

Issues for Discussion

Portfolio Structure versus the Investment Policy

The first point of business at each meeting between the client and an investment manager should be to review how the portfolio is structured in relation to the client's needs, how those needs may have changed, and anything which the investment manager sees as indicating that either the client's needs or the portfolio's structure in response to those needs may have changed. In other words, the fund's basic investment policies should be discussed at each meeting, with all of the investment policies described at the end of Chapter 3 being at least touched on. The manager should describe any changes in this structure that have taken place since the last meeting.

Portfolio Structure versus Economic and Market Forecasts

After the proper structuring of the portfolio relative to the client's long-term objective has been ensured, the next major question is to what extent the portfolio is consistent with the investment manager's economic and market observations. This area is fairly tangible, and sponsors should press hard to be sure that the portfolio manager's activities "make sense." It is surprising how frequently there can be an inconsistency between the way in which a portfolio is structured and the manager's view of the future market environment. The most classic example would be a manager who was bearish on stocks or bonds but was adding them to its portfolio. A sponsor should not tolerate such apparent inconsistencies without evidence that some other factor is making it appropriate for the manager to act opposite to its forecasts. For instance, a manager might indicate that its economic and stock market forecasts suggest that the stock market will be noticeably lower 12 months hence, but that it is buying a particular issue because the stock is extremely undervalued in light of new developments which have occurred. In view of its forecasts this manager might want to consider selling other, less-undervalued stocks in order to maintain an appropriate percentage in equities without missing the opportunity presented by the especially undervalued stock.

Since lower interest rates are generally helpful to both stock and bond portfolios, it is worth exploring why the manager sees a different outlook in this case.

The Manager's Measurement Standards for Determining Its Policy

The sponsor should be familiar with the variables that the manager is using to make decisions on the investment outlook. For instance, if the manager says that "long-term bonds will continue to do poorly," the sponsor should be aware of what category of long-term bonds the manager is talking about—all bonds, 10-year maturities, governments, corporates? A sponsor should also receive from the manager or from other sources information on historical yields, so that it can monitor the trend which is important to the investment manager. In no sense should the sponsor second-guess the manager, but if the manager is saying that the trend of interest rates is down and the sponsor's data show them to be up, then there is a need for further communication.

The Manager's Basis for Changing Its Policy

The investment manager should be pursuing a policy, but it should also have a predetermined standard for determining when that policy is wrong. In other words, if it is strongly bullish on the stock market, there must be some reason for this bullishness and some criteria which would indicate that this view was wrong. This is perhaps the area in which managers are the weakest and fund sponsors are most in the dark. A manager who was bearish because interest rates were rising, and consequently had a large cash position, should have some idea of what would be required to reverse its bearishness. It is easy for a manager to be lulled into a mistaken sense of security by having been right for a long time, only to find that the marketplace reverses itself, thus leaving the fund inappropriately structured for the coming market move. If, for instance, the manager has been bearish because of rising interest rates, a sponsor should be aware of the manager's criteria for changing this view. These criteria might include the volume of business loans (since a slackening of loan demand typically leads to lower interest rates), short-term interest rates (which typically lead long-term rates), or Federal Reserve policy.

Measuring the Manager's Previous Estimates

It is advisable for the sponsor to keep a record of the manager's predictions in order to measure its record, understand its thought processes, and see how those thought processes evolve. Certainly no one expects an investment manager to be a perfect predictor of the future, yet it does not seem to make much sense to have one who is excessively imperfect. The sponsor must try not to emphasize all of the manager's errors, of which there will be many in the area of forecasting. Of particular interest is the process by which a manager adjusts portfolios as new information suggests that past forecasts were in error. In many respects this is the acid test of an investor.

Although it is extremely important to follow the approach listed above, second-guessing must be avoided and the manager must be convinced that, though you are following his analysis, you are not expecting him to defend his previous forecasts. Rather, you are expecting him to make rational decisions in a rational way and to communicate those decisions to you. The worst thing that can happen is for a manager to feel that he must stay with a previous policy, even though he now thinks it is wrong, because he will come under more fire from the sponsor for changing his mind than for losing money with a bad policy. Although the sponsor must understand what the manager is doing, the sponsor must also make it clear to the manager that the main responsibility is with the manager and that it is perfectly appropriate to change one's mind when new facts become available. It is also appropriate, even admirable, to admit that one has been wrong.

Setting Objectives to Be Accomplished by the Next Meeting
As with any continuing process, at the end of the review meeting a summary should be made of what the meeting accomplished and of the objective to be accomplished prior to the next meeting. Further, specific responsibilities should be assigned, so that there is no doubt in anyone's mind as to what is to be done, who is to do it, and when it is to be done. As a final step, an approximate date for the next meeting should be established, so that the review process continues in an orderly fashion rather than languishing.

INTEGRATING MULTIPLE INVESTMENT MANAGERS

Controlling the investment management process is considerably more difficult for sponsors that have multiple investment managers. Further, it is more expensive to have multiple managers than to have a single manager, because virtually all investment managers charge a declining fee based on asset size. In addition, operating costs tend to be higher with multiple managers because multiple accounting and custodial systems are necessary and because the sponsor must deal with several groups rather than one. Thus, it is extremely important that sponsors choose their managers carefully and structure the way in which the managers are integrated and controlled. This chapter reviews the reasons for having multiple managers, when to consider adding a second manager, how to account for split portfolios, the criteria for deciding how to allocate new money among managers, the monitoring of multiple managers, and ways for keeping the activities of one manager from offsetting those of other managers.

Reasons for Having Multiple Managers

Three reasons for having multiple managers can be identified—for specialization, in order to diversify styles, and to diversify among organizations. Clearly, some managers have special skills which other managers do not. For instance, some managers specialize in stocks, whereas others specialize in bonds. Most sponsors feel they are unlikely to find the best bond manager and the best stock manager within the same firm, so they seek organizations which specialize in one asset category or another.

Diversification of styles is a second goal sought by sponsors which use multiple managers. Assume for a moment that half of all stocks are low-yielding growth companies, whereas the balance are high-yielding concerns with slow growth. A sponsor might wish to have representation in the entire market, but to own the best growth stocks and the best income stocks, and consequently it chooses one manager in each category.

The third goal, diversification among organizations, is indicated where managers with similar philosophies are chosen in order to minimize risks from a single manager. This practice is particularly common among large funds.

When Sponsor Should Consider Multiple Managers

There is very little tangible basis for deciding at what point, if any, a fund is better off being split among multiple managers instead of continuing to be invested solely with one manager. The most distinguishable factor is the desire for specialized skills, and this relates to the abilities of the current manager. If the current manager is unsuccessful in stocks but successful in bonds, the sponsor will tend to look to a specialty stock manager. Beyond such individual factors, most sponsors make decisions of this kind intuitively, based on the preferences of trustees or administrators. It is rare for an investment manager to indicate to a sponsor that a fund's assets have grown so large that the manager would prefer to have some of them diverted to other managers, though extremely large sponsors sometimes find small managers who will accept only relatively small amounts of money. At the other end of the spectrum, some managers are unwilling to accept accounts which are below certain minimum sizes. Although the acceptable minimum varies greatly it seems to be increasing, and it is frequently in the $5 million to $10 million range for all but the smallest investment managers. If a manager is willing to use commingled funds, almost no size is too small to be acceptable to the manager. This presumes that a commingled fund is available to the investment manager.

Criteria for Allocating New Money among Multiple Managers

Just as there is no firm basis for deciding when to have multiple managers, so there is no prescribed formula for deciding how to allocate new contributions among existing managers. Such allocations may be made equally, proportionally, according to performance, in order to maintain a risk policy, by funding a new manager, intuitively, to the most undervalued portfolio, and so on. Perhaps the simplest way to allocate new money is to give each manager an equal amount. However, this changes the proportions allocated among the managers (which may or may not be desirable). In order to keep the proportions the same, each manager can be given its pro rata share. It is also possible to divide new money by performance. Here there are two theories: give the money to the manager which has performed best or give it to the manager which has performed worst. The former theory suggests that the manager which has done a good job will continue to do well, or at least that the sponsor's odds are better if it sticks with the manager which has done well than if it goes with the manager which has done poorly. The contrary view is that the market moves in cycles and that the manager which has done well recently probably owes its success to the fact that the recent market cycle favored its investment philosophy. Since market cycles change, it is advisable to give the money to the manager which has done worst, since its poor performance was due to its participation in an unfavored sector of the market, though, hopefully, this sector will be more favored in the coming period.

New money can also be allocated to maintain a risk policy, such as the percentage in equities. If the policy is to be 60 percent in stocks and

40 percent in bonds, it makes sense to allocate 60 percent of new money to equity managers and 40 percent to fixed-income managers. Further, it is possible to allocate contributions to a new manager. Sponsors willing to make market judgments can find the manager whose portfolio style or asset category is most undervalued. The last basis, intuitive, suggests that a number of factors should be weighed and that in an informal way it should be decided where to place the new money. This is probably the way most new money is moved among managers.

The reverse process, finding a source for liquidating securities when the sponsor needs money from the fund, also presents problems. The criteria for allocating new money are also applicable to removing money. One caution is in order. During declining markets it is tempting to remove cash from the manager with the largest cash position. This may, in effect, penalize the manager who has been most successful in predicting the market's decline, and it may damage the fund by reducing the importance of the most successful manager.

Accounting for Multiple Managers

The use of multiple managers creates difficulties in accounting for assets and transactions. Although this problem is simple conceptually, the lack of uniform reporting can be a source of great frustration to a sponsor which is relying on this information for decision-making purposes. Difficulties arise in five areas: the information included in reports, the periods covered, comparisons, definitions, and the timing of receipt of reports. It is important that the information included be consistent, so that, for instance, all managers are reporting on equity and bond results as well as total portfolio returns. The period covered should also be consistent. If one manager is reporting on a moving one-year basis, whereas another manager is reporting on a "year-to-date" method, it is not possible to compare the managers.

The third area, comparisons, can also be a source of frustration. There should be uniformity in the market indexes utilized and uniform comparative universes. If one manager uses the Dow Jones average and another manager uses the S&P, or if one manager uses commingled fund comparisons and another manager uses separately managed funds, the sponsor's analytical task will be complicated. It is also necessary that consistent definitions of terms be utilized by all managers or that adjustments in definitions be made. The measurement of fixed-income performance should include or exclude accrued interest consistently, and convertible securities should be consistently defined as equities, bonds, or a separate category. Also, calculation formulas should be uniform, particularly for time-weighted returns, betas, and volatility. Finally, it is helpful for the timing of reports to be such that information on all fund managers is received at approximately the same time in order to simplify analysis.

There are three possible solutions to the problem of consistent accounting for multiple managers. The first, and the simplest, is to ask each manager to supply a summary page in a predetermined format. In this way the sponsor can determine what information is provided, the period being measured, and, to a certain extent, the comparisons, definitions, and timing. In addition, this enables the sponsor to determine the format rather than have an outside party make this decision. A sample format is given in Exhibit 15–2. The second alternative is to use outside consultant or monitoring firms which have an established format for use on all managers. Finally, a number of master trust custodial organizations provide uniform accounting facilities for multiply managed portfolios.

Monitoring Multiple Managers

Sponsors with multiple managers will probably want to measure each individual investment manager as well as the portfolio as a whole. As with the measurement of an individual portfolio, the key factors to be considered are the rates of return, risk, diversification, and the manager's contribution. Each of these factors can be looked at separately and in comparison to the market or other portfolios. The principal risk measurement that should be considered is the percentage in equities. For the overall fund this amount will depend not only on how each manager raises or lowers its exposure to the stock market but also on what the market does. Since stocks are more volatile than bonds, a rise in the stock market increases the percentage in equities. The risk level of individual sectors, such as the beta of the equity portfolio, should also be considered. Since diversification is an important reason many sponsors have multiple managers, it makes sense to measure the diversification levels of the individual parts of the portfolio as well as the diversification level of the portfolio as a whole. Finally, the contribution that each man-

EXHIBIT 15–2
Sample Format for Summary Sheet to Be Completed by Each
Investment Manager

Rates of Return

	Quarter Ending 12/91	Year Ending 12/91	Cumulative Period 12/87 – 12/91	
	Return	Return	Cumulative Return	Annual Equivalent Return
Total portfolio	5.9	22.5	75.0	11.8
Equities	8.0	32.8	96.8	14.5
S&P 500	8.4	30.4	104.0	15.3
Bonds	5.0	15.5	62.5	10.2
Salomon Bond Index	5.0	16.0	60.4	9.9
Cash and equivalents	1.7	7.1	47.6	8.1
U.S. Treasury bills	1.5	6.4	43.4	7.5

Asset allocation (as of 12/91)

	Value ($000)	Percentage of Portfolio
Equities	9,164	49.4
Bonds	6,524	35.2
Cash and equivalents	2,854	15.4
Total portfolio value	18,542	100.0

Courtesy of Merrill Lynch.

ager makes to the portfolio through securities selection and timing should be considered.

It would be useful to be able to determine each manager's contribution to the portfolio rate of return. However, this is not possible because of movements of cash both within sectors and from outside the portfolio. An alternative might be to perform a regression analysis (see Chapter 13 and Appendix) of the rates of return of each investment manager's portfolio against those of the composite portfolio for the entire fund. In this way it would be possible to see which managers were above or below the fund average in various measurements. However, though this is not conceptually difficult, it requires a fair amount of special effort. Most of this information can be obtained by looking at how the fund and each investment manager's section performed against the market rather than against the composite portfolio.

Interrelationships among Multiple Managers

One of the most frustrating aspects of having multiple managers is the knowledge that their activities occasionally tend to be offsetting. That is, manager A is increasing the percentage in equities while manager B is decreasing it, or manager C may even be buying General Motors stock while manager D is selling it. Frustrating as this may be, it is not clear what should be done about it. Sponsors do not want to see managers B and D offsetting managers A and C, except that, if B and D happen to be right, this is beneficial to the portfolio. Since there is no way of knowing which manager is correct, the sponsor cannot interfere to halt the incorrect trade. Sponsors which are concerned about this problem can do a number of things: use specialists, have mutually exclusive security lists, and require the managers to work as a team. If A manages equities and B manages bonds, it does not seem likely that the actions of these managers will offset each other.

Similarly, if growth stocks are being managed by one manager and income stocks by another, the portfolios of these managers will tend to be independent. Carrying this idea to an extreme, the managers could be assigned mutually exclusive security lists. For example, one manager could be limited to stocks A through L and another manager to stocks M through Z. Or, more logically, the two managers might themselves divide up the universe of stocks somehow, say by each taking half of the stocks in each industry or half of the industries. In all of these cases it is necessary for some control to be imposed as to the percentage in equities, or this policy decision will end up being made as a residual or leftover decision rather than through conscious choice.

Some sponsors have decided that their managers should work as a team rather than as individuals working independently or even competitively. In this case the managers meet with the sponsor, discuss policies, and establish strategies which are presumably in the interest of the sponsor and the fund. A key to the success of this method is the adoption of a payment procedure which does not penalize a manager for suggesting that his particular area of specialty is currently overvalued and that assets should therefore be taken away from him. Another problem with this method is suggested by the fact that few investment committees seem to have demonstrated greater investment ability than have individuals operating on their own. Due to the unfortunate tendency toward the herd instinct in all human affairs, including investing, this caution must be taken seriously.

Some investors have suggested, perhaps tongue in cheek, that there is one area in which it would be advisable to have managers offset one another's actions. It is known that most managers find it easier to buy securities than to sell them. Therefore, a sponsor might do well to have one investment manager making purchase decisions and another making sell decisions. It is claimed that investors have become emotionally involved with the securities which they have recommended and purchased on behalf of their clients and that they have tended to fall in love with them or they have become so used to defending them to clients that they find it impossible to sell them. This difficulty can be avoided by having a completely independent organization review the reasons for purchasing securities and giving it full discretion to sell them. Although most sponsors would find this an impractical method of operation, it is nonetheless an interesting way of trying to deal with the frequently discussed but seldom solved problem of how to get investment managers to sell securities at the proper time.

In summary, the control process utilized by a sponsor has a significant impact on the fund's success in supporting the organization. By carefully managing the review process, conducting meetings with investment managers, and integrating multiple managers, the control process can be made both comprehensive and simple. In this way the likelihood of the fund's success is greatly enhanced and all of the parties concerned will be much more comfortable about the way in which the fund is being administered.

CHAPTER 16

PRUDENCE IN MANAGING THE MANAGER: FRAUD, SPECULATION, AND BREACH OF FIDUCIARY RESPONSIBILITY

Get the facts and face the facts.

The sponsor must always keep in mind that it has control over an enormous amount of money, in the form of the fund, which, peculiarly, it has responsibility for but which does not belong to it. To make matters worse, the sponsor may not be technically qualified to make the decisions about the fund which practical necessity requires it to make, and there is substantial liability to the sponsor and some of its key employees for failure to conform properly. Therefore, it is necessary that the sponsor understand and recognize the forces which might unnecessarily "separate" the fund from its assets. These forces are fraud, speculation, and breach of fiduciary responsibility.

FRAUD

The available evidence indicates that it is relatively rare for pension funds to be defrauded. However, it is desirable to consider the possibilities of fraud, so that the sponsor can be aware of them. Perhaps the greatest potential losses might come from the massive misappropriation of securities. Since most funds do not physically hold securities, this problem exists more for the custodian than for the fund, but if securities were stolen from a custodian which did not have sufficient assets or insurance to cover the loss, the fund could lose money. Increasingly, as securities exist only as electronic bookkeeping entries, the risk of securities being physically stolen is reduced. However, the potential for computer fraud involving the misappropriation of securities may be as great as the previous potential for stealing securities.

A second area of potential fraud is the investment of fund assets at inflated prices or sale at below market value in nonarm's-length transactions For example, such as a fund invested in real estate mortgages which were based on overvaluation of the underlying asset. Following bankruptcy of the developer, there was insufficient equity in the real estate to protect the fund. In another case, stocks were bought at prices slightly in excess of the prevailing market price, with the differential illegally shared between a brokerage firm and the securities trader at the institution managing the pension funds.

A third potential area of fraud is the payment of brokerage commissions to brokers who may provide services to representatives of the investment manager or the fund sponsor rather than to the fund. Given that commission rates are negotiated, it is difficult for supervisors and auditors to determine the correct rate.

A final potential area of abuse is the purchase of unnecessary services or useful but excessively priced services. Again, though there have been extremely few instances of abuse, it is only sensible for the sponsor to be aware of ways in which people might take unfair advantage of the fund.

SPECULATION

For every dollar that is lost to pension funds through fraud, perhaps $10,000 will be lost through speculation. Speculation is probably as old as investing itself, and it is undoubtedly rooted in certain aspects of the human psyche which cause people to do what everyone else is doing and to seek something for nothing. Famous speculative binges of the past include the tulip bulb boom in Holland and the South Sea bubble in England. In the decade prior to 1929 there was tremendous speculation in commodity prices, stock prices, and Florida land prices.

EXHIBIT 16–1A

S&P 500: Quarterly Average Normalized Price/Earnings (1926 to Date)*

Median (14.6) ↓ (pointing to ~14.6)

5.0	6.0	7.0	8.0	8.5	9.0	9.5	10.0	10.5	11.0	11.5	12.0	12.5	13.0	13.5	14.0	14.5	15.0	15.5
						82-4												
						81-2												
						80-3												
						79-3												
						78-2												
						74-4												
						53-4												
						53-2												
						52-4												
						52-2												
						52-1					85-1							
					81-3	51-4	84-2	84-4			77-1				74-2	70-2	86-1	
					80-1	51-3	83-1	84-3			75-4			85-4	70-3	57-1	74-1	
					79-4	51-2	81-1	84-1			75-3			48-2	58-2	55-2	58-3	
					79-2	51-1	80-4	77-3	83-4	54-3	85-3	76-3	48-2	45-1	55-1	47-3	57-3	
					79-1	50-4	78-3	74-3	83-3	44-2	85-2	76-2	45-1	47-4	45-2	57-2		
					78-4	50-2	77-4	54-2	83-2	43-3	76-4	76-1	40-1					
					78-1	50-1	54-1	43-1	77-2	43-2	75-2	58-1	39-3	47-2	39-1	47-1		
	33-1				81-4	53-3	49-4	53-1	41-3	75-1	40-4	48-3	57-4	38-1	39-4	38-3	46-4	88-3
	32-4	82-3			80-2	50-3	42-4	52-3	41-1	48-4	40-2	48-1	54-4	33-4	27-1	37-4	45-3	70-4
	32-3	82-2	82-1	42-3	49-3	41-4	49-1	40-3	44-1	38-2	44-4	39-2	33-3	26-4	27-2	38-4	56-4	
32-2	32-1	31-4	42-2	42-1	49-2	33-2	41-2	31-3	43-4	31-2	44-3	30-4	31-1	26-4	26-3	26-1	27-3	

Decile Distribution

First decile	Below 9.7	} Stocks cheap
Second decile	9.7 to 10.5	
Third decile	10.5 to 11.8	
Fourth decile	11.8 to 13.2	
Fifth decile	13.2 to 14.6	
Sixth decile	14.6 to 16.2	
Seventh decile	16.2 to 17.3	
Eighth decile	17.3 to 18.6	} Stocks expensive
Ninth decile	18.6 to 20.6	
Now → Tenth decile	20.6 and above	

Median: 14.6

Average: 14.9

High quartile: 18.8x earnings and above

Low quartile: Below 11.1x earnings

*264 quarters.

1. The numbers on the table, such as "91-4," indicate 1991's fourth-quarter average normalized P/E (18.6).

2. "Normalized" earnings employed here are five-year average earnings, based on the last 20 quarters of earnings (4th quarter 1991 estimated). This is a simple way to iron out cyclical distortions. Since earnings are far more cyclical than book value or dividends, we think a smoothing technique is essential when making comparisons. In addition, errors in future earnings forecasts are not a factor.

			91-1																
		90-3	90-1																
		89-2	71-4																
90-4		86-4	71-1																
88-4	89-1	73-3	69-3			87-1													
88-2	87-4	69-4	66-4	90-2		72-3													
88-1	86-3	60-4	59-4	73-2	91-4	72-2	73-1												
70-1	86-2	60-3	59-3	71-3	91-3	72-1	68-3												
56-1	73-4	60-2	59-2	66-3	91-2	69-2	67-3				66-1		65-4						
55-4	58-4	60-1	46-3	62-4	89-4	69-1	67-2				65-3		65-2						
55-3	56-3	59-1	35-1	62-3	89-3	68-2	63-1	87-2			62-1		64-4						
30-3	56-2	45-4	30-1	46-1	71-2	67-4	62-2	72-4	63-3	87-3	37-3		64-3					37-1	
28-1	34-3	34-4	28-3	30-2	68-1	61-1	46-2	68-4	63-2	63-4	29-2	64-1	64-2	65-1				36-3	
27-4	34-1	34-2	28-2	29-4	67-1	35-2	28-4	66-2	61-2	61-3	29-1	61-4	35-3	37-2	29-3	35-4	36-2	36-1	36-4
16.0	16.5	17.0	17.5	18.0	18.5	19.0	19.5	20.0	20.5	21.0	21.5	22.0	22.5	23.0	24.0	25.0	26.0	27.0	28.0

Investors can benefit from having some feeling as to the level of securities prices compared to historical levels. Presumably, the higher the level currently, the more risk and the less expected return. The Leuthold Group provides useful information on a number of variables, including price earnings ratios, dividend yields, price to book value ratios, bond yields, and inflation rates (see Exhibit 16–1A through E).

Speculation can occur in high-quality securities as well as in more aggressive securities. It is interesting to note the surge in utility stock prices in the early 1960s, as shown in Exhibit 16–2.

Although speculation in individual securities is an everyday occurrence, it is fascinating to look at the case of silver, a commodity which moved far above any historical or rational value and then declined to its previous level. This is seen in Exhibit 16–3, where the price of silver presents one of the greatest examples in recent years of a speculative boom-and-bust.

It is admittedly difficult to distinguish between speculation and investment. Some cynics suggest that an investment is a speculation if the investor lost but an investment if he or she succeeded. Presumably

EXHIBIT 16–1B
S&P 500: Quarterly Average Yields (1926 to Date)*

```
                                                               Median
                                                               (4.25%)
                                                                  ↓
                                                               |85-3|
                                                               |85-2|
                                                               |83-4|
                                                               |83-3|
                                                               |83-2|
              |73-3|                                           |77-1|
              |71-3|                                           |75-4|
              |71-2|                        |90-3|             |75-3||84-4|
              |69-2|                        |88-4|             |75-2||84-3|
              |69-1|                        |88-3|             |58-1||84-2|
              |68-2|                        |88-2|             |39-1||83-1|
         |87-1||67-4||91-4|            |89-1||88-1|            |37-1||80-4|
         |73-2||67-3||91-3|            |87-4||86-1|      |85-4||36-4||85-1||77-3|
    |87-2||68-3||65-3||91-2|      |91-1||74-1||76-3||57-3||76-4||36-3||84-1||75-1|
    |72-1||66-1||63-4||71-4| |90-2||89-2||70-4||76-2||56-4||70-3||35-3||77-2||54-4|
    |68-4||65-4||63-3||71-1||89-3||89-4||60-4||70-1||76-1||56-3||70-2||33-3||57-4||47-1|
|87-3||64-3||65-2||61-1||68-1||73-4||86-4||60-3||66-4||57-2||56-2||90-4||58-2||30-2||55-1||39-3|
|73-1||62-1||65-1||59-4||67-2||69-3||86-3||60-2||66-3||55-1||56-1||74-2||55-2||30-1||45-3||33-4|
|72-4||61-4||64-4||59-3||66-2||67-1||86-2||60-1||62-4||46-2||55-3||57-1||46-3||29-4||45-2||30-3|
|72-3||61-3||64-2||59-2||63-2||63-1||69-4||29-2||62-3||36-1||46-1||45-4||36-2||28-3||34-2||27-4|
|72-2||61-2||64-1||29-3||59-1||62-2||58-4||29-1||58-3||35-4||28-4||38-4||34-1||28-2||28-1||27-3|

 2.5  2.6  2.7  2.8  2.9  3.0  3.1  3.2  3.3  3.4  3.5  3.6  3.7  3.8  3.9  4.0  4.2  4.4  4.6
```

Decile Distribution

First decile	7.09% and above	⎫ Stocks
Second decile	7.09% to 5.84%	⎬ cheap
Third decile	5.84% to 5.11%	⎭
Fourth decile	5.11% to 4.66%	
Fifth decile	4.66% to 4.25%	
Sixth decile	4.25% to 3.90%	
Seventh decile	3.90% to 3.64%	
Eighth decile	3.64% to 3.32%	⎫ Stocks
Ninth decile	3.32% to 3.06%	⎬ expensive
Now → Tenth decile	Below 3.06%	⎭

Median: 4.25%
Average: 4.43%
High quartile: 5.26% and above
Low quartile: 3.50% and below

*264 quarters.

The high yields in the early 1930s noted on the histogram are misleading and prevailed only momentarily, as dividends were cut sharply during the Depression. At the other end, the extreme low yields in 1972 were the product of nifty fifty frenzy. In 1987's third quarter, yields fell below even that extreme, recording an all time low!

4.8	5.0	5.2	5.4	5.6	5.8	6.0	6.2	6.4	6.6	6.8	7.0	7.25	7.50	.75	8.0	.25	.50	9.0+
		81-3																
		80-1																
		79-3																
		79-2																
		79-1																
		78-4																
		78-2																
		74-4																
	82-4	54-2																
	80-3	48-2																
81-2	78-3	47-3				82-3												
81-1	77-4	47-2	81-4			82-2												
74-3	44-4	44-2	80-2			53-4												
54-3	44-3	44-1	79-4			53-3												
46-4	43-3	43-4	78-1			52-2						51-2						
45-1	43-2	40-1	53-1	54-1	82-1	52-1						50-3						
39-2	39-4	35-1	48-3	52-4	53-2	51-4			51-3	50-1	51-1	42-3	50-4					
37-2	37-3	27-1	38-3	47-4	52-3	48-4	42-4		50-2	49-3	49-4	41-2	41-4					
35-2	34-4	26-4	33-2	43-1	30-4	48-1	40-4		49-1	41-3	49-2	38-1	33-2			42-2		32-2
34-3	27-2	26-3	26-1	31-1	26-2	40-2	31-2	31-3	40-3	41-1	37-4	32-4	33-1		42-1	32-3	31-4	32-1

the courts look at the reasoning process which went into recommending the investment rather than the results. Given sound business judgment behind the investment decision, no conflicts of interest, an adequately diversified portfolio, and appropriately addressed liquidity needs, the investor can feel confident that he or she is in fact investing rather than speculating.

Protection against speculation requires exercising common sense, which is perhaps the most valuable asset that any investor or investment manager can have. The sponsor watching over investment managers must attempt to understand what its managers are doing and to view those activities as objectively as possible. He must constantly ask the question, "Does this make sense?" Relative valuation yardsticks should be kept of such broad investment factors as stock market levels, price/earnings ratios (see Exhibit 16–1), and spreads and interest rate levels (Exhibit 16–4). It is unrealistic to expect the future to be exactly like the past, but clearly there is something to be learned from studying the past.

EXHIBIT 16–1C
S&P 400 Industrials: Quarterly Average Book Value Ratio (1926 to Date)*

Median (1.50) — arrow points down to the 1.50 column.

.40	.50	.60	.70	.80	.90	1.00	1.05	1.10	1.15	1.20	1.25	1.30	1.35	1.40	1.45	1.50	1.55	1.60
						81-4												
						79-4												
						79-3												
						79-2												
						79-1	81-3											
						78-4	80-1	82-4										
						53-4	78-2	80-3										
						53-2	77-4	78-3										
						50-4	54-1	75-1										
	49-3			82-3		48-2	52-4	74-3								83-4		
	49-2			82-2	80-2	47-4	52-2	53-1							83-2	83-3		
	49-1			82-1	78-1	47-2	52-1	52-3							84-3	76-3		
	42-4			50-3	74-4	44-4	51-4	51-3	81-2	83-1					84-2	76-2		
	41-4			50-1	53-3	44-3	51-2	47-1	81-1	80-4					84-1	76-1		
	41-2			48-1	50-2	44-2	51-1	46-4	77-3	77-2					77-1	74-2		
	42-3	35-1	49-4	43-1	48-3	43-3	47-3	40-1	54-2	75-4	75-2				84-4	58-2		
	42-2	34-4	48-4	41-3	44-1	43-2	45-1	39-3	45-3	75-3	54-3				76-4	54-4		
33-1	42-1	34-2	35-2	41-1	43-4	39-2	37-4	39-1	45-2	38-4	46-3			58-1	46-1			85-1
32-4	34-3	33-3	34-1	40-3	40-4	38-1	31-1	38-3	39-4	35-4	27-1			57-4	36-1			36-2
32-2	32-3	32-1	31-4	33-2	33-4	31-3	31-2	38-2	40-2	35-3	30-4	26-2	26-1	26-3	26-4	45-4	27-2	30-3

Decile Distribution

First decile	Below 1.05	⎫ Stocks
Second decile	1.05 to 1.18	⎬ cheap
Third decile	1.18 to 1.25	⎭
Fourth decile	1.25 to 1.33	
Fifth decile	1.33 to 1.50	
Sixth decile	1.50 to 1.68	
Seventh decile	1.68 to 1.89	
Eighth decile	1.89 to 2.03	⎫ Stocks
Ninth decile	2.03 to 2.20	⎬ expensive
Now → Tenth decile	2.20 and above	⎭

Median: 1.50
Average: 1.56
High quartile: 1.96 and above
Low quartile: Below 1.22

*264 quarters.

```
                              88-3
                              88-2
                              88-1
                              87-4
                              73-1
                    73-2      72-4
                    71-3 86-4 69-2
                    71-1 86-3 69-1
               86-1 69-4 86-2 68-3
               73-3 69-3 72-3 68-2
               71-4 67-1 72-2 67-4
85-3           70-1 63-4 72-1 67-3
85-2           59-4 63-3 71-2 66-1
74-1 85-4      73-4 59-1 61-3 68-1 65-4
70-3 60-4 70-4 66-4 56-4 61-2 67-2 65-3
70-2 60-3 60-2 62-2 56-1 66-3 59-3 66-2 65-2
63-1 57-2 58-4 60-1 36-4 63-2 56-3 64-1 65-1                90-1 90-3
58-3 62-4 57-1 57-3 55-4 30-2 61-1 37-1 62-1 64-4 88-4 90-4 89-2 89-4 91-1      91-4
55-1 62-3 36-3 37-3 55-3 30-1 59-2 29-4 61-4 64-3 68-4 89-1 29-2 89-3 90-2      91-3
46-2 55-2 27-3 37-2 27-4 28-1 56-2 28-2 28-3 64-2 28-4 87-1 29-1 87-2 29-3 87-3 91-2
─────────────────────────────────────────────────────────────────────────────────────
1.65 1.70 1.75 1.80 1.85 1.90 1.95 2.00 2.10 2.20 2.30 2.40 2.50 2.60 2.70 2.80 2.90 3.00 3.50
```

BREACH OF FIDUCIARY RESPONSIBILITY

To understand where abuses of fiduciary responsibility may arise and how the government views them, it is interesting to note the suits that have been filed by private individuals and by the government, principally the Secretary of Labor. Two areas of particular interest are imprudence in investing that results from poor judgment and from conflicts of interest. A brief review of cases on these topics appears below.

Imprudent Investment that Resulted from Poor Judgment

Inadequate Diversification and Speculation
A number of court cases have provided insight into the important but imprecisely defined section of ERISA which requires trustees to act in the interest of participants and beneficiaries "with the care, skill, prudence, and diligence" of a prudent, knowledgeable person and "by diversifying the investments of the plan so as to minimize the risk of large losses,

EXHIBIT 16–1D
Quality U.S. Corporate Bond Average Annual Yields (1790 to Date)*

Median (4.85%)

←— Low quartile —→

2.5%	.6	.7	.8	.9	3%	.25	.50	.75	4%	.25	.50	.75	5%	.25
													1960	
													1959	
													1875	
										1965			1858	
										1964		↓	1856	
										1962			1853	
							1956			1957			1852	1921
							1934			1932			1851	1920
							1910			1929	1961		1843	1872
						1953	1909		1963	1925	1919		1840	1871
						1935	1906		1933	1924	1918		1838	1868
						1905	1893	1958	1931	1923	1864		1837	1867
						1904	1892	1916	1930	1922	1863		1836	1857
					1955	1903	1891		1914	1928	1859		1832	1855
						1902	1896	1890	1912	1927	1876	1844	1831	1854
	1950					1901	1895	1888	1911	1926		1835	1830	1850
	1949				1952	1900	1894	1887	1908	1915	1827	1834	1823	1849
1946	1947			1954	1951	1899	1889	1886	1907	1913	1826	1833	1822	1845
1945	1943	1942		1948	1937	1898	1884	1883	1885	1879	1825	1829	1821	1839
1944	1941	1940	1939	1938	1936	1897	1882	1881	1880	1878	1824	1828	1792	1820
2.5%	**.6**	**.7**	**.8**	**.9**	**3%**	**.25**	**.50**	**.75**	**4%**	**.25**	**.50**	**.75**	**5%**	**.25**

Historical Decile Distribution of High Quality Bond Yields

200 years of average annual yields

First decile	7.70% and above
Second decile	6.00% to 7.70%
Third decile	5.50% to 6.00%
Fourth decile	5.10% to 5.50%
Fifth decile	4.85% to 5.10%
Sixth decile	4.55% to 4.85%
Seventh decile	4.15% to 4.55%
Eighth decile	3.70% to 4.15%
Ninth decile	3.20% to 3.70%
Now → Tenth decile	Below 3.20%

Median: 4.25%
Average: 4.43%

High quartile: 5.26% and above
Low quartile: 3.50% and below

*202 Year Average: 5.22%

1. Over this entire period, the median yield is 4.85%, the average 5.22% and the mode 5%. There are two periods in the chart that are clearly outliers, very abnormal.

2. At one extreme is the period 1939–1950. For much of this period the Treasury and the Federal Reserve Bank Board kept interest rates pegged, fixing long term government bonds at 2.5% and T-bills at 0.38%.

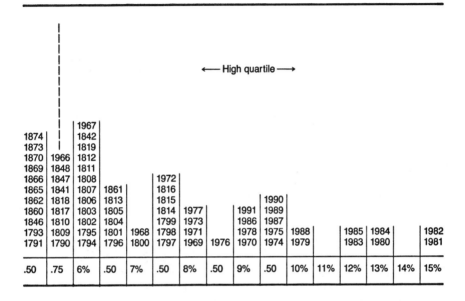

3. The other extreme occurred over the last 20 years when the rates have been in excess of 8%. Never before in the U.S. history have high quality credits paid interest at these levels. One bond index of Railroad bonds did approach 10% levels in the 1860s, but many of the Railroad bonds included in that index were high bankruptcy risks not quality credits. (We used New England Municipals as the quality index during this period.)

4. Sidney Homer's classic tome *A History of Interest Rates*, tracking interest rate history back over 1,000 years, confirms that rates exceeding 8% have prevailed only in nations experiencing hyperinflation or in situations involving poor credit risks. Historically, 6% has been a pretty high rate of interest to pay or receive.

unless under the circumstances it is clearly prudent not to do so." [Section 404(B).] The case of *Ray Marshall, Secretary of the U.S. Department of Labor* v. *Teamsters Local 282 Pension Trust Fund* is of interest because it provides some authority on two areas, speculation and lack of diversification. In this case the Secretary of Labor brought action to stop the trustees of a pension fund from making a proposed loan. The fund had intended to lend $20 million under a construction-permanent mortgage to finance a hotel and gambling casino in Las Vegas. The fund had assets of $55 million, which was less than its actuarial liabilities. Further, its current contributions were less than its current actuarial costs. The loan could not be made because the court ruled that the project

EXHIBIT 16–1E
Annual Inflation Rates (%) (1792 to 1991)

Median (1.20%)

−16	−14	−12	−10	−8	−7	−6	−5	−4	−3	−2	−1	0	1	2
														1965
														1960
										1938		1955		1952
										1930		1954		1945
										1927		1936		1944
										1891		1929		1935
										1889		1924		1925
										1886		1911	1986	1923
										1885		1909	1964	1901
										1883		1905	1963	1900
										1879		1904	1962	1897
										1874		1896	1961	1890
										1873		1893	1959	1888
										1860		1865	1956	1887
										1859	1949	1851	1953	1882
										1856	1939	1837	1950	1857
										1843	1928	1833	1940	1855
							1933			1838	1913	1832	1926	1846
			1932				1876			1834	1892	1829	1915	1844
			1921	1931		1922	1875	1877	1908	1810	1871	1821	1914	1839
			1858	1894		1884	1866	1868	1869	1808	1867	1817	1898	1823
1840		1870	1820	1828	1807	1878	1848	1841	1849	1806	1861		1872	1803
1802	1816	1815	1819	1826	1797	1824	1795	1830	1842	1798	1818	1799	1852	1800

← Deflation   Inflation →

Decile Distribution

	First decile	−5.8% and below
	Second decile	−5.8% to −2.2%
	Third decile	−2.2% to −1.0%
	Fourth decile	−1.0% to +0.3%
	Fifth decile	+0.3% to +1.2%
	Sixth decile	+1.2% to +2.1%
Now →	Seventh decile	+2.1% to +3.9%
	Eighth decile	+3.9% to +5.8%
	Ninth decile	+5.8% to +9.4%
	Tenth decile	+9.4% and above

Average: +1.73%
Median: +1.20%

1. Inflation is now accepted by most as a fact of life. The lowest inflation in recent years was 1986's +1.2%. Prior to this, 1955 had "zero" inflation. The most recent "deflation" year as measured by the CPI was 1949.

2. Historically, 32.5% of the years on the histogram are "deflation" years, while another 11% are "zero" inflation years. Price stability (2% deflation to 2% inflation) has prevailed almost half the time (46%) in our history.

3	4	5	6	7	8	9	10	12	14	16	18	20	30	40
	1988													
	1987													
	1985													
	1984													
	1983													
	1982													
	1971													
1991	1968													
1972	1957	1989	1990											
1967	1937	1969	1977			1981								
1966	1910	1941	1976			1978								
1958	1907	1850	1973		1951	1975								
1934	1906	1825	1970	1899	1948	1836		1980	1979		1918			
1912	1903	1811	1943	1831	1946	1835		1814	1947		1917			
1847	1902	1796	1881	1812	1916	1827	1974	1809	1919	1920	1863			
1845	1854	1792	1880	1801	1804	1805	1942	1794	1853	1813	1862		1793	1864
3	**4**	**5**	**6**	**7**	**8**	**9**	**10**	**12**	**14**	**16**	**18**	**20**	**30**	**40**

was excessively risky, that the proposed mortgage rate of 9¾ percent was only fractionally above that carried by "Ginnie Mae" securities guaranteed by the U.S. government, and that the loan represented too large a portion of the fund's assets.

Expected Return Inadequate Relative to Risk
In *Marshall* v. *Fitzsimmons et al.*, the Secretary of Labor sued various trustees and related parties of the Central States Teamsters' Pension Fund for, among other things, making a $30 million loan secured by a casino in Las Vegas. The interest rate was deemed inadequate relative to the risk taken.

Failure to Collect Loans in Default
In *Marshall* v. *Wilson et al.* and *Marshall* v. *Fitzsimmons et al.*, the Secretary of Labor filed suit under ERISA, claiming that the trustees had not taken action to collect loans in default.

EXHIBIT 16–2

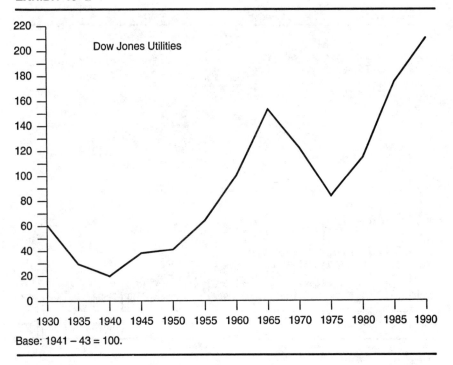

Dow Jones Utilities

Base: 1941 – 43 = 100.

Source: Dow Jones & Company

The case of *Marshall* v. *Fitzsimmons et al.* contains other charges which might be viewed as representing poor judgment in the investment area. These include:

Failure to obtain an independent and reliable appraisal of properties prior to making a loan.

Failure to obtain sufficient reliable information regarding the financial condition of the borrower before the loan was made and before granting a moratorium on payments following a delinquency in receipt of interest.

Failure to enforce the right of the plan to the assignment of rents when interest payments were delinquent.

EXHIBIT 16–3
Index of Silver Prices

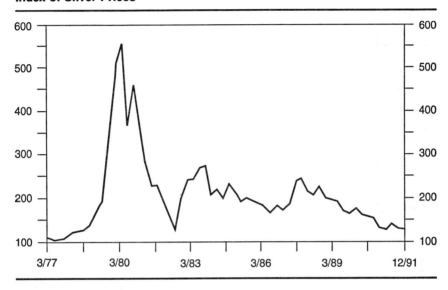

Source: Comex Closing Prices December 31, 1976 = 100

EXHIBIT 16–4
Long-Term Bond Yields Quarterly Averages (percent per annum)

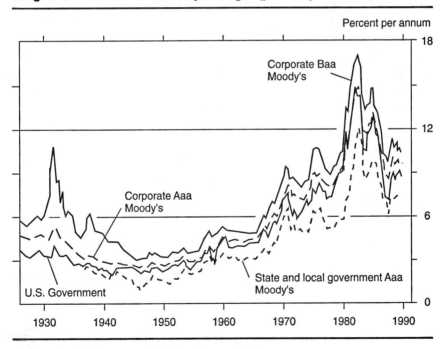

Source: Board of Governors of the Federal Reserve System

Failure to monitor the borrower's performance adequately under the terms of the loan agreement.

Failure to cease making loans when the value of the security and the likelihood of repayment were such that further disbursements were imprudent.

Making a loan to a cable TV company without adequately assessing the economic feasibility of the operation.

Failure to pursue the guarantor of the defaulted loan.

Imprudent Investment that Resulted from Conflicts of Interest

Usery (Secretary of Labor) v. Penn
In this case the buyer of a company had been made the trustee of its profit-sharing plan, at which time he immediately used the assets of the plan to purchase 97 percent of the shares outstanding from the company's former owner.

O'Neil v. Marriott Corp.
The trustees of a plan were officers and major shareholders of the sponsor, and the major asset of the plan was shares of the sponsor. The plaintiffs charged that the trustees of the plan were in a position of conflict of interest since they were insiders to the activities of the company and were also major company shareholders themselves. For both of these reasons the trustees were said to be inhibited from acting in the sole interest of the plan participants.

Marshall (Secretary of Labor) v. Snyder et al.
In this case the officers of the union controlled the pension plans and the firm which was the administrative agent of the plan. The complaint alleged that the plan trustees permitted the unwarranted expenditure of plan assets, including a $1 million loan to one defendant, a $380,000 outlay to refurbish the union headquarters, and $300,000 to purchase stock from the administrative agent. These other interesting points of law were noted in this case:

1. Just because a previous consent order established maximum compensation to be paid to parties of interest, these amounts were not necessarily reasonable. The trustees still had a fidu-

ciary responsibility to see that only reasonable fees were paid for services rendered.

2. The burden of proof as to the appropriateness of a transaction between a party in interest and the fund is on the person involved in a transaction, not on the person challenging it.

3. A fiduciary who serves as an employee, agent, or other representative of a party in interest still remains subject to the party in interest prohibitions of ERISA.

4. It is not necessarily sufficient for a fiduciary who breaches his duties to make good the losses resulting from the breach. Other remedies may also be appropriate. In this case a receiver was appointed to take over responsibility from the trustees who were charged with breach of duty.

Additional Cases Showing Conflicts of Interest

In the case of *Marshall* v. *Deep South Electric et al.* the preponderance of the fund's assets was in receivables, of which over 90 percent were based on loans made to the plan sponsor, with the remainder attributable to loans to a company owned by the plan trustee. Interestingly, since the loans had been negotiated before the effective date of ERISA, the Labor Department acknowledged that there was no duty under ERISA to see that they were adequately secured. However, the Labor Department felt that the trustees had a fiduciary responsibility to seek repayment of the loans once they were in default and ERISA had taken effect.

One of the most unusual cases brought by the Labor Department was *Marshall* v. *Conser et al.*, in which the plaintiff was alleged to have failed to act in the best interests of the plan participants because the fiduciary attempted to resign without appointing a successor trustee. The court recognized the severity of the problem, but instead of stopping the trustee from resigning, it approved a new trustee to serve the plan.

Conflicts of interest arise because of the ERISA requirement that employee benefit plans be operated "solely in the interest of participants and beneficiaries, and for the exclusive purpose of providing benefits to participants and beneficiaries and defraying reasonable expenses of plan administration."

The case against the Central States Teamsters contains a number of accusations of breach of fiduciary responsibility which serve aptly to demonstrate various problem areas. This is demonstrated in the following sentence:

7. Defendants, during their respective tenure as plan fiduciaries, breached their fiduciary obligations by failing to discharge their duties with respect to the plan solely in the interest of its participants and beneficiaries, and for the exclusive purpose of providing benefits to participants and beneficiaries and defraying reasonable expenses of plan administration, and with the care, skill, prudence, and diligence under the circumstances then prevailing that a prudent man acting in a like capacity and familiar with such matters would use in the conduct of an enterprise of a like character and with like aims, in violation of ERISA §§404(a)(1)(A) and (B), 29 U.S.C. §§1104(a)(1)(A) and (B), by, among other things:

a. failing to adhere to procedures designed to and which would in fact ensure that adequate information was available to them for consideration in connection with decisions concerning the management of plan assets;

b. failing to employ, retain, and consult with an adequate staff of persons whose professional background, skill, and experience would enable them to make appropriate recommendations with respect to the management of plan assets;

c. entering into commitments to disburse and disbursing plan assets for ventures as to which they had, at the time of such action, insufficient information to make a prudent judgment as to the economic feasibility of such ventures, the degree of risk thereof, and the probable security of plan assets devoted thereto;

d. entering into commitments to disburse and disbursing plan assets in transactions which were imprudent because the plan's expected return in or as a result of such transactions was not commensurate with the plan's risk of loss therein;

e. failing to enforce the plan's right to compliance, by persons who were borrowers of plan assets, with the terms of loan agreements, security agreements, and other undertakings, when compliance with such undertakings by the borrowers would have tended to benefit the plan;

f. surrendering rights, security interests, and other assets of the plan in exchange for no consideration or inadequate consideration to the plan;

g. granting modifications of agreements controlling the obligations of borrowers of plan assets, granting moratoria on the payment of principal and interest required by such original agreements, making new extensions of credit and otherwise restructuring the terms of such agreements to the advantage of borrowers and the disadvantage of the plan, when such modifications were not calculated to increase the likelihood of repayment, the value of the plan's security, or the return on its investment;

h. failing to monitor the use of loan proceeds by borrowers of plan assets, when loan agreements required that such use be limited to specific purposes related to improvements on property in which the plan held security interests;

i. failing to act diligently and promptly to secure protection of the plan's tangible property from damage, enforce the plan's right to have borrowers obtain insurance for and pay taxes relating to property held as collateral, and record mortgage instruments on property held as collateral for loans;

j. failing to exercise the plan's options to demand payment of loans from borrowers, to cease making advances to borrowers in default on their obligations, and to demand payment from guarantors;

k. causing the payment of plan assets to persons and on behalf of persons having no claims against the plan and without consideration to the plan; and

l. failing to pursue claims of restitution on behalf of the plan against persons who have diverted plan assets or otherwise unlawfully derived benefit from the plan to the plan's detriment.[1]

THE BLIND FIDUCIARY

The importance of being careful, prudent, and thoughtful should be emphasized. But it should not be the only factor in making decisions. Sponsors should be responsible fiduciaries, not blind fiduciaries. The blind fiduciary views the world from only one point of view, that of the person who claims to be looking out for beneficiaries but who is actually looking out for himself or herself.

That person has the following characteristics:

Does only what others do.

Sees only risk and not return.

Prefers short-run stability of principal to long-run growth.

Ignores inflation.

Reads into ERISA prohibitions which do not exist, such as against use of futures, leverage, short selling, and alternative investments.

---

[1]U.S. Department of Labor Complaint against Teamsters Central States Pension Fund, Civil Action 78C342; quoted from *BNA Pension Fund Reporter* Bureau of National Affairs, Inc., February 6, 1978, no. 174, p. R-1

Hires only big firms with deep pockets, in case things go badly. Hires only firms with good recent track records, regardless of how overvalued their styles are or how undervalued other styles are.

APPENDIX

CHECKLIST OF FIDUCIARY RESPONSIBILITY

To ensure that a fund is being properly managed and to help satisfy fiduciary obligations, sponsors should ask themselves whether they have exercised prudence in:

1. Analyzing what it is that the organization wants from the fund.   Yes____ No____
2. Assigning responsibility for the fund to a person or group within the organization, including degrees of responsibility and authority.   Yes____ No____
3. Analyzing the fund's needs and stating an investment policy.
Yes____ No____
4. Periodically reviewing those needs and the policy (at least annually).   Yes____ No____
5. Hiring investment managers, including an analysis of how the investment managers' particular skills are applicable to the fund's specific needs.   Yes____ No____
6. Delegating investment responsibility to the investment managers and securing their acknowledgment that they are fiduciaries under ERISA.   Yes____ No____
7. Continuing the use of investment managers, including an analysis of whether the fund has met its financial goals and of how the fund's performance compares to appropriate indexes and universes on an absolute basis and on a risk-adjusted basis.   Yes____ No____
8. Reviewing fund assets to be sure that the portfolio is adequately diversified.   Yes____ No____
9. Providing adequate information for the investment manager about the fund's policies, objectives, and measurement standards.   Yes____ No____

10. Establishing procedures of communication between the investment manager and the sponsor. Yes_____ No_____

11. Being sure that all interested parties (sponsor's representative, investment manager, actuary, lawyer, accountant, etc.) are operating with the same guidelines. Yes_____ No_____

12. When making direct loans of the fund's assets, establishing and continuing to monitor the economic feasibility of the venture, the adequacy of the security, the record of the borrower as to past success, and the financial condition of the borrower. Yes_____ No_____

13. Being aware of the activities of cofiduciaries and of any potential conflicts of interest or other breaches. Yes_____ No_____

14. Taking action when this is warranted by conditions. Yes_____ No_____

15. Documenting all activities, so that a historical record indicates adequate analysis and prudence for all decisions. Yes_____ No_____

CHAPTER 17

MANAGING THE CUSTODIAL PROCESS

ANALYSIS

Although the choice of the investment manager has a far greater impact on the fund than the choice of the custodian, the fund sponsor's daily life will be much simpler if the custodian is operating efficiently. Consequently, it is advisable that great care be exercised in choosing a custodian. The key factors in an organization's ability to provide effective custodial service are:

1. The financial stability of the organization.
2. The adequacy of security procedures.
3. The accuracy of recordkeeping.
4. The scope of recordkeeping/analysis.
5. Timeliness.
6. Consulting and other special services.
7. Cost.

Financial Stability

Since the cash in the sponsor's portfolio is commingled, at least temporarily, with that of other customers of the custodian, as well as with the funds of the custodial organization itself, it is essential that the custodial organization have sufficient capital, antifraud safety procedures, management controls, and insurance to provide safety for the sponsor's assets.

Although it is hoped that the appropriate regulatory authorities will take adequate care in overseeing custodial organizations, nonetheless the sponsor should consider these factors before choosing a custodian.

Adequacy of Security Procedures

Safekeeping of the physical securities owned by trusts has become less important with the growth of the Depository Trust Company and other central depositories. The DTC holds vast amounts of securities and issues electronic records against them, much as a bank issues statements against a checking account. The development of the DTC helps eliminate wasteful and costly effort and minimizes security risks. Presumably, at some point in the future, few physical securities will exist and most transactions in securities will be carried out without physically transferring the securities. Nevertheless, the sponsor should consider the adequacy of security procedures in choosing a custodian.

Accuracy of Recordkeeping

No matter how complete and timely, the records provided by the custodian to the fund sponsor have little value unless they are credible to all parties. Therefore, it is extremely important that the custodial organization provide accurate information. Sponsors can take two steps in order to gain confidence that accurate information will be provided, though typically they only use a third method. The third method is to ask the custodial organization whether its process produces accurate information. A more reliable method is to discuss the custodial organization's error-checking procedures with its representative. Details should be obtained regarding manual checks and checks built into computer programs which produce custodial reports, including exception reports which are printed when unusual results occur. Finally, existing customers can be questioned as to the success of the custodian in this all-important area of accurate reporting.

Scope of Recordkeeping/Analysis

This area can be further broken down into basic recordkeeping, regulatory information, analysis, and comparison. The basic recordkeeping information required is periodic positions and transaction statements. A beginning balance of cash and securities in the account is shown as the initial position. Following that, every transaction which affects the cash balance or the securities held is reported in the cash or transaction statements. Finally, an ending position is shown.

Items affecting cash are the receipt of income, purchases and sales, and contributions and withdrawals. Factors affecting the balance of securities, in addition to purchases and sales, are stock splits and stock dividends and contributions and withdrawals of securities "in kind." Position statements can be provided at book value or at both book value and market value. Position statements at book value permit reconciling all positions through changes in book value that arise from purchases and sales. Market valuations permit assessment of the fund based on the true value of its assets as of a point in time. The usefulness of such valuations may be affected by the sources of the prices used to arrive at them. Although this is typically not a problem with common stocks, it is a problem with bonds, which, unlike stocks, are not traded in a central marketplace.

Even more difficult to price are private placements and mortgages, for which there are generally no public markets. Some care should be used in noting the sources of valuations, especially if the custodian also serves as the investment manager. Summaries of the information provided in the transaction statements can be very helpful. Such summaries might include listings of all dividends received, all interest received, all common stock purchases, and so on. This information is required in order to make performance calculations and other analyses, and the extent to which it is provided and broken down determines the level of analysis that is possible.

Regarding regulatory information, reporting requirements for both endowment funds and ERISA funds have been established by regulatory authorities, and the custodian is in an excellent position to provide this information at relatively little cost. Among the information of an analytical nature which the custodian might provide to the fund sponsor are performance measurement (both time-weighted and dollar-weighted rates of return), risk analysis, beta, alpha, and R^2. The custodian might also furnish comparisons of the fund's performance with stock and bond market indexes and the performance of commingled and separately managed funds. Since this information is analyzed in the chapters discussing performance measurement, no further analysis of them will be made here.

Timeliness

The usefulness of any recordkeeping or analytical tool is partly a function of the time lapse between the period reported on and the receipt of the report by the appropriate official. Although it might seem that statements should be available a day or two after the close of an accounting period, there are valid reasons why it usually takes one to three weeks to supply them. First, if the custodian is not the investment manager for the complete portfolio, time must be allowed for any transactions made near month-end to be reported to the custodian and input into the custodian's accounting system. Second, if the sponsor's portfolio holds commingled funds as part of its assets, the commingled funds must be valued before the final valuation can be provided on the portfolio. Since most funds invest in short-term instruments through commingled portfolios, this delay is likely to impact a high percentage of all accounts. Third, depending on the periods covered and on the policies of the custodian and the sponsor, there may be a need to audit the statements prior to their issuance. Finally, assuming that the custodian is valuing the positions, information regarding the prices of the securities held must be received and input. All of these factors tend to delay the preparation of custodial reports beyond the processing and mailing or electronic transmission times which are inherent to any reporting system.

Consulting and Other Special Services

Since custodians have a wealth of information about the investments of individual clients and groups of clients, they are in a position to provide assistance to clients. In order to do so, they may need to offer consulting services. Since consulting is a customized service, it will likely involve separate charges.

Cost

As with the services offered by custodians, large variations exist among the costs charged for those services. The sponsor should carefully assess its needs to be sure it receives, and pays for, the services it most needs.

MONITORING

A number of firms have developed in-depth services for monitoring the effectiveness of the custodial process. Typical factors monitored are the accuracy and timeliness with which dividend and interest income are credited, the correctness of calculations of accrued interest on the purchase and sale of bonds, the efficiency with which free cash balances are invested in short-term securities, and stock execution prices outside the reported daily highs and lows. Since audits by certified public accountants typically do not go into great detail in these areas, such analyses of each transaction within a portfolio can be quite useful. In addition, since all transaction information is captured in the monitoring audit, the data obtained in this way can be used for ERISA reporting (such as the reporting of a party in interest transaction) and for analyses of individual transactions or portfolio components.

CHAPTER 18

UNDERSTANDING PENSION FUNDING

While this book is primarily dedicated to the subject of investing, those associated with investments—as sponsors, investment managers, or administrators—can best serve their constituents if they understand the needs of the organizations they serve. For pension funds, the process generating cash inflow and outflow is quite complex. Therefore, this chapter is devoted to discussing, as simply as possible, the techniques actuaries use to determine the amount of money to be set aside for payment of pension benefits. The chapter begins with a brief summary of benefit design considerations, then discusses the funding of defined benefit plans.

BENEFIT DESIGN

There are two fundamental questions to be answered in plan design: what benefits are to be provided and who is to receive them (eligibility). The number and variety of retirement benefits are very large. However, they can be divided into two general types. *Defined contribution plans* are those where benefits are provided based upon the amount accumulated on behalf of the employee. The ultimate benefit will vary depending upon the investment results of the fund, with the employee bearing the risk as to the success of these investment results.

Defined benefit plans, on the other hand, describe the pension amount to be received by the employee upon retirement. While the amount of money in the fund at the time of the employee's retirement is related to investment results, as with the defined contribution plan, in defined benefit plans the benefit is established irrespective of the level of assets in the fund. Thus, in a defined contribution plan, the benefit is based upon the assets available for each employee at retirement, whereas in a defined benefit plan the benefit is fixed by the formula prescribed by the plan so it is up to the employer to allocate sufficient funds to pay the promised benefit.

An exception to the above structure is the Taft-Hartley or jointly trusteed defined benefit plan established by a number of employers in conjunction with their unions. These plans typically are funded by contributions from the employer based upon the number of hours each individual employee works. In this sense, they look like defined contribution plans. However, the benefit is prescribed by an agreement. Unlike corporate or public pension funds, however, there is no employer who is responsible for meeting benefits promised. Rather, the assets in the pension fund must be sufficient in and of themselves to meet pension benefits, or the plan will default on its obligations.

If the plan is to have defined contributions, funding issues are minimal. Thus, this chapter is primarily concerned with funding defined benefit plans.

After the sponsor decides the plan is to have defined benefits, the next question is what these benefits are and who should receive them. ERISA and the Internal Revenue Service impose restrictions on eligibility to ensure that pension plans are not used solely as compensation schemes for managers and key shareholders. As a rule, employees who have reached the age of 21 years and have at least one year of service must be included in the plan.

A number of other decisions must be made as to benefit levels, retirement age, vesting schedule, provisions for early retirement and disability, and any provision for increases in postretirement benefits due to inflation. Most plans base the benefit on either average salary earned during the career or some form of final average such as last five years prior to retirement. A frequent benefit for salaried employees is 1 percent of average salary up to a specified "integration level" plus 1.5 percent of average salary in excess of the integration level, all times the employee's years of service. So a 40-year employee might receive an annual pension of between 40 percent and 60 percent of his or her average salary.

Vesting is the required period of service to the fund sponsor before benefit rights are earned. Most corporations choose the option under ERISA which provides for no vesting until five years of service and then 100 percent vesting.

While inflation has subsided from the high levels of the late 1970s, nonetheless it represents a major threat to the purchasing power of pension benefits. Inflation has been addressed by many companies by changing to final-average as opposed to career-average compensation formulas, wherein benefits are based on the salary of a period such as the last five years rather than of the entire career. However, for most retirees, cost-of-living benefits are at the discretion of the company rather than being built into the retirement formula. Social security benefits and benefits to retired federal employees are conspicuous exceptions.

FUNDING

Once the benefit package has been designed, the sponsor and its actuary turn to the question of funding benefits. While some pension plans, especially public plans, are contributory, most corporate and jointly trusteed plans are not. The discussion of pension funding in this chapter assumes the plan is not contributory.

Funding is really a budgeting process. Although in common parlance people speak of actuaries as determining the cost of a pension plan, this is not true. The ultimate cost of the plan is determined by the benefits provided for in the plan document, and the expenses of running the retirement program. The basic formula describing this process is:

Contributions + Investment return = Benefits + Expenses

For a given level of benefits applied to a group of employees, the only way to impact cost is through investing especially successfully or by lowering expenses. The actuary's job is to help management understand the cost associated with the plan, and develop methods for allocating these costs to specific years. While differences in actuarial approaches can change the incidence of costs and funding from earlier to later years, or vice versa, the ultimate cost of a plan will not be impacted by these decisions.

Why fund a defined benefit plan? In some countries pension plans are not funded, but rather are treated as any other liability, reflected on the books of the company, but with no specified fund of assets set aside to meet pension benefits. In the United States, funding of defined benefit plans (putting aside investible funds to provide for future benefits) is considered appropriate because:

1. ERISA requires funding for private plans.
2. For qualified plans, the Internal Revenue Code permits tax deductions for funding of a qualified plan without the employee concurrently paying taxes on the funds contributed on his or her behalf.
3. Employees, employers, and regulators feel more confident about the likelihood that benefits will be paid if plans are funded.
4. Funding establishes the proper allocation of cost, in a cash flow sense, to the employees and periods of service over which benefits were earned.

Funding a Defined Benefit Pension Plan

Funding a plan for retirement at normal retirement age involves, conceptually:

1. Estimating a benefit at retirement.
2. Calculating the value of that benefit, as measured by the value of an annuity purchased at normal retirement age which will pay the annual benefit to the employee for life (and for the spouse's life if the plan has survivor benefits).
3. Calculating the present value of that annuity, discounted at the assumed rate of return.
4. Reducing this amount by the probability that the employee will not be employed at retirement due to death, disability, termination of employment, or early retirement (the decrement assumptions).
5. Allocating this benefit cost, based on the funding method employed, to past, current, and future years.

For example, for a benefit of $20,000 per year an annuity at age 65 would cost about 8.14244 × $20,000, or $162,849 based on the 1971 group annuity mortality table and an 8 percent interest assumption. For an employee aged 30, the present value of this benefit is $162,849 divided by 1.08 to the 35th power, or $11,014. If the employee has only a 30 percent probability of still being employed by this employer at age 65, the expected cost of this benefit is 0.3 × $11,014, or $3,304. This amount is then allocated to the appropriate time periods.

For a group of employees, the process starts with analyzing the benefits under the plan and then analyzing the employee population as to number, age, salary, sex, and years of service. Actuaries must recognize that the eligible base of employees could diminish for four reasons. These reasons, called decrements, are termination of employment, death, disability, and early retirement, all of which trigger different benefit payouts and therefore an adjustment to the amount of funds to be accumulated for payment of benefits.

Once the demographics of the plan are understood, the cost of the plan is determined by making assumptions about future salaries, investment returns, and probabilities for the decrements. Consideration must be given to current service and, if benefits are provided for service prior to the formation of the plan, the cost of this past service. Through the choice of a funding method, the costs are allocated to each year, past and present. Finally, the funding process also requires a method of adjusting funding to account for errors made in earlier assumptions.

Assumptions

Because planning for an employee's retirement spans a number of years, assumptions must be made about how the future will unfold in order to estimate the amount of money which must be contributed to the fund.

The two most important assumptions actuaries and their clients must make are as to the growth in salaries and the rate of return on investments, the economic assumptions. If the benefit calls for payment based upon final salary, projections must be made of salaries over the employee's career in order to estimate benefits. If benefits are based upon average salary, or on hours worked, the actuary need only estimate future salaries if the funding method is one which spreads costs or benefits over the employee's life, as opposed to recognizing just the current year's benefits. For all funds, the actuary must estimate the return which will be earned on those funds. Other important assumptions relate to the decrements—the timing and number of employees who will terminate employment before retirement, die, become disabled, or retire early.

It is common to view salary increases as having three components: inflation, productivity, and merit, each of which can be estimated and added to determine the expected progression of salaries over the years for the population of employees under consideration. Similarly, an investment return estimate can be made from a projection of future inflation, any real return expected for riskless investments, and a risk premium attributable to the risk category of assets owned.

Assumptions Taken as a Whole

ERISA requires that actuarial assumptions must be reasonable when taken as a group (i.e., in the aggregate), and it makes determination of the assumptions the sole responsibility of the actuary. However, in practice the actuary and the plan sponsor work together on the assumption selection process.

The actuary and plan sponsor have two approaches to choose from. Under the first approach, which is referred to as explicit, the actuary attempts to make his best estimate of each individual assumption based upon currently available information. Alternatively, under the implicit approach the actuary views certain assumptions in combination, usually the rate of return on investments and the rate of salary increases, such that the effect of the use of an overly conservative assumption offsets the effect of the use of another assumption which may be too liberal. For instance, the actuary may use an assumption as to salary growth of 2 or 3 percent, when a higher rate is expected, while at the same time using an investment return of 7 percent, while 10 percent appears more likely. The low salary increase assumption will provide for too low a level of funding, whereas the low investment return assumption will lead to funding which is too high. Together, the factors may offset each other.

Use of implicit assumptions enables the actuary to avoid frequent changes in assumptions, to take a very long-term view, and to provide a way of applying judgment rather than pure facts in what is an art as well as a science. Changes introduced by the Omnibus Budget Reconciliation Act of 1987 have caused most plan sponsors and their actuaries to adopt the explicit approach. Under that Act, actuaries must use either assumptions which are individually reasonable, or assumptions which are reasonable in the aggregate but produce the same results as assumptions which are individually reasonable. As a result of this new requirement, it has become increasingly common to use the explicit approach for selecting assumptions.

Correcting for Errors and Changes

With so many assumptions about the future inherent in the funding process, it is inevitable that actual experience will differ from expectations.

These differences, which can be either positive or negative, create the need for a formal system of continuing mid-course correction. If, for instance, the plan is funded based on the assumption that invested funds will earn 7 percent and 10 percent is actually earned, an actuarial or experience gain will have occurred. If, on the other hand, employees do not terminate (leave voluntarily or involuntarily) to the extent anticipated, then an actuarial or experience loss will have been realized, since more employees with longer service than was anticipated will receive benefits. These gains and losses are then amortized over a number of years, to smooth the impact on any one year.

After a number of years, the annual cost for a plan will consist of the current year's cost, plus past service costs, and each year's amortization of gains and losses.

Funding Methods

The funding method is the procedure used to allocate costs to each year and measure liabilities for prior years. As such it is used to calculate the amount of money which should be funded for the current period, but it also can be used to calculate the expense to be charged to the company's books for reporting purposes, the tax expense for calculation of income taxes, or the amount to be credited to the ERISA Funding Standard Account, the monitoring device the government uses to be sure pension funds are being adequately funded. A different funding method, as well as different assumptions, can be used for different purposes, although a consistent method and assumptions must be used to calculate the minimum contribution required by ERISA and the maximum tax-deductible contribution.

The funding method also provides a means for determining progress to date in the accumulation of assets relative to the need for assets.

In general, the funding methods can be classified according to whether benefits or costs are allocated to each year. The unit credit family allocates benefits while the entry age normal family allocates costs.

The unit credit method, in its purest or standard form, addresses only the cost of the benefit accrued during the current year. An alternative, the projected unit credit method, projects salaries and benefits to be earned over the employee's career, then allocates the benefits equally to each year. The cost of each year's benefit is then charged to that year. Plans which calculate benefits as a percentage of final average salary are precluded from using the unit credit method; they must use the projected unit credit alternative.

Under the entry age normal method the value of the benefit projected at the time the employee enters the plan is determined and is then allocated to each year of the employee's service, usually by expressing cost as a level percentage of payroll or a level annual dollar amount.

Unit Credit

For instance, if an employee is earning $31,180 per year now and, at a 6 percent growth rate, is projected to earn $100,000 per year at retirement 20 years from now, and his pension is to be 50 percent of final salary, his retirement benefit is $50,000 per year. To purchase an annuity which pays $50,000 per year, approximately $500,000 is needed at retirement. Therefore, the funding target for this employee is $500,000 at retirement age. If this benefit is allocated pro rata according to service, ¹⁄₂₀ or $25,000 is allocated to each year. The cost of this benefit is then charged to each year, but is not equal each year for two reasons. First, because of compound interest, far less than $25,000 is required now in order to have $25,000 20 years from now. Each year the cost of having $25,000 at some specific year in the future will increase. Second, decrements must be considered. If the employee leaves the company, becomes disabled, dies, or retires early, his benefits will be reduced or eliminated. Thus, the probability of the employee's reaching retirement age is different each year, increasing over time. (This is not only because employees with long tenure tend to stay with their companies, but rather more for purely statistical reasons. Whereas an employee who is aged 30 may leave the company at ages 31, 32, and so forth, the probability is zero that an employee of age 40 will leave the company at those ages.)

Entry Age Normal

The entry age normal methods allocate cost rather than benefits. In the above example, the $500,000 cost of an annuity purchased at age 65 would be allocated such that each year's cost would be the same percentage of the employee's salary.

The unit credit method would, in general, produce an upward sloping cost curve as time goes on since the cost of providing the level benefit rises for the reasons just cited. Because the entry age normal method provides a level cost, its cost is normally higher than the unit credit method in earlier years and less in later years. Some observers have drawn an analogy between term life insurance and the unit credit method, and whole life insurance and entry age normal. The former provide only for cost as incurred in the current year, which is low at an early age and high at a later age. Whole life insurance and entry age normal both level the annual premium or cost by building a reserve in earlier years which, together with the interest on the reserve, can be used to meet costs in later years.

Whether the unit credit method or the entry age normal method is used, when evaluated at a time after the plan sponsor's initiation of business, part of the costs will be allocable to prior years of service of employees. The accumulated actuarial value of these past amounts is sometimes referred to as the actuarial reserve or accrued liability. The unfunded accrued liability is the excess of the accrued liability over the plan's asset value. At the inception of a plan, when there are not yet any plan assets, the two amounts are equal. An element of cost, called annual past service cost, is involved when either the unit credit or the entry age normal method is used. This is determined by amortizing the initial unfunded accrued liability over a period, such as 30 years, much like a mortgage.

Two variations of the entry age normal method are the frozen initial liability and the aggregate methods.

The *frozen initial liability method* calculates costs during the first year of the plan in the same manner as does the entry age normal method. The unfunded accrued liability calculated at this point is then frozen and amortized as a level dollar amount. Annual reassignments of past service cost based upon actual experience are not made, but rather the effects of such experience are assigned only to future years by increasing or decreasing the percentage of payroll or constant flat dollar costs. Under this method, if there is no plan amendment or change of assumptions during a given year, the past service cost will remain level in amount from one year to the next. But the normal costs will increase or decrease to reflect the fact that an actuarial loss or gain was experienced, and has been assigned to future years.

The *aggregate method* is similar to the frozen initial liability method, except that under the aggregate method, the unfunded liability is set to zero. With the aggregate method, all costs for remaining future unfunded benefits of the plan—normal costs, experience gains and losses, and past service costs—are treated together and spread over future years of service. Thus, there is no separately identified unfunded liability due to past service costs or experience gains and losses.

Amortization of Past Service Costs and Costs Associated with Plan Modifications, Changes in Methods or Assumptions, and Experience Gains and Losses

The preceding section related principally to ways of allocating normal costs, the costs for the current period based upon current plan benefits, and assuming that methods and assumptions are appropriate and that assumptions are in fact realized. However, as observed earlier, there are additional sources of cost in a pension plan. For instance, when a pension plan is started, or when benefits are improved, it is common to provide benefits retroactively. Since these costs were not considered during previous calculations of cost, it becomes necessary to supplement the nominal cost or provide for these costs for past service.

A need to change the amount being allocated also results from changes in assumptions or methods. If, for example, it is decided that the investment return assumption should be 8 percent, not 7 percent, an immediate reduction in the present value of liabilities, and hence in the need for contributions, occurs. To smooth this impact over a number of years, and to prevent manipulation of earnings or funding based on changes in assumptions, this gain would be amortized over a period of years. Similarly, if a change in method occurred, any gain or loss from doing so would also be amortized over a number of years. Finally, experience will provide gains and losses from existing assumptions, as actual experience deviates from that which was assumed. Gains and losses from these experience factors are also amortized.

As with the normal costs, there are various methods which can be used to allocate supplemental costs. Either a level or declining cost curve typically results from allocation of supplemental costs since these costs are based on a known value to be allocated, and do not reflect growth factors such as salaries which could lead normal costs to grow each year.

Amortization Period

The period over which the unfunded portion of the actuarial reserve is amortized varies depending upon the source of the unfunded amount and when it arose. Until ERISA was enacted, it was not necessary to fund the unfunded portion of the actuarial reserve; a plan sponsor needed only to pay the normal cost plus interest on the unfunded portion of the actuarial reserve at the assumed rate of return. Under ERISA, unfunded actuarial liabilities must be amortized over no more than a certain prescribed number of years, as follows:

	Amortization Period— Minimum Funding Purposes
Unfunded actuarial reserve as of beginning of 1976 plan year	40 years
Increase or decrease in unfunded actuarial reserve arising after 1976 on account of plan adoption or plan amendments	30 years
Increase or decrease in unfunded actuarial reserve arising from a change in assumptions	10 years
Increase or decrease in unfunded actuarial reserve due to actuarial experience (gains or losses)	5 years
Increase or decrease in unfunded actuarial reserve due to a change in actuarial method	30 years*

*30 years for an increase, but the larger of 30 years or the balance remaining from the 1976 amortization period (i.e., starting in 1986, 30 years for increases or decreases).

At the other extreme, the Internal Revenue Service permits tax deductions only for amounts that fund costs in 10 years or more, to prevent excessive loss of revenue to the Treasury.

It should be noted that the amortization schedule includes interest, as in the case of a mortgage. If a $1.5 million actuarial loss is experienced by a plan because, for instance, salaries increased faster than expected or investments grew more slowly than expected, an actuarial or experience loss must be recognized. This loss must be funded over at most five years. This does not mean, however, that the fund must charge only $300,000 to the current year's expense. Under the original assumption, the plan would now have an extra $1.5 million liability compared to what it had before the loss. Five years from now this $1.5 million would have accumulated to an amount as though the fund earned the actuarial investment return each year, compounded, on this sum. If a 10 percent rate is used, this amount is $2,415,765. Therefore, the current year's amortization must include not only the $300,000, but sufficient interest such that the total payment for each year will accumulate to $2,415,765 in five years. This amount is approximately $360,000 per year.

A series of examples, provided by Hewitt Associates, appears in this chapter's appendix to assist readers who wish to study examples of the workings of various actuarial methods.

Valuing Assets

Pension fund assets are typically not valued at the current market value for purposes of funding. Although ERISA requires that market value be reflected in some reasonable way, using current market value directly would result in widely varying costs from year to year. Just as actuaries smooth the impact of experience gains and losses, they use a smoothing technique for valuing assets. A common approach is to use a moving average of market value over a period of three to five years. The IRS requires that the actuarial value be at least 80 percent and at most 120 percent of the fund's actual market value.

Ancillary Benefits

Most pension plans have benefits other than pure pensions for the employee. Many plans have disability benefits, which provide payment for workers who are unable to continue working; early retirement benefits, for those who stop working before the normal retirement age; life insurance; surviving spouse benefit; and in a few cases cost-of-living adjustments. The cost of each of these benefits must be added to the pure costs of a pension benefit. Adjustments to the costs accrued to meet these benefits will also be made as experience differs from that assumed.

Social Security Integration

Many pension plans are "integrated" with Social Security, meaning that the benefit provided—expressed as a percentage of the employee's pay—is higher at higher pay levels. This is done to partially offset the fact that Social Security benefits are higher, as a percentage of pay, at lower pay levels. Before the 1986 Tax Reform Act, integration was frequently achieved by subtracting a percentage of the employee's Social Security benefit (for example, a typical formula was 1.5 percent of final average salary minus 1.5 percent of the Social Security benefit, times years of service). Under current law, integration is most frequently achieved by providing different accruals above and below an integration level (for example, 1 percent of final average salary up to $20,000 plus 1.5 percent of final average salary in excess of $20,000, all times years of service).

Plan Assets and Unfunded Liabilities

The preceding discussion of funding dealt with the calculation of benefits and how the cost of these benefits can be allocated to each year. Another important use of the funding process is to measure the funded status of a plan, that is, its assets relative to the plan's liabilities or promises to pay future benefits. While the plan's asset valuation is subject to some minor interpretation, considerable confusion can arise from attempts to measure the plan's liabilities. This confusion results from different definitions of liabilities, depending upon the use to which the information is put, and different ways of calculating them, depending on the funding method and assumptions employed.

Liabilities can be viewed in terms of present value of benefits to be paid in the future, or normal costs accumulated to date. For a given employee at retirement age, these two figures will be the same, but at any point during his career there can be a difference.

Present Value of Future Benefits

It may be helpful to distinguish four definitions of liabilities associated with future benefits, as illustrated by the attached bar charts (see Exhibit 18–1). The differences relate, in the first three cases, to promises to pay benefits upon plan termination and in the fourth to liabilities if the plan continues.

A distinction can be drawn between vested and accrued benefits:

- Vested benefits are benefits to which the employee would be entitled if he or she were to terminate employment.
- Accrued benefits are total benefits earned to date, including vested benefits and nonvested benefits. Nonvested benefits are benefits which would be forfeited if the employee were to terminate employment.

Generally, if a plan is terminated, all accrued benefits become vested irrespective of whether or not an employee has satisfied the plan's

EXHIBIT 18-1
Alternative Measurements of Pension Plan Liabilities

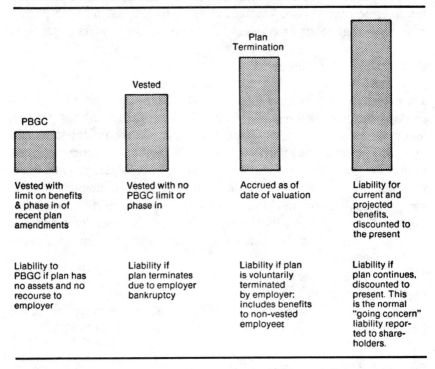

PBGC	Vested	Plan Termination	
Vested with limit on benefits & phase in of recent plan amendments	Vested with no PBGC limit or phase in	Accrued as of date of valuation	Liability for current and projected benefits, discounted to the present
Liability to PBGC if plan has no assets and no recourse to employer	Liability if plan terminates due to employer bankruptcy	Liability if plan is voluntarily terminated by employer; includes benefits to non-vested employees	Liability if plan continues, discounted to present. This is the normal "going concern" liability reported to shareholders.

vesting requirement (typically five years of service). If the plan is terminated voluntarily by the plan sponsor, the sponsor is generally required to fund all accrued benefits, whether or not they are vested. If the plan termination is the result of the company's bankruptcy, to the extent that plan assets are insufficient to provide accrued benefits, the Pension Benefit Guaranty Corporation (PBGC) will guarantee certain benefits. The PBGC will guarantee benefits up to a certain level only; so employees with very large benefits will not have their full benefits protected. Further, plan improvements occurring within the five-year period preceding the plan termination will be only partially protected by the PBGC. The PBGC liability is represented by the left-hand bar. The second bar reflects this liability plus vested benefits for employees who are entitled to more than the minimum amount provided by the PBGC and adjustment for the five-year phase-in. If the plan terminates, for instance, through bankruptcy of the employer, and plan assets are sufficient, then all vested benefits will be paid at retirement. These two sets of liabilities apply only to benefits which are vested under the plan, usually applying to employees who have five or more years of service. However, even employees who have less than five years of service (or are otherwise not vested) have accrued benefits which would eventually become vested after the employee's tenure reaches a certain point. If the employer voluntarily terminates the plan, accrued but nonvested liabilities automatically become vested to the extent funded. These accrued liabilities are displayed in bar number three.

All of the preceding calculations assume the plan will be terminated. The amount of benefit earned by the employee will be fixed at the time of termination, since even if the plan is terminated but the company continues, future service will not be credited toward pension benefits. Thus, the measure of these liabilities is only a function of benefits promised in the plan document and earned to the date of termination and assumptions as to future investment return and mortality. If, on the other hand, the plan continues, the benefits to employees will increase because salaries and years of service will have increased. Even though these years of service have not yet been credited and benefits have not been earned for them, the value of benefits to be paid in the future is calculated assuming additional service will be credited to employees, and salaries will be higher, in future years. The liability calculated under this approach is called the actuarial reserve and is represented, as a present value, in bar four.

For all four of these measures of liabilities, a comparison can be made with the market value or actuarial value of assets to determine the funded or unfunded amount or ratio.

Liabilities Compared to Accumulated Cost

There is a completely different way of viewing plan liabilities in relation to assets. In the four examples demonstrated above, liabilities are calculated based on benefits earned. Alternatively, liabilities can be expressed relative to the asset target which is inherent in the funding method. Each of the funding methods (unit credit, entry age normal, etc.) describes a cost to be charged to past and current years. The sum of the charges for past years represents the asset target. Assets can be compared to this asset target to measure unfunded liability. The fund may not be funded relative to the asset target if, of course, assets have not achieved an adequate return. Even assuming investment return was realized precisely, the asset target thus calculated would not be equal to current plan assets if the fund had not fully amortized supplemental costs arising from benefits granted for service prior to the formation of the plan, retroactive improvements in the plan, or costs associated with changes of funding method or assumptions, or of experience gains and losses. Because the normal cost charged to each year is dependent upon the funding method and assumptions, unfunded liabilities viewed in this way are dependent on the funding method and assumptions chosen. This severely limits the comparability among various plans of measurements of funding status.

Limitations of Actuarial Methodology

The actuary typically looks at a plan with two serious limitations, both of which are caused in part by IRS restrictions on deductibility of contributions. First, no estimate is made for changes in the work force due to new employees entering the plan. Second, no funding occurs for projected increases in benefits unless they are provided for in the plan document. Companies that wish to avoid sharply higher future costs due to these factors may choose conservative funding methods or assumptions. For instance, if the sponsor would normally assume 8 percent as the expected investment return, it can fund a greater amount by assuming only a 7.5 percent return, thus providing funding for the larger benefits expected in the future. But be careful! The IRS can disqualify corporate tax deductions if the actuarial assumptions are considered overly conservative.

Conclusion

While not overly complicated conceptually, the actual mechanics of actuarial science are complex to the point where very few laymen will find it possible or worthwhile to learn the many intricacies of this artful science. Nonetheless, those associated with pension plans or investment of pension plans will be well served to be at least broadly familiar with actuarial terminology and precepts.

APPENDIX

EXAMPLES OF PENSION FUNDING

In these examples, the four actuarial cost methods explained in "Paying for Pensions—A Primer for Executives" are illustrated. Thirty-year contributions for a plan with two participants are calculated using each of the methods. For simplicity, contributions have been calculated only for the retirement benefit. Calculations associated with vesting, death, or disability benefits have not been illustrated. Employee characteristics, the benefit formula, and the actuarial assumptions are shown below.

Work force: 2 employees

	Date of birth	Date of hire
Employee 1	1/1/50	1/1/80
Employee 2	1/1/30	1/1/70

Plan benefit: $10 per month for each year of service.

Assumptions:
1. Effective Date of Plan: January 1, 1980
2. Interest: 8 percent
3. Mortality: 1971 Group Annuity Mortality Table
4. Withdrawal: 4.4 percent at age 30, decreasing to 0.0 percent at age 60
5. Assets: Market Value

Calculations have been rounded to the nearest dollar. Because of this, certain results vary by several dollars from what the arithmetic indicates would be obtained. Earnings on the first-year assets include interest at the assumed rate plus an additional $50.

	Year 1		Year 2	
	Employee 1	*Employee 2*	*Employee 1*	*Employee 2*
Entry age normal				
Present value of benefits				
Projected benefit: $10 per month × 12 months × Projected years of service	$ 4,200	$ 3,000	$ 4,200	$ 3,000
× Age 65 annuity factor	× 8.14244	× 8.14244	× 8.14244	× 8.14244

= Money needed for retiree at age 65	$ 34,198	$ 24,427	$ 34,198	$ 24,427
÷ Interest factor	÷(1.08)^{35}	÷(1.08)^{15}	÷(1.08)^{34}	÷(1.08)^{14}
= Money needed today if employee remains in service to retirement	$ 2,313	$ 7,700	$ 2,498	$ 8,316
× Probability of remaining in service to retirement	× .474	× .803	× .496	× .815
= Present value of benefits on valuation date	$ 1,096	$ 6,183	$ 1,239	$ 6,778
Plan total		$7,279		$8,017

Normal cost

Projected benefit	$ 4,200	$ 3,000		
× Age 65 annuity factor	×8.14244	×8.14244		
= Money needed for retiree at age 65	$ 34,198	$ 24,427		
÷ Interest factor	÷(1.08)^{35}	÷(1.08)^{25}		
× Probability of remaining in service from hire date to retirement	× .474	× .666		
= (1) Present value of benefits on hire date	$ 1,096	$ 2,376		
(2) A contribution of $1 each year from hire to retirement as a present value of	9.57466	9.99817		
Normal Cost = (1) ÷ (2)	$ 114	$ 238	$ 114	$ 238
Plan total		$352		$352

Accrued liability

(1) Present value of benefits on valuation date	$ 1,096	$ 6,183	$ 1,239	$ 6,778
(2) Normal cost	$ 114	$ 238	$ 114	$ 238
(3) A contribution of $1 each year from valuation date to retirement has present value of	9.5747	8.5501	9.6847	8.2805
(4) Present value of future normal costs = (2) × (3)	$ 1,096	$ 2,035	$ 1,104	$ 1,971
Accrued liability = (1) − (4)	$ 0	$ 4,148	$ 135	$ 4,807
Plan total		$4,148		$4,942

	Year 1	Year 2
Gain and loss analysis		
(1) 1/1/80 unfunded accrued liability		$ 4,148
(2) 1/1/80 normal cost		352
(3) 1/1/80 contribution		693
(4) One year's interest on (1) and (2)		360
(5) One year's interest on (3)		55

(6) Expected unfunded accrued
  liability = (1) + (2) − (3) + (4)
  − (5) $4,112
(7) Actual unfunded accrued
  liability (accrued liability of
  $4,942 less assets of $798) $4,144
  Loss = (7) − (6) $ 32

Expected interest was $55; actual interest was $105 ($798 − $693), resulting in an asset gain of $50. The 1/1/80 unfunded accrued liability of $4,148 is based on probabilities of remaining to retirement of .474 and .803 for the two employees. The 1/1/81 unfunded accrued liability is based on probabilities of .496 and .815. This implies a probability of

$$1 - \frac{.474}{.496} = 4.435\% \text{ and } 1 - \frac{.803}{.815} = 1.472\%$$ that the employees would not remain in service until January 1, 1981.

Thus we would have "expected" to lose (4.435% × $135) + (1.472% × $4,807) = $82 in liabilities. Since we did not lose these liabilities, we have an $82 turnover loss.

30-year contribution	*Year 1*	*Year 2*
Normal cost	$352	$352
30-year amortization of initial unfunded accrued liability	341	341
15-year amortization of gains or losses		3
30-year contribution (beginning of year)	$693	$696

	Year 1		*Year 2*	
	Employee 1	*Employee 2*	*Employee 1*	*Employee 2*
Aggregate				
Present value of benefits				
Projected benefit: $10 per month × 12 months × Projected years of service	$ 4,200	$ 3,000	$ 4,200	$ 3,000
× Age 65 annuity factor	× 8.14244	× 8.14244	× 8.14244	× 8.14244
= Money needed for retiree at age 65	$ 34,198	$ 24,427	$ 34,198	$ 24,427
÷ Interest factor	÷$(1.08)^{35}$	÷$(1.08)^{15}$	÷$(1.08)^{34}$	÷$(1.08)^{14}$
= Money needed today if employee remains in service to retirement	$ 2,313	$ 7,700	$ 2,498	$ 8,316
× Probability of remaining in service to retirement	× .474	× .803	× .496	× .815
= Present value of benefits on valuation date	$ 1,096	$ 6,183	$ 1,239	$ 6,778
Plan total		$7,279		$8,017

Normal cost

	Employee 1	Employee 2	Employee 1	Employee 2
Present value of benefits on valuation date	$ 1,096	$ 6,183	$ 1,239	$ 6,778
(1) Plan total	$7,279		$8,017	
(2) Assets	0		917	
(3) Present value of future normal costs = (1) − (2)	$7,279		$7,100	
A contribution of $1 each year from valuation date to retirement has present value of	9.5747	8.5501	9.6847	8.2805
(4) Plan total	18.1248		17.9652	
(5) Normal cost per employee (3) ÷ (4)	$401.60		$395.21	
Normal cost = (5) × Number of employees	$803		$790	

	Year 1		Year 2	
	Employee 1	*Employee 2*	*Employee 1*	*Employee 2*
Frozen initial liability *Present value of benefits* Projected benefit: $10 per month × 12 months × Projected years of service	$ 4,200	$ 3,000	$ 4,200	$ 3,000
× Age 65 annuity factor	× 8.14244	× 8.14244	× 8.14244	× 8.14244
= Money needed for retiree at age 65	$ 34,198	$ 24,427	$ 34,198	$ 24,427
÷ Interest factor	$\div(1.08)^{35}$	$\div(1.08)^{15}$	$\div(1.08)^{34}$	$\div(1.08)^{14}$
= Money needed today if employee remains in service to retirement	$ 2,313	$ 7,700	$ 2,498	$ 8,316
× Probability of remaining in service to retirement	× .474	× .803	× .496	× .815
= Present value of benefits on valuation date	$ 1,096	$ 6,183	$ 1,239	$ 6,778
Plan total	$7,279		$8,017	

Normal cost

	Employee 1	Employee 2	Employee 1	Employee 2
Present value of benefits on valuation date	$ 1,096	$ 6,183	$ 1,239	$ 6,778
(1) Plan total	$7,279		$8,017	
Present value of future normal costs (see entry age normal for development)	$1,096	$2,035		
(2) Plan total	$3,131			
(3) Accrued liability = (1) − (2)	$4,148			
(4) Assets	$ 0		$ 791	
(5) Unfunded frozen initial liability on 1/1/80 = (3) − (4)	$4,148		$4,148	

(6) Amortization payment		341
(7) Interest on (5) less interest on (6)		305
(8) Unfunded frozen initial liability on 1/1/81 = (5) − (6) + (7)	N/A	$4,112
(9) Unfunded frozen initial liability on valuation date	$4,148	$4,112
(10) Present value of future normal costs = (1) − (4) − (9)	$3,131	$3,114

A contribution of $1 each year from valuation date to retirement has present value of	9.5747	8.5501	9.6847	8.2805
(11) Plan total		18.1248		17.9652
(12) Normal cost per employee = (10) ÷ (11)		$172.75		$173.34
Normal cost = (12) × Number of employees		$345		$347
30-year contribution				
Normal cost		$345		$347
30-year amortization of unfunded frozen initial liability		341		341
30-year contribution (beginning of year)		$686		$688

	Year 1		Year 2	
	Employee 1	*Employee 2*	*Employee 1*	*Employee 2*
Standard unit credit				
Normal cost				
Benefit earned in current year $10 per month × 12 months	$ 120	$ 120	$ 120	$ 120
× Age 65 annuity factor	× 8.14244	× 8.14244	× 8.14244	× 8.14244
= Money needed at retirement for benefit earned in current year	$ 977	$ 977	$ 977	$ 977
÷ Interest factor	÷$(1.08)^{35}$	÷$(1.08)^{15}$	÷$(1.08)^{34}$	÷$(1.08)^{14}$
× Probability of remaining in service to retirement	× .474	× .803	× .496	× .815
= Normal cost	$ 31	$ 247	$ 35	$ 271
Plan total	$278		$306	
Accrued liability				
Benefit earned prior to current year $10 per month × 12 months × Number of years of service	$ 0	$ 1,200	$ 120	$ 1,320

× Age 65 annuity factor	× 8.14244	× 8.14244	× 8.14244	× 8.14244
= Money needed at retirement for benefit earned in prior years	$ 0	$ 9,771	$ 977	$ 10,748
÷ Interest factor	$\div(1.08)^{35}$	$\div(1.08)^{15}$	$\div(1.08)^{34}$	$\div(1.08)^{14}$
× Probability of remaining in service to retirement	× .474	× .803	× .496	× .815
= Accrued liability	$ 0	$ 2,473	$ 35	$ 2,982
Plan total		$2,473		$3,017

Gain and loss analysis

(1) 1/1/80 unfunded accrued liability	$ 2,473
(2) 1/1/80 normal cost	278
(3) 1/1/80 contribution	481
(4) One year's interest on (1) and (2)	220
(5) One year's interest on (3)	38
(6) Expected unfunded accrued liability = (1) + (2) − (3) + (4) − (5)	$ 2,452
(7) Actual unfunded accrued liability (accrued liability of $3,017 less assets of $569)	$ 2,448
Gain = (6) − (7)	$ 4

Expected interest was $38; actual interest was $88 ($569 − $481), resulting in an asset gain of $50. The 1/1/80 unfunded accrued liability of $2,473 is based on probabilities of remaining to retirement of .474 and .803 for the two employees. The 1/1/81 unfunded accrued liability is based on probabilities of .496 and .815. This implies a probability of $1 - \dfrac{.474}{.496} = 4.435\%$ and $1 - \dfrac{.803}{.815} = 1.472\%$ that the employees would not remain in service until January 1, 1981.

Thus we would have "expected" to lose (4.435% × $35) + (1.472% × $2,982) = $46 in liabilities. Since we did not lose these liabilities, we have a $46 turnover loss.

30-year contribution	*Year 1*	*Year 2*
Normal cost	$278	$306
30-year amortization of initial unfunded accrued liability	203	203
15-year amortization of gains or losses		(1)
30-year contribution (beginning of year)	$481	$508

	Summary					
	Year 1			Year 2		
	Normal Cost	*Unfunded Accrued Liability*	*Contri- bution*	*Normal Cost*	*Unfunded Accrued Liability*	*Contri- bution*
1. Entry age normal	$352	$4,148	$693	$352	$4,144	$696
2. Aggregate	$803	—	$803	$790	—	$790
3. Frozen initial liability	$345	$4,148	$686	$347	$4,112	$688
4. Standard unit credit	$278	$2,473	$481	$306	$2,448	$508

Source: Hewitt Associates.

CHAPTER 19

THE ART OF BEING
A GOOD CLIENT

One of the difficult things about managing money is that clients tend to have absolute objectives in bear markets and relative objectives in bull markets.

Previous chapters have discussed the investment and administrative process from the sponsor's point of view. This chapter, like the others, attempts to provide insight for the sponsor, only this time by presenting the point of view of those who provide services to the sponsor. If the sponsor's representatives have a better understanding of the problems encountered by the people who serve them, they will be in a better position to derive the maximum benefit from those people. As the chapter title implies, there is no precise method of achieving this goal. Being a good client is more an art than a science, with empathy and common sense being important factors.

BEING A GOOD CLIENT OF AN INVESTMENT MANAGER

The do's and don'ts of being a good client of an investment manager are as follows:

1. State your goals. If the investment manager is going to help you achieve your goals, it must know what they are. (This, of course, assumes that you do, which point has been addressed elsewhere in this book.)

2. State your goals precisely. Everyone wants high returns with no risk. Try to be as specific as possible.

3. Don't change your goals too frequently. It is important to monitor the progress of the fund in terms of its goals and in terms of how the sponsor's needs change over time. However, investing is a long-term process, requiring a time horizon of several years, and the investment manager cannot be expected to shift the portfolio back and forth within shorter periods. Also, goals cannot be shifted between relative and absolute standards. As the chapter opening quotation indicates, most sponsors would like to meet their assumed rate of return when the market falls apart and rank number one when the market is rising sharply. These goals are inconsistent. If your objective is to meet your assumed rate of return, you can't complain if you are up 10 percent when the market is up 50 percent. On the other hand, if you want to be up 50 percent when the market is up 50 percent, you have to be prepared to be down 20 percent when it is down 20 percent.

4. Don't compare yourself to others with different goals. If you decide that you can meet your plan's needs by investing in long-term U.S. government bonds, don't be shocked that an equity-oriented fund outperformed yours in a rising stock market.

5. Provide your manager with cash flow projections. Give it as much information as possible about the plan's liquidity requirements in future years. This will help it establish both cash flow and risk objectives.

6. Don't make surprise contributions or withdrawals. This greatly frustrates the investment manager, who may have put considerable effort into establishing an appropriate portfolio only to have it become inappropriate because of the fund's new cash situation.

7. Confide in your manager about internal preferences, utilities, and politics. If your plan has very little ability to bear risk but the chief executive of the organization is a crapshooter, the investment manager should know this. It may want to spend more time educating the chief executive; it may try to walk the fine line between the two extremes; or it may simply resign the account.

8. Don't fall for every fad. One investment strategy pursued consistently and successfully will produce better results than 10 different strategies pursued in succession. The manager should be hired to perform a specific function and should be left pretty much alone to carry it out.

9. Don't believe the performance figures of every person who walks in the door. Some investment managers feel that their biggest threat is not their inability to meet client needs but their inability to outperform the standards set by the marketing representatives of other investment management organizations.

10. Don't expect miracles. If the market is not completely efficient, it is pretty close. It is not realistic to expect an investment manager to consistently outperform peers who are working with substantially the same tools that it uses. If your investment manager achieves at least average performance, takes the time to understand you and your organization, is responsive to requests, and even anticipates them, you are probably deriving about as much as you can expect from your relationship with it.

BEING A GOOD CLIENT OF A CUSTODIAN

An organization providing custodial services would appreciate the following:

1. Regarding the timeliness of reports, please recognize that if you own commingled funds, they must be valued before your portfolio can be valued, and that both your fund and the commingled funds are frequently audited before the custodian's final valuations are issued. These factors delay the submission of reports.

2. Your custodial organization does its best to assure accuracy, but mistakes do happen. Therefore, please try to review reports as soon as you receive them rather than waiting until the day before the board of directors meeting.

BEING A GOOD CLIENT OF A PERFORMANCE MEASUREMENT CONSULTANT

1. Your consultant's reports cannot be produced until statements are received from the bank custodian. Please recognize this and, in addition, use your influence to see that the custodian's statements are produced and delivered promptly.

2. In order to compare your results with those of other funds, it is necessary that those funds be measured first. Obviously, this delays the processing of your comparative report.

3. Measuring performance is different from creating accounting reports. If your accounting procedures are inadequate, you should correct that problem instead of expecting your consultant to do so.

CHAPTER 20

APPLYING THE "MANAGING YOUR MANAGER" TECHNIQUES TO PORTFOLIOS OF INDIVIDUALS AND TRUSTS

It seems to make sense. Let's try it with our own money.

It is ironic that millions of dollars per year are spent organizing and managing the investment process for pension and endowment funds, yet individuals, even those with vast wealth, do not appear to have taken advantage of the rapidly developing science of managing the investment manager. Given the significant benefits in investment results and administration which can accrue to those applying these techniques, it is only a matter of time until wealthy individuals use this knowledge to their own benefit, for the benefit of future generations of their families, and for their charitable foundations.

In terms of personal assets, the process of managing the investment manager can be viewed with respect to assets owned directly, and to those held in trust. The latter is particularly important since most families of substantial means establish trusts in order to pass assets to future generations with reduced transfer tax liability.

TRUSTS

One of the most challenging tasks in establishing a trust is choosing one or more trustees. This, in turn, leads to the question as to whether to have corporate or individual trustees. A corporate trustee, typically a bank trust department, usually has two significant advantages. First, bank trust departments are not dependent upon specific individuals, but rather are institutions which continue beyond the lives of individual trust officers. Second, bank trust departments typically have significant resources which are designed to fulfill the trust function, including investment, custody, reporting, and tax preparation facilities. The very significant drawback of a corporate trustee is the lack of flexibility provided in investing. The corporate trustee will feel obliged to make the investment decisions for the trust, whether its facilities are top-notch or otherwise. Similarly, whereas the trust company continues indefinitely, high-caliber investment departments frequently do not. Investors who are successful in one period are not necessarily successful in others. People are the key to success in any endeavor, and competent people are often attracted to new organizations. Bank trust departments are particularly susceptible to losing people to organizations which have more lucrative compensation programs and greater investment flexibility. This certainly gives pause to the person who is considering entrusting his hard-earned net worth to a single organization without any chance of flexibility for generations to come.

As a compromise between the flexibility offered by individual trustees and the stability provided by corporate trustees, a useful combination for many families is to have multiple co-trustees, each having an expertise which can benefit the trust, yet each being supported by others—corporate or individual—who have the necessary skills to fill the needs of the trust. For instance, a corporate trustee could provide custody, recordkeeping, and tax preparation, as well as fiduciary oversight to be sure the trust document and all relevant laws are followed. At the same time, a competent individual co-trustee could handle the selection of the investment advisor or investment manager. If the investment manager or advisor was not satisfactory, it could be replaced, without court approval and without disruption of the custody and historical recordkeeping activities of the corporate trustee. It would even be possible to have the investment advisory arm of the corporate trustee serve as a hired investment manager, which, like an independent investment manager, could be discharged by the trustees.

The principal duties of trustees are to hold the assets and invest them prudently. They must exercise these duties with care and loyalty to the beneficiary whose assets have been placed under their control by the grantor. In many states, the trustees cannot delegate discretionary authority over the trust, since investment of funds is fundamental to the office of trustee and fundamental authority cannot be delegated. If the trustees are the primary source of investment advice, this will be no problem. However, if the trustees have chosen an outside investment manager, a problem may exist since most investment managers would prefer to have discretionary authority over an account, and some even point to superior investment results for their discretionary accounts relative to their nondiscretionary accounts. For large investment management organizations, it is easy to see how a new investment recommendation can be purchased immediately for discretionary accounts, with the result that the price of the security is pushed upward. By the time authority is received from the advisory accounts, the price may be higher.

This problem can be addressed in a number of ways. The trustees can invest in commingled or mutual funds which in turn can make specific investments on a discretionary basis. The investment advisor can telephone the trustees for oral approval of transactions before they are executed, normally with written follow-up. Although it involves some risk to the investment manager, conceivably the trustees could give the investment manager discretion to purchase subject to approval, within a day or two, of the transaction. If the trustees rejected the security, they would not permit the custodian to pay for it. Obviously, this would work only in an environment in which the manager had a very clear understanding of the trustees' criteria for approval.

The trustees could also review the entire "approved for purchase" list of the investment manager and eliminate from consideration those companies which the trustees feel are inappropriate.

Regardless of the method used, to the extent that the trustees can articulate their opinions as to the types of securities which are appropriate, this whole process is greatly facilitated.

Another problem which arises for trustees is the distinction between income and principal investments. With most pension and other tax-exempt funds, there is no distinction between the two since the sponsoring fund has rights to both and since no taxes are paid. However, for personal assets and trusts, the distinction can be very significant. Many, if not most, trusts are established such that the income accrues to a life beneficiary while the principal eventually is distributed to remaindermen, the simplest case being when a man dies and leaves his estate such that his wife receives the income and his children the corpus of the trust upon the death of the wife.

SETTING INVESTMENT OBJECTIVES

The overall process for establishing objectives, asset types, and managers is the same for all portfolios. What is the purpose of the portfolio—what goals must be met in terms of current income, future income, capital appreciation, liquidity, and safety? Does the owner of the assets know what he or she wants? Does he or she recognize the implications on future income and assets of high current income? Does he or she understand the volatility of common stocks and long-term bonds, and the trade-off between income risk and principal risk as the time to maturity of a fixed-income portfolio is increased?

Just as with pension funds, if the portfolio is to achieve the goal required, it is necessary to articulate the purpose for the fund, then set objectives which will meet this purpose. In the most frequent (and perhaps most difficult) case, income flows to the current generation and principal to future generations. This requires the trustee, in setting the investment objectives, to balance both income and principal objectives. In the case of a trust of modest size, and with legal advice, a high income objective might be established under the assumption that most people would prefer to satisfy the basic income needs of their widows rather than provide greater capital to their children. However, in trusts of larger size, an attempt must be made to balance both objectives equally. Defining exactly what "equally" means in terms of choosing assets and managers can be quite difficult. Perhaps it is useful to think in terms of the two possible extremes which prudent trustees might consider in investing trust assets. A trust which had income as its objective might be totally invested in tax-exempt bonds. On the other hand, a portfolio which had no specific income need might invest in a portfolio of high-quality growth stocks, without regard to income. Since the equity portfolio is of high quality, in order to meet the prudent standards of the trust most of the stocks would undoubtedly pay a dividend. A portfolio having a yield equal to that of a portfolio invested half in bonds and half in growth stocks is a reasonable way to satisfy this objective.

One of the important factors to consider in a personal or trust portfolio, which is not as important in an institutional portfolio, is the time horizon of the investment. Individuals have life expectancies and trusts have termination points, either in time or in terms of the death of donors or beneficiaries. Identifying the time horizon is vital because of the volatility of markets and the relationship between expected return and volatility. An investor with a time horizon of several years should not purchase risky or illiquid investments. Rather, investments should be concentrated in relatively short-term fixed-income securities whose ultimate value can be determined with a high degree of certainty at the time of purchase. The longer the time horizon, the more appropriate it is to seek higher returns by sacrificing short-term stability and liquidity. Of course, this assumes that income and the need for stability of principal can be met principally with common stocks.

After setting goals, the next step is to answer the five questions associated with choice of investment policy (see page 103 for further explanation). These decisions are: what asset categories are appropriate, in what proportions, at what risk level, at what diversification level, and how much discretion should the investment manager have in changing these policies?

CHOOSING ASSET CATEGORIES

In fixed-income investing, the individual portfolio or personal trust portfolio will probably have a bias toward tax-exempt bonds and notes, since most individuals with substantial assets are in a tax bracket where it is sensible to own tax-free securities. However, the trustees and investment managers should not automatically assume tax-exempts are appropriate, but should look rather at alternative yields of similar quality and maturity fixed-income investments in both taxable and tax-free areas, and choose the one which provides the higher after-tax return for the safety and liquidity levels required. State, local, and federal taxes should be considered.

The balance of the portfolio should logically be invested in equity securities of reasonably high quality. An individual who has a substantial net worth might question whether or not a trust's investment should go beyond stocks and bonds to real estate, venture capital, or energy investments, for the goal of income or appreciation. These investments, in most cases, are not appropriate for a trust, depending upon the needs of the beneficiaries and the similarity of their investment objectives. The liquidity needs of the trust are also an important consideration as these asset types tend to be quite illiquid. If there is much distinction in the investment sophistication, age, net worth, and/or income of the beneficiaries, it is advisable for the trust to invest in higher quality marketable assets and to let those beneficiaries who so desire buy less-liquid and more-risky investments in their own portfolios.

In other words, each individual should look at his or her total financial situation and try to achieve the income and risk characteristics appropriate for him or her. Part of his or her assets and income will flow from the trust, and these should be considered just as any other assets, with the overall portfolio being designed to meet the investor's needs. In addition to this structure providing some comfort to the trustees, it also provides comfort to the individuals, since they can have some assurance that, if their direct investments are unsuccessful, at least the trust will be a stable source of income and capital.

INVESTMENT MANAGERS

Choosing investment managers for individuals or personal trusts is similar to choosing them for tax-free portfolios. The only differences relate to taxes and time horizons. The investment manager would normally try very hard to seek long-term capital gains, so it must be attentive to the holding period. In addition, income from most investments is taxable, so after-tax yields must be considered when reviewing both taxable and tax-exempt securities. The horizon period of individuals and trusts may differ from those of the pension fund, which typically has an indefinite time horizon, on the one hand, but which is usually managed by a pension director with a much shorter perspective. To the extent that a long time horizon exists for a trust or an individual, the investment manager can lean toward more-volatile and less-liquid assets in order to seek a higher long-run capital appreciation and higher ultimate income.

As to the manager's characteristics, it is important when interviewing a prospective manager to be sure its performance record has been generated in a way consistent with the trust's needs. Since pension funds now dominate the investment management market, techniques which ignore holding period and taxes are appropriate for many managers. However, a trustee may not be comfortable with high turnover and certainly the economics of paying high transaction costs and taxes must be considered in the ultimate measurement of results. Therefore, a manager which achieves its performance by careful selection of securities whose value accumulates over the years would be preferable to one which has a shorter perspective.

MEASURING INVESTMENT MANAGERS AND COMPARING INVESTMENT RESULTS

Measurement techniques are similar for all types of portfolios, so little elaboration is required in this area. Comparison is different, though, for personal and trust assets. Since tax considerations apply, tax-free bond indexes should be used and comparisons should be made against taxable portfolios. Regrettably, no investment performance results for taxable clients are available in significant volume as of this date.

CUSTODY, RECORDKEEPING, AND ADMINISTRATION

Custody requirements for taxable individuals and personal trusts are similar to those required for pension funds, and, for large portfolios with multiple managers, the master custodian which provides compositing (consolidation) and sophisticated recordkeeping is very helpful. In addition, the trust will require tax preparation beyond or certainly different from that required for pension funds. Tax lot accounting will also be required. This means distinguishing individual purchases of securities so that at the time of sale a specific purchase lot can be referenced. If a security was purchased at a number of different prices, it is normally desirable to sell the highest cost security first (assuming there is no distinction in holding period), in order to minimize the current tax bill. Typically, the master custodian can be of assistance in this area. The custodian or manager keeping records should also be able to provide information required by courts or by beneficiaries.

COMMUNICATION WITH BENEFICIARIES

As with the pension fund, the assets in a trust or personal account frequently do not belong to the people managing and administering them. However, in the case of a pension fund, the managers and administrators are under the control of the people who control the fund sponsor. In the case of a personal trust, especially a testamentary trust, the trustee is independent of the donor and beneficiaries, and needs only answer to the court in the jurisdiction in which the trust was established. Nonetheless, good business practice and courtesy suggest that most beneficiaries should receive reports on their assets. The amount and frequency of reporting depend on the state law under which the trust was established, the requirements of the trust document, and any agreement made by the beneficiaries and trustees. It further depends upon the interest and sophistication levels of the beneficiaries, and how the trustees feel the interests of beneficiaries are best served.

STANDARDS OF PRUDENCE

Trustees are held to very high standards, and must be careful to be prudent in all their activities. Whereas pension trusts typically do not come under the jurisdiction of the states in which they are established, personal trusts do. State laws typically fall into one of two categories: legal list and prudent man. Legal list states provide lists of securities in which trustees can invest without fear of personal liability. Prudent man states allow trustees to invest as would a "prudent man." The definition of the actions of a "prudent man" have come under court scrutiny and been revised in many states in the last few years. While no hard and fast rules can be drawn, the fiduciary checklist shown at the end of Chapter 16 can be quite helpful to trustees of personal trusts as well as to those of pension funds.

An important area of concern is the extent to which courts will view portfolios as a whole rather than looking at the prudence of each investment. Portfolios *should* be viewed in aggregate, but if local law dictates otherwise, a trustee could be "surcharged" or sued for loss in an individual investment despite great success of the overall portfolio. Causing further concern is the fact that trust law does not consider loss of purchasing power, so a trustee which has maintained its principal may be devastated by inflation. The trustee would be considered prudent, but the beneficiary would be broke.

APPENDIX

Mathematics Refresher

There is no need for representatives of fund sponsors to be statisticians or mathematical wizards. On the other hand, the trend toward increasing the measurement of all business activities is strong, and this trend will continue. Thus, it is desirable for sponsors' representatives to be familiar with quantitative techniques. This appendix is directed at people who would like to go beyond the measured results to determine how they are calculated, or who want to be able to make their own calculations. Three areas of measurement will be discussed: measures of central tendency (averages), measures of dispersion around the average (variabilities), and measures which show the relationship between two or more variables (correlations). In addition, the appendix will discuss calculations of dollar-weighted rates of return, time-weighted rates of return, and the "linking" of returns from one period to another.

MEASURES OF CENTRAL TENDENCY

Two measures of central tendency are used in the investment area. The *arithmetic mean* is the traditional average, and it is calculated by adding up all the numbers and dividing the total by the number of observations. The *median* is the number midway between the high point and the low. Columns A and B below show two series of numbers and their respective means and medians. It is worth noting that the mean and median for a series can be the same, but they need not be, and that either can be greater than the other. In series A the mean is smaller than the median because the number 1 is not as close to the median as is the number 6. In distribution B the mean and the median are equal. Distributions in which the mean and median are close to each other are considered to be "normal" distributions. A distribution in which the mean is different from the median is considered to be "skewed" to either the right or the left.

	A	B
	6	6
	5	5
	1	4
	──	──
Total	12	15
Mean	4	5
Median	5	5

Additional measures of central tendency include the *mode* (the number which appears the most times) and the *geometric mean* (which is calculated by multiplying all numbers in the series together and taking the *n*th root of the product).

MEASURES OF DISPERSION

Just as it is frequently desirable to know something about the "average" of a series, it is also useful to know how the results are distributed around the mean. For instance, 10 is the average of 11 and 9 and it is also the average of 0 and 20. The quality control inspector in a pharmaceutical plant would want to know not only the average amount of medication in each capsule but also whether or not there was a wide dispersion around the average. If 10 grains were the desired average, 9 or 11 might be tolerable, but certainly 0 and 20 would not be. Measurements of dispersion to be discussed are range, mean absolute deviation, standard deviation, variance, and semivariance. In order to show examples of each calculation, the series in column C will be used.

Measures of Dispersion

	C
	30
	26
	20
	15
	12
	7
	2

$$\text{Mean} = \frac{\Sigma 2 \ldots 30}{7} = \frac{112}{7} = 16$$

Median = Halfway point between high and low = 15

Range = High − Low = 30 − 2 = 28

Mean absolute
deviation = Average of the absolute difference between each observation and the average of all observations ("absolute" means without regard to sign; 3 and -3 both have the absolute value of 3; the sign for absolute value is $\|$, such that $\|-3 = 3$
$= \|(30 - 16) + \|(26 - 16) + \|(20 - 16) +$
$\|(15 - 16) + \|(12 - 16) + \|(7 - 16) +$
$\|(2 - 16)$
$= 14 + 10 + 4 + 1 + 4 + 9 + 14 = 56$

$56 \div 7 = 8$

Variance = Sum of the squares of the differences between each observation and the average, divided by the number of observations
$= 14^2 + 10^2 + 4^2 + 1^2 + 4^2 + 9^2 + 14^2$
$= 196 + 100 + 16 + 1 + 16 + 81 + 196 = 606$

$\dfrac{606}{7} = 86.6$

Standard
deviation = Square root of variance = $\sqrt{86.6} = 9.3$

Semivariance = Sum of the squares of the differences between the mean and each observation that is smaller than the mean, divided by the number of observations that are smaller than the mean.
$= 1 + 16 + 81 + 196 = 294 \div 4 = 73.5$

Range. The range shows the difference between the high and the low of the series and thus gives a rough idea of how representative of the distribution the mean is.

Mean absolute deviation. Whereas the range looks only at the two extreme points, the mean absolute deviation considers every observation and its relation to the average. "Absolute" deviations are shown (i.e., minus signs are ignored), since otherwise pluses and minuses would cancel out, thus showing no deviation.

Variance. The variance is a true measure of the width of the distribution. Like the mean absolute deviation, the variance relates each observation to the average. Unlike the mean absolute deviation, which solves the problem of minus signs by ignoring them, the variance solves this problem by squaring each number (multiplying a negative number by itself produces a positive number).

Standard deviation. This measure, also referred to by the Greek letter sigma (σ), is the square root of the variance. The standard deviation is a useful and widely used measure because it has the interesting characteristic that, for a normal, or bellshaped, distribution, 68 percent of the observations fall within ± 1 standard deviation and 95 percent fall within two standard deviations. Since it is usually reasonable to suggest that distributions in finance are normal, a good estimate of the dispersion of a distribution around its average is provided by the standard deviation measure.

Semivariance. This measure considers only downside dispersion. Since measures of dispersion are frequently used to measure risk in securities and portfolios, the amount of uncertainty as to future value is one definition of risk. Some investors find this definition difficult to accept because they feel that only below-average expectations represent risk. If an investor expects a stock to rise from 10 to 12, and it actually goes to 13, the extra point is not risk (though it is clearly uncertainty). Thus, these investors are more comfortable with the semivariance measure. However, as a practical matter, both variance and semivariance lead to very similar results.

MEASURES RELATING TWO OR MORE VARIABLES

By far the most common technique for determining the statistical relationship between two variables is regression analysis (also called correlation analysis). This procedure was described in considerable detail in Chapter 8 as the beta analysis for measuring equity portfolios. In more general terms, the simple regression analysis attempts to measure the relationship between any two variables. It takes the form of the equation:

$$y = a + bx + c$$

Here, y is the variable to be predicted based on knowledge of the current value of x plus the historical relationship between x and y. The term b is key because it tells us how many x's equal one y. If b is 0.5, for every increase by one unit of x, y increases by one-half unit. The term a is a constant, and c represents an error term. That is, if a and b do not completely account for the movement of y, then some additional factor has to be considered, and this is represented by c. The following example illustrates the use of this technique in estimating the total costs of production in a widget factory. (In Greek "a" is alpha and "b" is beta, hence the terms used in Modern Portfolio Theory.) If overhead, such as rent, heat, light, and the boss's salary, costs $10,000 per month, and it costs $1 to produce each widget, the total costs of producing the widgets will equal $10,000 plus $1 times the number of widgets produced. If in a certain month 20,000 widgets were produced, the total costs would be as follows:

$$\text{Total costs} = \text{Fixed costs} + \text{Number of units produced}$$
$$\times \text{ Variable costs} + \text{Unforeseen costs}$$
$$y = \$10,000 + 20,000 \times \$1 + c$$
$$y = \$30,000 + c$$

The preceding is an example of a "simple" "linear" regression. The regression is "simple" in that only one independent variable, x, was used. It is possible to utilize more complex equations in which more than one independent variable helps explain the y term. For instance, in the preceding example it would have been possible to consider additional costs which impact the total costs. The experience level of employees, number of new employees to be trained, absentee rate, changes in material costs, and so on, all could have been related to the total costs.

The relationship is called "linear" because the line drawn on a scatter diagram relating the variables is straight. This can be seen in chart A. Chart B shows an exponential relationship, such that y equals x^2. In this case the line curves sharply upward. Other more complex measurement techniques permit the consideration of relationships which are nonlinear.

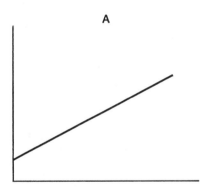

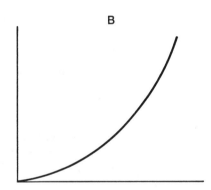

TIME-WEIGHTED, DOLLAR-WEIGHTED, AND LINKED RATES OF RETURN

There are several ways of computing the total rate of return on a portfolio. Each means something slightly different. We will examine three such ways.

The time-weighted rate of return.   The time-weighted rate of return is the most effective way to compare the returns of different portfolios. It counts each period equally, and thus it assumes no control over the size and timing of cash flows by the portfolio manager. It requires a knowledge of the value of the portfolio at the time of each cash flow. Assume three time periods. At each we have a known value for the portfolio.

Time beginning of	Value before cash flow	Cash flow
Year 1) = T_0	100 = V_0	10 = C_0
Year 2) = T_1	130 = V_1	5 = C_1
Year 3) = T_2	150 = V_2	

For the return between T_0 and T_1 (during year 1),

$$r_1 = [V_1/(V_0 + C_0) - 1] \times 100$$
$$r_1 = [(130/110) - 1] \times 100, \text{ or } 18.2\%$$

For the return between T_1 and T_2 (during year 2),

$$r_2 = [V_2/V_1 + C_1) - 1] \times 100$$
$$r_2 = [(150/135) - 1] \times 100, \text{ or } 11.1\%$$

To find the time-weighted rate for the total period (year 1 and year 2) we link r_1 and r_2:

$$1 + r_T = (1 + r_1)(1 + r_2)$$

This is what we mean by linking. Therefore, the total rate

$$r_T = [(1.182)(1.111) - 1] \times 100$$
$$= 31.32\% \text{ for two years}$$

Note that each interval of the same time period has the same impact on the total, no matter how much is in the portfolio during that period. Therefore, the annual rate is computed by $\sqrt{1 + r_T} - 1$, = 14.6%, the annual time-weighted This is the amount which, when linked with itself, yields 31.3 percent.

Note also that in most cases in which the cash flows as a percentage of the portfolio value are small, the time-weighted and the dollar-weighted rates are similar (14.6 compared to 14.5). However, if the cash flows are large or if the number of periods being measured is great, the differences can be significant.

The dollar-weighted rate of return. This rate is often called the internal rate of return or the discounted cash flow. It assigns more importance to the cumulative rate of return of periods when the portfolio is worth more. It may be a meaningful measure of a manager's performance if he has complete control of cash flows. It does not require knowledge of the value of the portfolio at each cash flow, but only at the beginning and ending of the measurement period. The essential form in an n-period model of the rate of return is reflected in the formula:

$$V_n = V_0(1 + r)^{T_0} + C_0(1 + r)^{T_1} + C_1(1 + r)T_2$$
$$+ \cdots C_n(1 + r)^{T_n}$$

where r is the internal rate of return.

In our year 1 to year 3 sample

$$V_2 + V_0(1 + r)^2 + C_0(1 + r)^2 + C_1(1 + r),$$
$$\text{or } 150 = 100(1 + r)^2 + 10(1 + r)^2 + 5(1 + r)$$

Note that this becomes a quadratic equation. We can solve it by using the quadratic formula or by using different values of r (trial and error, or "iteration"), and we find that $r = 14.5$ is the annual dollar-weighted rate of return.

The linked internal rate of return.   The linked internal method is an approximation of the time-weighted return and a hybrid of the dollar-weighted and time-weighted rates. The internal rate is used to find returns for shorter intervals within a larger period of time, and these internal rates are linked together to find the time-weighted rate of return for the entire period. For instance, the internal rate may be used to find quarterly rates of return which are then linked together to find the annual rate. If the quarterly returns are called r_1, r_2, r_3, and r_4, then the annual return is found by the formula $(1 + r) = (1 + r_1)(1 + r_2)(1 + r_3)$ $(1 + r_4)$. From the resultant $1 + r$ we subtract 1 and multiply by 100 to find the percentage return for the full period.

Assume that the dollar-weighted rates per quarter were 5 percent, -10 percent, 20 percent, and 4 percent, respectively. Then the linked annual rate would be:

$$[(1 + 0.05)(1 - 0.10)(1 + 0.20)(1 + 0.04)] - 1 \times 100 = 17.9\%$$

This method is used to approximate the time-weighted rate when more frequent valuations are not available.

INDEX